BLACK LEGACY PRESS™
WWW.BLACKLEGACYPRESS.ORG

SLAVE NARRATIVES

VOLUME IV
GEORGIA NARRATIVES
PART 3

By
United States.
Work Projects Administration

Copyright © 2024 by BLACKLEGACYPRESS.ORG

All rights reserved. No part of this publication may be reproduced or transmitted in any form or by any means electronic or mechanical, including information storage and retrieval systems without permission in writing from the publisher, except for student research using the appropriate citations.

ISBN: 978-1-63652-222-7

SLAVE NARRATIVES

A Folk History of Slavery in the United States.
From Interviews with Former Slaves

**UNITED STATES.
WORK PROJECTS ADMINISTRATION**

TYPEWRITTEN RECORDS PREPARED BY
THE FEDERAL WRITERS' PROJECT
1936-1938
ASSEMBLED BY
THE LIBRARY OF CONGRESS PROJECT
WORK PROJECTS ADMINISTRATION
FOR THE DISTRICT OF COLUMBIA
SPONSORED BY THE LIBRARY OF
CONGRESS

WASHINGTON 1941

VOLUME IV
GEORGIA NARRATIVES
PART 3

Prepared by
The Federal Writers' Project of
The Works Progress Administration
For the State of Georgia

CONTENTS

JENNIE KENDRICKS	1
EMMALINE KILPATRICK	9
FRANCES KIMBROUGH	15
CHARLIE KING	17
NICEY KINNEY	23
JULIA LARKEN	33
GEORGE LEWIS	43
MIRRIAMMCCOMMONS	49
ED MCCREE	53
LUCY MCCULLOUGH,	63
AMANDA MCDANIEL	67
TOM MCGRUDER	73
SUSAN MCINTOSH	77
MATILDA MCKINNEY	87
WILLIAMMCWHORTER	91
MOLLIE MALONE	103
CARRIE MASON	107
SUSAN MATTHEWS	113
EMILY MAYS	117
LIZA MENTION	121
HARRIET MILLER	125
MOLLIE MITCHELL	131
BOB MOBLEY	135

FANNY NIX	139
HENRY NIX	143
LEWIS OGLETREE	147
RICHARD ORFORD	151
ANNA PARKES	157
G.W. PATTILLO	169
ALEC POPE	175
ANNIE PRICE	183
CHARLIE PYE	191
CHARLOTTE RAINES	197
FANNY RANDOLPH	201
SHADE RICHARDS	205
DORA ROBERTS	211
FEREBE ROGERS	215
HENRY ROGERS	223
JULIA RUSH	233
NANCY SETTLES	239
WILL SHEETS	243
ROBERT SHEPHERD	251
TOM SINGLETON	269
CHARLIE TYE SMITH	279
GEORGIA SMITH	283
MARY SMITH	289
MELVIN SMITH	291
NANCY SMITH	301
NELLIE SMITH	311
PAUL SMITH	327

EMELINE STEPNEY 343
AMANDA STYLES 347

[HW: Dist 5
Ex-Slave #63]

Whitley,
1-22-36
Driskell

EX SLAVE
JENNIE KENDRICKS
[Date Stamp: MAY 8 1937]

JENNIE KENDRICKS

Jennie Kendricks, the oldest of 7 children, was born in Sheram, Georgia in 1855. Her parents were Martha and Henry Bell. She says that the first thing she remembers is being whipped by her mother.

Jennie Kendricks' grandmother and her ten children lived on this plantation. The grandmother had been brought to Georgia from Virginia: "She used to tell me how the slave dealers brought her and a group of other children along much the same as they would a herd of cattle," said the ex-slave, "when they reached a town all of them had to dance through the streets and act lively so that the chances for selling them would be greater".

When asked to tell about Mr. Moore, her owner, and his family Jennie Kendricks stated that although her master owned and operated a large plantation, he was not considered a wealthy man. He owned only two other slaves besides her immediate family and these were men.

"In Mr. Moores family were his mother, his wife, and six children (four boys and two girls). This family lived very comfortably in a two storied weatherboard house. With the exception of our grandmother who cooked for the owner's family and slaves, and assisted her mistress with housework all the slaves worked in the fields where they cultivated cotton and the corn, as well as the other produce grown there. Every morning at sunrise they had to get up and go to the fields where they worked until it was too dark to see. At noon each day they were permitted to come to the kitchen, located just a short distance in the rear of the master's house, where they were served dinner. During the course of the day's work the women shared all the men's work except plowing. All of them picked cotton when it was time to gather the crops. Some nights they were required to spin and to help Mrs. Moore, who did all of the weaving. They used to do their own personal work, at night also." Jennie Kendricks says she remembers how her mother and the older girls would go to the spring at night where they washed their clothes and then left them to dry on the surrounding bushes.

As a little girl Jennie Kendricks spent all of her time in the master's house where she played with the young white children. Sometimes she and Mrs. Moore's youngest child, a little boy, would fight because it appeared to one that the other was receiving more attention from Mrs. Moore than the other. As she grew older she was kept in the house as a playmate to the Moore children so she never had to work in the field a single day.

She stated that they all wore good clothing and that all of it was made on the plantation with one exception. The servants spun the thread and Mrs. Moore and her daughters did all of the weaving as well as the making of the dresses that were worn on this particular plantation. "The way they made this cloth", she continued, "was to wind a certain amount of thread known as a "cut" onto a reel. When a certain number of cuts were reached they were placed on the loom. This cloth was colored with a dye made from the bark of trees or with a dye that was made from the indigo berry cultivated on the plantation. The dresses that the women wore on working days were made of striped or checked materials while those worn on Sunday were usually white."

She does not know what the men wore on work days as she never came in contact with them. Stockings for all were knitted on the place. The shoes, which were the one exception mentioned above, were made by one Bill Jacobs, an elderly white man who made the shoes for all the plantations in the community. The grown people wore heavy shoes called "Brogans" while those worn by the children were not so heavy and were called "Pekers" because of their narrow appearance. For Sunday wear, all had shoes bought for this purpose. Mr. Moore's mother was a tailoress and at times, when the men were able to get the necessary material, she made their suits.

There was always enough feed for everybody on the Moore plantation. Mrs. Moore once told Jennie's mother to always see that her children had sufficient to eat so that they would not have to steal and would therefore grow up to be honorable. As the Grandmother did all of the cooking, none of the other servants ever had to cook, not even on Sundays or other holidays such as the Fourth of July. There was no stove in this plantation kitchen, all the cooking was done at the large fireplace where there were a number of hooks called potracks. The pots, in which the cooking was done, hung from these hooks directly over the fire.

The meals served during the week consisted of vegetables, salt bacon, corn bread, pot liquor, and milk. On Sunday they were served milk, biscuits, vegetables, and sometimes chicken. Jennie Kendricks ate all of her meals in the master's house and says that her food was even better. She was also permitted to go to the kitchen to get food at any time during the day. Sometimes when the boys went hunting everyone was given roast 'possum and other small game. The two male slaves were often permitted to accompany them but were not allowed to handle the guns. None of the slaves had individual gardens of their own as food sufficient for their needs was raised in the master's garden.

The houses that they lived in were one-roomed structures made of heavy plank instead of logs, with planer [HW: ?] floors. At one end of this one-roomed cabin there was a large chimney and fireplace made of rocks, mud, and dirt. In addition to the one door, there was a window at the back. Only one family could live in a cabin as the space was so limited. The furnishings of each cabin consisted of a bed and one or two chairs. The beds were well constructed, a great deal better than some of the beds the ex-slave saw during these days. Regarding mattresses she said, "We took some tick and stuffed it with cotton and corn husks, which had been torn into small pieces and when we got through sewing it looked like a mattress that was bought in a store."

Light was furnished by lightwood torches and sometimes by the homemade tallow candles. The hot tallow was poured into a candle mold, which was then dipped into a pan of cold water, when the tallow had hardened, the finished product was removed.

Whenever there was sickness, a doctor was always called. As a child Gussie was rather sickly, and a doctor was always called to attend to her. In addition to the doctor's prescriptions there was heart leaf tea and a warm remedy of garlic tea prepared by her grandmother.

If any of the slaves ever pretended sickness to avoid work, she knows nothing about it.

As a general rule, slaves were not permitted to learn to read or write, but the younger Moore children tried to teach her to spell, read, and write. When she used to stand around Mrs. Moore when she was sewing she appeared to be interested and so she was taught to sew.

Every Sunday afternoon they were all permitted to go to town where a colored pastor preached to them. This same minister performed all marriages after the candidates had secured the permission of the master.

There was only one time when Mr. Moore found it necessary to sell any of his slaves. On this occasion he had to sell two; he saw that they were sold to another kind master.

The whipping on most plantation were administered by the [HW: over]seers and in some cases punishment was rather severe. There was no overseer on this plantation. Only one of Mr. Moore's sons told the field hands what to do. When this son went to war it became necessary to hire an overseer. Once he attempted to whip one of the women but when she refused to allow him to whip her he never tried to whip any of the others. Jennie Kendricks' husband, who was also a slave, once told her his master was so mean that he often whipped his slaves until blood ran in their shoes.

There was a group of men, known as the "Patter-Rollers", whose duty it was to see that slaves were not allowed to leave their individual plantations without passes which [HW: they] were supposed to receive from their masters. "A heap of them got whippings for being caught off without these passes," she stated, adding that "sometimes a few of them were fortunate enough to escape from the Patter-Rollers". She knew of one boy who, after having outrun the "Patter-Rollers", proceeded to make fun of them after he was safe behind his master's fence. Another man whom the Patter-Rollers had pursued any number of times but who had always managed to escape, was finally caught one day and told to pray before he was given his whipping. As he obeyed he noticed that he was not being closely observed, whereupon he made a break that resulted in his escape from them again.

The treatment on some of the other plantations was so severe that slaves often ran away, Jennie Kendricks told of one man [HW: who was] [TR: "being" crossed out] lashed [HW: and who] ran away but was finally caught. When his master brought him back he was locked in a room until he could be punished. When the master finally came to administer the whipping, Lash had cut his own throat in a last effort to secure his freedom. He was not successful; his life was saved by quick action on the part of his master. Sometime later after rough handling Lash finally killed his master [HW: and] was burned at the stake for this crime.

Other slaves were more successful at escape, some being able to remain away for as long as three years at a time. At nights, they slipped to the plantation where they stole hogs and other food. Their shelters were usually caves, some times holes dug in the ground. Whenever they were caught, they were severely whipped.

A slave might secure his freedom without running away. This is true in the case of Jennie Kendricks' grandfather who, after hiring his time out for a number of years, was able to save enough money with which to purchase himself from his master.

Jennie Kendricks remembers very little of the talk between her master and mistress concerning the war. She does remember being taken to see the Confederate soldiers drill a short distance from the house. She says "I though it was very pretty, 'course I did'nt know what was causing this or what the results would be". Mr. Moore's oldest sons went to war [HW: but he] himself did not enlist until the war was nearly over. She was told that the Yankee soldiers burned all the gin houses and took all live stock that they saw while on the march, but no soldiers passed near their plantation.

After the war ended and all the slaves had been set free, some did not know it, [HW: as] they were not told by their masters. [HW: A number of them] were tricked into signing contracts which bound them to their masters for several years longer.

As for herself and her grandmother, they remained on the Moore property where her grandmother finally died. Her mother moved away when freedom was declared and started working for someone else. It was about this time that Mr. Moore began to prosper, he and his brother Marvin gone into business together.

According to Jennie Kendricks, she has lived to reach such a ripe old age because she has always been obedient and because she has always been a firm believer in God.

[HW: Dist 1
Ex-Slave #62]

EX-SLAVE INTERVIEW:
EMMALINE KILPATRICK, Age 74
Born a slave on the plantation of
Judge William Watson Moore,
White Plains, (Greene County) Georgia

BY: SARAH H. HALL
ATHENS, GA.
[Date Stamp: MAY 8 1937]

EMMALINE KILPATRICK

One morning in October, as I finished planting hyacinth bulbs on my cemetery lot, I saw an old negro woman approaching. She was Emmaline Kilpatrick, born in 1863, on my grandfather's plantation.

"Mawnin' Miss Sarah," she began, "Ah seed yer out hyar in de graveyard, en I cum right erlong fer ter git yer ter read yo' Aunt Willie's birthday, offen her toomstone, en put it in writin' fer me."

"I don't mind doing that for you, Emmaline," I replied, "but why do you want to know my aunt's birthday?"

"Well," answered the old ex-slave, "I can't rightly tell mah age no udder way. My mammy, she tole me, I wuz bawned de same night ez Miss Willie wuz, en mammy allus tole me effen I ever want ter know how ole I is, jes' ask my white folks how ole Miss Willie is."

When I had pencilled the birthdate on a scrap of paper torn from my note book and she had tucked it carefully away in a pocket in her clean blue checked gingham apron, Emmaline began to talk of the old days on my grandfather's farm.

"Miss Sarah, Ah sho did love yo' aunt Willie. We wuz chilluns growin' up tergedder on Marse Billie's place. You mought not know it, but black chilluns gits grown heap faster den white chilluns, en whilst us played 'round de yard, en orchards, en pastures out dar, I wuz sposed ter take care er Miss Willie en not let her git hurt, er nuthin' happen ter her."

"My mammy say dat whan Marse Billie cum hom' frum de War, he call all his niggers tergedder en tell 'am dey is free, en doan b'long ter nobody no mo'. He say dat eny uf 'um dat want to, kin go 'way and live whar dey laks, en do lak dey wanter. Howsome ebber, he do say effen enybody wants ter stay wid him, en live right on in de same cabins, dey kin do it, effen dey promise him ter be good niggers en mine him lak dey allus done."

"Most all de niggers stayed wid Marse Billie, 'ceppen two er thee brash, good fer nuthin's."

Standing there in the cemetery, as I listened to old Emmaline tell of the old days, I could see cotton being loaded on freight cars at the depot. I asked Emmaline to tell what she could remember of the days whan we had no railroad to haul the cotton to market.

"Well," she said, "Fore dis hyar railroad wuz made, dey hauled de cotton ter de Pint (She meant Union Point) en sold it dar. De Pint's jes' 'bout twelve miles fum hyar.

Fo' day had er railroad thu de Pint, Marse Billie used ter haul his cotton clear down ter Jools ter sell it. My manny say dat long fo' de War he used ter wait twel all de cotton wuz picked in de fall, en den he would have it all loaded on his waggins. Not long fo' sundown he wud start de waggins off, wid yo' unker Anderson bossin' 'em, on de all night long ride towards Jools. 'Bout fo' in de mawnin' Marse Billie en yo' grammaw, Miss Margie, 'ud start off in de surrey, driving de bays, en fo' dem waggins git ter Jools Marse Billie done cotch up wid em. He drive er head en lead em on ter de cotton mill in Jools, whar he sell all his cotton. Den him en Miss Margie, dey go ter de mill sto' en buy white sugar en udder things dey doan raise on de plantation, en load 'em on de waggins en start back home."

"But Emmaline," I interrupted, "Sherman's army passed through Jewels and burned the houses and destroyed the property there. How did the people market their cotton then?"

Emmaline scratched her head. "Ah 'members somepin 'bout dat," she declared. "Yassum, I sho' does 'member my mammy sayin' dat folks sed when de Fed'rals wuz bunnin' up evvy thing 'bout Jools, dey wuz settin' fire ter de mill, when de boss uv dem sojers look up en see er sign up over er upstairs window. Hit wuz de Mason's sign up day, kaze dat wuz de Mason's lodge hall up over de mill. De sojer boss, he meks de udder sojers put out de fire. He say him er Mason hisself en he ain' gwine see nobuddy burn up er Masonic Hall. Dey kinder tears up some uv de fixin's er de Mill wuks, but dey dassent burn down de mill house kaze he ain't let 'em do nuthin' ter de Masonic Hall. Yar knows, Miss Sarah, Ah wuz jes' 'bout two years ole when dat happen, but I ain't heered nuffin' 'bout no time when dey didden' take cotton ter Jools ever year twel de railroad come hyar."

"Did yer ax me who mah'ed my maw an paw? Why, Marse Billie did, cose he did! He wuz Jedge Moore, Marse Billie wuz, en he wone gwine hev no foolis'mant 'mongst 'is niggers. Fo' de War en durin' de War, de niggers went ter de same church whar dare white folks went. Only de niggers, dey set en de gallery."

"Marse Billie made all his niggers wuk moughty hard, but he sho' tuk good keer uv 'em. Miss Margie allus made 'em send fer her when de chilluns wuz bawned in de slave cabins. My mammy, she say, Ise 'bout de onliest slave baby Miss Margie diden' look after de bawnin, on dat plantation. When any nigger on dat farm wuz sick, Marse Billie seed dat he had medicine an lookin' atter, en ef he wuz bad sick Marse Billie had da white folks doctor come see 'bout 'im."

"Did us hev shoes? Yas Ma'am us had shoes. Dat wuz all ole Pegleg wuz good fer, jes ter mek shoes, en fix shoes atter dey wuz 'bout ter give out. Pegleg made de evvy day shoes for Marse Billie's own chilluns, 'cept now en den Marse Billie fetched 'em home some sto' bought shoes fun Jools."

"Yassum, us sho' wuz skeered er ghosts. Dem days when de War won't long gone, niggers sho' wus skert er graveyards. Mos' evvy nigger kep' er rabbit foot, kaze ghosties wone gwine bodder nobuddy dat hed er lef' hind foot frum er graveyard rabbit. Dem days dar wuz mos' allus woods 'round de graveyards, en it uz easy ter ketch er rabbit az he loped outer er graveyard. Lawsy, Miss

Sarah, dose days Ah sho' wouldn't er been standin' hyar in no graveyard talkin' ter ennybody, eben in wide open daytime."

"En you ax wuz dey enny thing else uz wuz skert uv? Yassum, us allus did git moughty oneasy ef er scritch owl hollered et night. Pappy ud hop right out er his bed en stick de fire shovel en de coals. Effen he did dat rat quick, an look over 'is lef' shoulder whilst de shovel gittin' hot, den maybe no no nigger gwine die dat week on dat plantation. En us nebber did lak ter fine er hawse tail hair en de hawse trough, kaze us wuz sho' ter meet er snake fo' long."

"Yassum, us had chawms fer heap er things. Us got 'em fum er ole Injun 'oman dat lived crost de crick. Her sold us chawms ter mek de mens lak us, en chawms dat would git er boy baby, er anudder kind er chawms effen yer want er gal baby. Miss Margie allus scold 'bout de chawms, en mek us shamed ter wear 'em, 'cept she doan mine ef us wear asserfitidy chawms ter keep off fevers, en she doan say nuffin when my mammy wear er nutmeg on a wool string 'round her neck ter keep off de rheumatiz.

"En is you got ter git on home now, Miss Sarah? Lemme tote dat hoe en trowel ter yer car fer yer. Yer gwine ter take me home in yer car wid yer, so ez I kin weed yer flower gyarden fo' night? Yassum, I sho' will be proud ter do it fer de black dress you wo' las' year. Ah gwine ter git evvy speck er grass outer yo' flowers, kaze ain' you jes' lak yo' grammaw—my Miss Margie."

United States. Work Projects Administration

[HW: Dist 6
Ex Slave #65]

J.R. Jones

FRANCES KIMBROUGH, EX-SLAVE
Place of birth: On Kimbrough plantation, Harries County, near Cataula, Georgia
Date of birth: About 1854
Present residence: 1639-5th Avenue, Columbus, Georgia
Interviewed: August 7, 1936
[Date Stamp: MAY 8 --]

FRANCES KIMBROUGH

"A unt Frances" story reveals that, her young "marster" was Dr. Jessie Kimbrough—a man who died when she was about eighteen years of age. But a few weeks later, while working in the field one day, she saw "Marse Jessie's" ghost leaning against a pine "watchin us free Niggers wuckin."

When she was about twenty-two years of age, "a jealous Nigger oman" "tricked" her. The "spell" cast by this "bad oman" affected the victim's left arm and hand. Both became numb and gave her great "misery". A peculiar feature of this visitation of the "conjurer's" spite was: if a friend or any one massaged or even touched the sufferer's afflicted arm or hand, that person was also similarly stricken the following day, always recovering, however, on the second day.

Finally, "Aunt" Frances got in touch with a "hoodoo" doctor, a man who lived in Muscogee County—about twenty-five miles distant from her. This man paid the patient one visit, then gave her absent treatment for several weeks, at the end of which time she recovered the full use of her arm and hand. Neither ever gave her any trouble again.

For her old-time "white fokes", "Aunt" Frances entertains an almost worshipful memory. Also, in her old age, she reflects the superstitious type of her race.

Being so young when freedom was declared, emancipation did not have as much significance for "Aunt" Frances as it did for the older colored people. In truth, she had no true conception of what it "wuz all about" until several years later. But she does know that she had better food and clothes before the slaves were freed than she had in the years immediately following.

She is deeply religious, as most ex-slaves are, but— as typical of the majority of aged Negroes—associates "hants" and superstition with her religion.

[HW: Dist 6
Ex-Slave #64]

Mary A. Crawford
Re-Search Worker

CHARLIE KING—EX-SLAVE
Interviewed
435 E. Taylor Street, Griffin, Georgia
September 16, 1936

CHARLIE KING

Charlie was born in Sandtown, (now Woodbury) Meriwether County, Georgia, eighty-five or six years ago. He does not know his exact age because his "age got burned up" when the house in which his parents lived was burned to the ground.

The old man's parents, Ned and Ann King, [TR: "were slaves of" crossed out] Mr. John King, who owned a big plantation near Sandtown [TR: "also about two hundred slaves" crossed out]. [TR: HW corrections are too faint to read.]

Charlie's parents were married by the "broom stick ceremony." The Master and Mistress were present at the wedding. The broom was laid down on the floor, the couple held each other's hands and stepped backward over it, then the Master told the crowd that the couple were man and wife.

This marriage lasted for over fifty years and they "allus treated each other right."

Charlie said that all the "Niggers" on "ole Master's place" had to work, "even chillun over seven or eight years of age."

The first work that Charlie remembered was "toting cawn" for his mother "to drap", and sweeping the yards up at the "big house". He also recalls that many times when he was in the yard at the "big house", "Ole Miss" would call him in and give him a buttered biscuit.

The Master and Mistress always named the Negro babies and usually gave them Bible names.

When the Negroes were sick, "Ole Master" and "Ole Miss" did the doctoring, sometimes giving them salts or oil, and if [HW: a Negro] refused it, they used the raw hide "whup."

When a member of a Negro family died, the master permitted all the Negroes to stop work and go to the funeral. The slave was buried in the slave grave yard. Sometimes a white minister read the Bible service, but usually a Negro preacher [HW: "officiated"].

The Negroes on this plantation had to work from sun up till sun down, except Saturday and Sunday; those were free.

The master blew on a big conch shell every morning at four o'clock, and when the first long blast was heard the lights "'gin to twinkle in every "Nigger" cabin." Charlie, chuckling, recalled that "ole Master" blowed that shell so it could-a-been heard for five miles." Some of the

"Niggers" went to feed the mules and horses, some to milk the cows, some to cook the breakfast in the big house, some to chop the wood, while others were busy cleaning up the "big house."

When asked if he believed in signs, Charlie replied: "I sho does for dis reason. Once jest befo my baby brother died, ole screech owl, he done come and set up in the big oak tree right at the doah by de bed and fo' the next twelve hours passed, my brother was dead. Screech owls allus holler 'round the house before death."

The slaves always had plenty to eat and wear, and therefore did not know what it was to be hungry.

The Master planted many acres of cotton, corn, wheat, peas, and all kinds of garden things. Every "Nigger family was required to raise plenty of sweet potatoes, the Master giving them a patch." "My 'ole Master' trained his smartest 'Niggers' to do certain kinds of work. My mother was a good weaver, and [HW: she] wove all the cloth for her own family, and bossed the weaving of all the other weavers on the plantation."

Charlie and all of his ten brothers and sisters helped to card and spin the cotton for the looms. Sometimes they worked all night, Charlie often going to sleep while carding, when his mother would crack him on the head with the carder handle and wake him up. Each child had a night for carding and spinning, so they all would get a chance to sleep.

Every Saturday night, the Negroes had a "breakdown," often dancing all night long. About twelve o'clock they had a big supper, everybody bringing a box of all kinds of good things to eat, and putting it on a long table.

On Sunday, all the darkies had to go to church. Sometimes the Master had a house on his plantation for preaching, and sometimes the slaves had to go ten or twelve miles to preaching. When they went so far the slaves could use 'ole' Master's' mules and wagons.

Charlie recalls very well when the Yankees came through. The first thing they did when they reached 'ole Master's' place was to break open the smokehouse and throw the best hams and shoulders out to the darkies, but as soon as the Yankees passed, the white folks made the "Niggers" take "all dey had'nt et up" back to the smokehouse. "Yes, Miss, we had plenty of liquor. Ole Master always kept kegs of it in the cellar and big 'Jimmy-john's' full in the house, and every Saturday night he'd give us darkies a dram, but nobody nevah seed no drunk Nigger lak dey does now."

Charlie's mother used to give her "chillun" "burnt whiskey" every morning "to start the day off." This burnt whiskey gave them "long life".

Another thing that Charlie recalls about the Yankees coming through, was that they took the saddles off their "old sore back horses", turned them loose, and caught some of Master's fine "hosses", threw the saddles over them and rode away.

Charlie said though "ole Marster" "whupped" when it was necessary, but he was not "onmerciful" like some of the other "ole Marsters" were, but the "paterolers" would sho lay it on if they caught a Nigger off his home plantation without a pass." The passes were written statements or permits signed by the darkies' owner, or the plantation overseer.

Charlie is very feeble and unable to work. The Griffin Relief Association [TR: "furnishes him his sustenance" crossed out, "sees to him" or possibly "supports him" written in.]

United States. Work Projects Administration

PLANTATION LIFE AS VIEWED BY EX-SLAVE
NICEY KINNEY, Age 86
R.F.D. #3
Athens, Ga.

Written by:
Miss Grace McCune
Athens

Edited by:
Mrs. Sarah H. Hall
Athens
and
John N. Booth
District Supervisor
Federal Writers' Proj.
Res. 6 & 7
Augusta, Ga.

Sept. 28, 1938

NICEY KINNEY

A narrow path under large water oaks led through a well-kept yard where a profusion of summer flowers surrounded Nicey Kinney's two-story frame house. The porch floor and a large portion of the roof had rotted down, and even the old stone chimney at one end of the structure seemed to sag. The middle-aged mulatto woman who answered the door shook her head when asked if she was Nicey Kinney. "No, mam," she protested, "but dat's my mother and she's sick in bed. She gits mighty lonesome lyin' dar in de bed and she sho does love to talk. Us would be mighty proud if you would come in and see her."

Nicey was propped up in bed and, although the heat of the September day was oppressive, the sick woman wore a black shoulder cape over her thick flannel nightgown; heavy quilts and blankets were piled close about her thin form, and the window at the side of her bed was tightly closed. Not a lock of her hair escaped the nightcap that enveloped her head. The daughter removed an empty food tray and announced, "Mammy, dis lady's come to see you and I 'spects you is gwine to lak her fine 'cause she wants to hear 'bout dem old days dat you loves so good to tell about." Nicey smiled. "I'se so glad you come to see me," she said, "'cause I gits so lonesome; jus' got to stay here in dis bed, day in and day out. I'se done wore out wid all de hard wuk I'se had to do, and now I'se a aged 'oman, done played out and sufferin' wid de high blood pressur'. But I kin talk and I does love to bring back dem good old days a-fore de war."

Newspapers had been pasted on the walls of Nicey's room. In one corner an enclosed staircase was cut off from the room by a door at the head of the third step; the space underneath the stair was in use as a closet. The marble topped bureau, two double beds, a couple of small tables, and some old chairs were all of a period prior to the current century. A pot of peas was perched on a pair of "firedogs" over the coals of a wood fire in the open fireplace. On a bed of red coals a thick iron pan held a large pone of cornbread, and the tantalizing aroma of coffee drew attention to a steaming coffeepot on a trivet in one corner of the hearth. Nicey's daughter turned the bread over and said, "Missy, I jus' bet you ain't never seed nobody cookin' dis way. Us is got a stove back in de kitchen, but our somepin t'eat seems to taste better fixed dis 'way; it brings back dem old days when us was chillun and all of us was at home wid mammy." Nicey grinned. "Missy," she said, "Annie—dat's dis gal of mine here—laughs at de way I laks dem old ways of livin', but she's jus' as bad 'bout 'em as I is, 'specially 'bout dat sort of cookin'; somepin t'eat cooked in dat old black pot is sho good.

"Marse Gerald Sharp and his wife, Miss Annie, owned us and, Child, dey was grand folks. Deir old home was 'way up in Jackson County 'twixt Athens and Jefferson. Dat big old plantation run plumb back down to de Oconee River. Yes, mam, all dem rich river bottoms was Marse Gerald's.

"Mammy's name was Ca'line and she b'longed to Marse Gerald, but Marse Hatton David owned my daddy—his name was Phineas. De David place warn't but 'bout a mile from our plantation and daddy was 'lowed to stay wid his fambly most evvy night; he was allus wid us on Sundays. Marse Gerald didn't have no slaves but my mammy and her chillun, and he was sho mighty good to us.

"Marse Gerald had a nice four-room house wid a hall all de way through it. It even had two big old fireplaces on one chimbly. No, mam, it warn't a rock chimbly; dat chimbly was made out of home-made bricks. Marster's fambly had deir cookin' done in a open fireplace lak evvybody else for a long time and den jus' 'fore de big war he bought a stove. Yes, mam, Marse Gerald bought a cook stove and us felt plumb rich 'cause dere warn't many folks dat had stoves back in dem days.

"Mammy lived in de old kitchen close by de big house 'til dere got to be too many of us; den Marse Gerald built us a house jus' a little piece off from de big house. It was jus' a log house, but Marster had all dem cracks chinked tight wid red mud, and he even had one of dem franklin-back chimblies built to keep our little cabin nice and warm. Why, Child, ain't you never seed none of dem old chimblies? Deir backs sloped out in de middle to throw out de heat into de room and keep too much of it from gwine straight up de flue. Our beds in our cabin was corded jus' lak dem up at de big house, but us slept on straw ticks and, let me tell you, dey sho slept good atter a hard days's wuk.

"De bestest water dat ever was come from a spring right nigh our cabin and us had long-handled gourds to drink it out of. Some of dem gourds hung by de spring all de time and dere was allus one or two of 'em hangin' by de side of our old cedar waterbucket. Sho', us had a cedar bucket and it had brass hoops on it; dat was some job to keep dem hoops scrubbed wid sand to make 'em bright and shiny, and dey had to be clean and pretty all de time or mammy would git right in behind us wid a switch. Marse Gerald raised all dem long-handled gourds dat us used 'stid of de tin dippers folks has now, but dem warn't de onliest kinds of gourds he growed on his place. Dere was gourds mos' as big as waterbuckets, and dey had short handles dat was bent whilst de gourds was green, so us could hang 'em on a limb of a tree in de shade to keep water cool for us when us was wukin' in de field durin' hot weather.

"I never done much field wuk 'til de war come on, 'cause Mistess was larnin' me to be a housemaid. Marse

Gerald and Miss Annie never had no chillun 'cause she warn't no bearin' 'oman, but dey was both mighty fond of little folks. On Sunday mornin's mammy used to fix us all up nice and clean and take us up to de big house for Marse Gerald to play wid. Dey was good christian folks and tuk de mostest pains to larn us chillun how to live right. Marster used to 'low as how he had done paid $500 for Ca'line but he sho wouldn't sell her for no price.

"Evvything us needed was raised on dat plantation 'cept cotton. Nary a stalk of cotton was growed dar, but jus' de same our clothes was made out of cloth dat Mistess and my mammy wove out of thread us chillun spun, and Mistess tuk a heap of pains makin' up our dresses. Durin' de war evvybody had to wear homespun, but dere didn't nobody have no better or prettier dresses den ours, 'cause Mistess knowed more'n anybody 'bout dyein' cloth. When time come to make up a batch of clothes Mistess would say, 'Ca'line holp me git up my things for dyein',' and us would fetch dogwood bark, sumach, poison ivy, and sweetgum bark. That poison ivy made the best black of anything us ever tried, and Mistess could dye the prettiest sort of purple wid sweetgum bark. Cop'ras was used to keep de colors from fadin', and she knowed so well how to handle it dat you could wash cloth what she had dyed all day long and it wouldn't fade a speck.

"Marster was too old to go to de war, so he had to stay home and he sho seed dat us done our wuk raisin' somepin t'eat. He had us plant all our cleared ground, and I sho has done some hard wuk down in dem old bottom lands, plowin', hoein', pullin' corn and fodder, and I'se even cut cordwood and split rails. Dem was hard times and evvybody had to wuk.

"Sometimes Marse Gerald would be away a week at a time when he went to court at Jefferson, and de very last thing he said 'fore he driv off allus was, 'Ca'line, you and de chillun take good care of Mistess.' He most allus fetched us new shoes when he come back, 'cause he never kept no shoemaker man on our place, and all our shoes was store-bought. Dey was jus' brogans wid brass toes, but us felt powerful dressed up when us got 'em on, 'specially when dey was new and de brass was bright and shiny. Dere was nine of us chillun, four boys and five gals. Us gals had plain cotton dresses made wid long sleeves and us wore big sunbonnets. What would gals say now if dey had to wear dem sort of clothes and do wuk lak what us done? Little boys didn't wear nothin' but long shirts in summertime, but come winter evvybody had good warm clothes made out of wool off of Marse Gerald's own sheep, and boys, even little tiny boys, had britches in winter.

"Did you ever see folks shear sheep, Child? Well, it was a sight in dem days. Marster would tie a sheep on de scaffold, what he had done built for dat job, and den he would have me set on de sheep's head whilst he cut off de wool. He sont it to de factory to have it carded into bats and us chillun spun de thread at home and mammy and Mistess wove it into cloth for our winter clothes. Nobody warn't fixed up better on church days dan Marster's Niggers and he was sho proud of dat.

"Us went to church wid our white folks 'cause dere warn't no colored churches dem days. None of de churches 'round our part of de country had meetin' evvy Sunday, so us went to three diffunt meetin' houses. On de fust Sunday us went to Captain Crick Baptist church, to Sandy Crick Presbyterian church on second Sundays, and on third Sundays meetin' was at Antioch Methodist church whar Marster and Mistess was members. Dey put me under de watchkeer of deir church when I was a mighty little gal, 'cause my white folks sho b'lieved in de church and in livin' for God; de larnin' dat dem two good old folks gimme is done stayed right wid me all through life, so far, and I aims to live by it to de end. I didn't sho 'nough jine up wid no church 'til I was done growed up and had left Marse Gerald; den I jined de Cedar Grove Baptist church and was baptized dar, and dar's whar I b'longs yit.

"Marster was too old to wuk when dey sot us free, so for a long time us jus' stayed dar and run his place for him. I never seed none of dem Yankee sojers but one time. Marster was off in Jefferson and while I was down at de washplace I seed 'bout 12 men come ridin' over de hill. I was sho skeered and when I run and told Mistess she made us all come inside her house and lock all de doors. Dem Yankee mens jus' rode on through our yard down to de river and stayed dar a little while; den dey turned around and rid back through our yard and on down de big road, and us never seed 'em no more.

"Soon atter dey was sot free Niggers started up churches of dey own and it was some sight to see and hear 'em on meetin' days. Dey would go in big crowds and sometimes dey would go to meetin's a fur piece off. Dey was all fixed up in deir Sunday clothes and dey walked barfoots wid deir shoes acrost deir shoulders to keep 'em from gittin' dirty. Jus' 'fore dey got to de church dey stopped and put on deir shoes and den dey was ready to git together to hear de preacher.

"Folks don't know nothin' 'bout hard times now, 'specially young folks; dey is on de gravy train and don't know it, but dey is headed straight for 'struction and perdition; dey's gwine to land in dat burnin' fire if dey don't mind what dey's about. Jus' trust in de Lord, Honey, and cast your troubles on Him and He'll stay wid you, but if you turns your back on Him, den you is lost, plumb gone, jus' as sho as shelled corn.

"When us left Marse Gerald and moved nigh Athens he got a old Nigger named Egypt, what had a big fambly, to live on his place and do all de wuk. Old Marster didn't last long atter us was gone. One night he had done let his farm hands have a big cornshuckin' and had seed dat dey had plenty of supper and liquor to go wid it and, as was de custom dem days, some of dem Niggers got Old Marster up on deir shoulders and toted him up to de big house, singin' as dey went along. He was jus' as gay as dey was, and joked de boys. When dey put him down on de big house porch he told Old Mistess he didn't want no supper 'cept a little coffee and bread, and he strangled on de fust bite. Mistess sont for de doctor but he was too nigh gone, and it warn't long 'fore he had done gone into de glory of de next world. He was 'bout 95 years old when he died and he had sho been a good man. One of my nieces and her husband went dar atter Marse Gerald died and tuk keer of Mistess 'til she went home to glory too.

"Mammy followed Old Mistess to glory in 'bout 3 years. Us was livin' on de Johnson place den, and it warn't long 'fore me and George Kinney got married. A white preacher married us, but us didn't have no weddin' celebration. Us moved to de Joe Langford place in Oconee County, but didn't stay dar but one year; den us moved 'crost de crick into Clarke County and atter us farmed dar 9 years, us moved on to dis here place whar us has been ever since. Plain old farmin' is de most us is ever done, but George used to make some mighty nice cheers to sell to de white folks. He made 'em out of hick'ry what he seasoned jus' right and put rye split bottoms in 'em. Dem cheers lasted a lifetime; when dey got dirty you jus' washed 'em good and sot 'em in de sun to dry and dey was good as new. George made and sold a lot of rugs and mats dat he made out of plaited shucks. Most evvybody kep' a shuck footmat 'fore deir front doors. Dem sunhats made out of shucks and bulrushes was mighty fine to wear in de field when de sun was hot. Not long atter all ten of our chillun was borned, George died out and left me wid dem five boys and five gals.

"Some old witch-man conjured me into marryin' Jordan Jackson. Dat's de blessed truth, Honey; a fortune-teller is done told me how it was done. I didn't want to have nothin' to do wid Jordan 'cause I knowed he was jus' a no 'count old drinkin' man dat jus' wanted my land and stuff. When he couldn't git me to pay him no heed hisself, he went to a old conjure man and got him to put a spell on me. Honey, didn't you know dey could do dat back in dem days? I knows dey could, 'cause I never woulda run round wid no Nigger and married him if I hadn't been witched by dat conjure business. De good Lord sho punishes folks for deir sins on dis earth and dat old man what put dat spell on me died and went down to burnin' hell, and it warn't long den 'fore de spell left me.

"Right den I showed dat no 'count Jordan Jackson dat I was a good 'oman, a powerful sight above him, and dat he warn't gwine to git none of dis land what my chillun's daddy had done left 'em. When I jus' stood right up to him and showed him he warn't gwine to out whack me, he up and left me and I don't even use his name no more 'cause I don't want it in my business no way a t'all. Jordan's done paid his debt now since he died and went down in dat big old burnin' hell 'long wid de old witch man dat conjured me for him.

"Yes, Honey, de Lord done put it on record dat dere is sho a burnin' place for torment, and didn't my Marster and Mistess larn me de same thing? I sho does thank 'em to dis day for de pains dey tuk wid de little Nigger gal dat growed up to be me, tryin' to show her de right road to travel. Oh! If I could jus' see 'em one more time, but dey can look down from de glory land and see dat I'se still tryin' to follow de road dat leads to whar dey is, and when I gits to dat good and better world I jus' knows de Good Lord will let dis aged 'oman be wid her dear Marster and Mistess all through de time to come.

"Trust God, Honey, and He will lead you home to glory. I'se sho enjoyed talkin' to you, and I thanks you for comin'. I'se gwine to ax Him to take good keer of you and let you come back to cheer up old Nicey again."

PLANTATION LIFE AS VIEWED BY AN EX-SLAVE

JULIA LARKEN, Age 76
693 Meigs Street
Athens, Georgia

Written by:
Miss Grace McCune
Athens

Edited by:
Mrs. Sarah H. Hall
Athens

and
John N. Booth
District Supervisor
Federal Writers' Project
Residencies 6 & 7
Augusta, Georgia

JULIA LARKEN

Julia's small three-room cottage is a servant house at the rear of a white family's residence. A gate through an old-fashioned picket fence led into a spacious yard where dense shade from tall pecan trees was particularly inviting after a long walk in the sweltering heat.

An aged mulatto woman was seated on the narrow porch. Her straight white hair was arranged in braids, and her faded print dress and enormous checked apron were clean and carefully patched. A pair of dark colored tennis shoes completed her costume. She arose, tall and erect, to greet her visitor. "Yessum, dis here's Julia Larken," she said with a friendly smile. "Come right in, Chile, and set here and rest on my nice cool porch. I knows you's tired plumb out. You shouldn't be out walkin' 'round in dis hot sun—It ain't good for you. It'll make you have brain fever 'fore you knows it."

When asked for the story of her life, Julia replied: "Lordy, Chile, did you do all dis walkin', hot as it is today, jus' to hear dis old Nigger talk? Well, jus' let me tell you, dem days back yonder 'fore de war was de happiest time of my whole life.

"I don't know much 'bout slavery, 'cause I was jus' a little gal when de war ended. I was borned in war times on Marse Payton Sails' plantation, way off down in Lincoln County. My Ma was borned and bred right dar on dat same place. Marster bought my Daddy and his Mammy from Captain LeMars, and dey tuk de name of Sails atter dey come to live on his place. Mammy's name was Betsy Sails and Daddy was named Sam'l. Dey was married soon atter Marster fetched Daddy dar.

"Dere ain't no tellin' how big Marster's old plantation was. His house set right on top of a high hill. His plantation road circled 'round dat hill two or three times gittin' from de big road to de top of de hill. Dere was a great deep well in de yard whar dey got de water for de big house. Marster's room was upstairs and had steps on de outside dat come down into de yard. On one side of his house was a fine apple orchard, so big dat it went all de way down de hill to de big road.

"On de other side of de house was a large gyarden whar us raised evvything in de way of good veg'tables; dere was beans, corn, peas, turnips, collards, 'taters, and onions. Why dey had a big patch of nothin' but onions. Us did love onions. Dere was allus plenty of good meat in Marster's big old smokehouse dat stood close by de well. Marster, he believed in raisin' heaps of meat. He had cows, hogs, goats, and sheep, not to mention his chickens and turkeys.

"All de cloth for slaves' clothes was made at home. Mammy was one of de cooks up at de big house, and she made cloth too. Daddy was de shoe man. He made de shoes for all de folks on de plantation.

"De log cabins what de slaves lived in was off a piece from de big house. Dem cabins had rock chimblies, put together wid red mud. Dere warn't no glass in de windows and doors of dem cabins—jus' plain old home-made wooden shutters and doors." Julia laughed as she told of their beds. "Us called 'em four posters, and dat's what dey was, but dey was jus' plain old pine posties what one of de men on de plantation made up. Two posties at de head and two at de foot wid pine rails betwixt 'em was de way dey made dem beds. Dere warn't no sto'-bought steel springs dem days, not even for de white folks, but dem old cord springs went a long ways towards makin' de beds comfortable and dey helped to hold de bed together. De four poster beds de white folks slept on was corded too, but deir posties warn't made out of pine. Dey used oak and walnut and sometimes real mahogany, and dey carved 'em up pretty. Some of dem big old posties to de white folkses beds was six inches thick.

"Slaves all et up at de big house in dat long old kitchen. I kin jus' see dat kitchen now. It warn't built on to de big house, 'cept it was at de end of a big porch dat went from it to de big house. A great big fireplace was 'most all de way 'cross one end of dat kitchen, and it had racks and cranes for de pots and pans and ovens but, jus' let me tell you, our Marster had a cookstove too. Yessum, it was a real sho' 'nough iron cookstove. No'm, it warn't 'zactly lak de stoves us uses now. It was jus' a long, low stove, widout much laigs, jus' flat on top wid eyes to cook on. De oven was at de bottom. Mammy and Grandma Mary was mighty proud of dat stove, 'cause dere warn't nobody else 'round dar what had a cookstove so us was jus' plumb rich folks.

"Slaves didn't come to de house for dinner when dey was wukin' a fur piece off in de fields. It was sont to 'em, and dat was what kilt one of my brothers. Whilst it was hot, de cooks would set de bucket of dinner on his haid and tell him to run to de field wid it fore it got cold. He died wid brain fever, and de doctor said it was from totin' all dem hot victuals on his haid. Pore Brudder John, he sho' died out, and ever since den I been skeered of gittin' too hot on top of de haid.

"Dere was twelve of Mammy's chillun in all, countin' Little Peter who died out when he was a baby. De other boys was John, Tramer, Sam'l, George, and Scott. De only one of my brothers left now is George, leastwise I reckon he's livin' yet. De last 'count I had of him he was in Chicago, and he must be 'bout a hundred years old now. De gals was me and Mary, 'Merica, Hannah, Betsy, and Emma.

"'Fore Grandma Mary got too old to do all de cookin', Mammy wuked in de field. Mammy said she allus woke up early, and she could hear Marster when he started gittin' up. She would hurry and git out 'fore he had time to call 'em. Sometimes she cotch her hoss and rid to the field ahead of de others, 'cause Marster never laked for nobody to be late in de mornin'. One time he got atter one of his young slaves out in de field and told him he was a good mind to have him whupped. Dat night de young Nigger was tellin' a old slave 'bout it, and de old man jus' laughed and said: 'When Marster pesters me dat way I jus' rise up and cuss him out.' Dat young fellow 'cided he would try it out and de next time Marster got atter him dey had a rukus what I ain't never gwine to forgit. Us was all out in de yard at de big house, skeered to git a good breath when us heared Marster tell him to do somepin, 'cause us knowed what he was meanin' to do. He didn't go right ahead and mind Marster lak he had allus been used to doin'. Marster called to him again, and den dat fool Nigger cut loose and he evermore did cuss Marster out. Lordy, Chile, Marster jus' fairly tuk de hide off dat Nigger's back. When he tried to talk to dat old slave 'bout it de old man laughed and said: 'Shucks, I allus waits 'til I gits to de field to cuss Marster so he won't hear me.'

"Marster didn't have but two boys and one of 'em got kilt in de war. Dat sho'ly did hurt our good old Marster, but dat was de onliest diffunce de war made on our place. When it was over and dey said us was free, all de slaves stayed right on wid de Marster; dat was all dey knowed to do. Marster told 'em dey could stay on jus' as long as dey wanted to, and dey was right dar on dat hill 'til Marster had done died out and gone to Glory.

"Us chillun thought hog killin' time wes de best time of all de year. Us would hang 'round de pots whar dey was rendin' up de lard and all day us et dem good old browned skin cracklin's and ash roasted 'taters. Marster allus kilt from 50 to 60 hogs at a time. It tuk dat much meat to feed all de folks dat had to eat from his kitchen. Little chillun never had nothin' much to do 'cept eat and sleep and play, but now, jus' let me tell you for sho', dere warn't no runnin' 'round nights lak dey does now. Not long 'fore sundown dey give evvy slave chile a wooden bowl of buttermilk and cornpone and a wooden spoon to eat it wid. Us knowed us had to finish eatin' in time to be in bed by de time it got dark.

"Our homespun dresses had plain waisties wid long skirts gathered on to 'em. In hot weather chillun wore jus' one piece; dat was a plain slip, but in cold weather us had plenty of good warm clothes. Dey wove cotton and wool together to make warm cloth for our winter clothes and made shoes for us to wear in winter too. Marster evermore did believe in takin' good keer of his Niggers.

"I kin ricollect dat 'fore dere was any churches right in our neighborhood, slaves would walk 8 and 10 miles to church. Dey would git up 'way 'fore dawn on meetin' day, so as to git dar on time. Us wouldn't wear our shoes on dem long walks, but jus' went barfoots 'til us got nearly to de meetin' house. I jus' kin 'member dat, for chillun warn't 'lowed to try to walk dat fur a piece, but us could git up early in de mornin' and see de grown folks start off. Dey was dressed in deir best Sunday go-to-meetin' clothes and deir shoes, all shined up, was tied together and hung over deir shoulders to keep 'em from gittin' dust on 'em. [HW in margin: Sunday clothing] Men folks had on plain homespun shirts and jeans pants. De jeans what deir pants was made out of was homespun too. Some of de 'omans wore homespun dresses, but most of 'em had a calico dress what was saved special for Sunday meetin' wear. 'Omans wore two or three petticoats all ruffled and starched 'til one or dem underskirts would stand by itself. Dey went barfoots wid deir shoes hung over deir shoulders, jus' lak de mens, and evvy 'oman pinned up her dress and evvy one of her petticoats but one to keep 'em from gittin' muddy. Dresses and underskirts was made long enough to touch de ground dem days. Dey allus went off singin', and us chillun would be wishin' for de time when us would be old enough to wear long dresses wid starched petticoats and go to meetin'. Us chillun tried our best to stay 'wake 'til dey got home so us could hear 'em talk 'bout de preachin' and singin' and testifyin' for de Lord, and us allus axed how many had done jined de church dat day.

"Long 'fore I was old enough to make dat trip on foot, dey built a Baptist church nearby. It was de white folkses church, but dey let deir own Niggers join dar too, and how us chillun did love to play 'round it. No'm, us never broke out no windows or hurt nothin' playin' dar. Us warn't never 'lowed to throw no rocks when us was on de church grounds. De church was up on top of a high hill and at de bottom of dat hill was de creek whar de white folks had a fine pool for baptizin'. Dey had wooden steps to go down into it and a long wooden trough leadin' from de creek to fill up de pool whenever dere was baptizin' to be done. Dey had real sermons in dat church and folks come from miles around to see dem baptizin's. White folks was baptized fust and den de Niggers. When de time come for to baptize dem Niggers you could hear 'em singin' and shoutin' a long ways off.

"It jus' don't seem lak folks has de same sort of 'ligion now dey had dem days, 'specially when somebody dies. Den de neighbors all went to de house whar de corpse was and sung and prayed wid de fambly. De coffins had to be made atter folks was done dead. Dey measured de corpse and made de coffin 'cordin'ly. Most of 'em was made out of plain pine wood, lined wid black calico, and sometimes dey painted 'em black on de outside. Dey didn't have no 'balmers on de plantations so dey couldn't keep dead folks out long; dey had to bury 'em de very next day atter dey died. Dey put de corpse in one wagon and de fambly rode in another, but all de other folks walked to de graveyard. When dey put de coffin in de grave dey didn't have no sep'rate box to place it in, but dey did lay planks 'cross de top of it 'fore de dirt was put in. De preacher said a prayer and de folks sung _Harps from de Tomb_. Maybe several months later dey would have de funeral preached some Sunday.

"Us had all sorts of big doin's at harvest time. Dere was cornshuckin's, logrollin's, syrup makin's, and cotton pickin's. Dey tuk time about from one big plantation to another. Evvy place whar dey was a-goin' to celebrate tuk time off to cook up a lot of tasty eatments, 'specially to barbecue plenty of good meat. De Marsters at dem diffunt places allus seed dat dere was plenty of liquor passed 'round and when de wuk was done and de Niggers et all dey wanted, dey danced and played 'most all night. What us chillun laked most 'bout it was de eatin'. What I 'member best of all is de good old corn risin' lightbread. Did you ever see any of it, Chile? Why, my Mammy and Grandma Mary could bake dat bread so good it would jus' melt in your mouth.

"Mammy died whilst I was still little and Daddy married again. I guess his second wife had a time wid all of us chillun. She tried to be good to us, but I was skeered of her for a long time atter she come to our cabin. She larnt me how to make my dresses, and de fust one I made all by myself was a long sight too big for me. I tried it on and was plumb sick 'bout it bein' so big, den she said; 'Never mind, you'll grow to it.' Let me tell you, I got dat dress off in a hurry 'cause I was 'most skeered to death for fear dat if I kept it on it would grow to my skin lak I thought she meant. [HW in margin: Humor] I never put dat dress on no more for a long time and dat was atter I found out dat she jus' meant dat my dress would fit me atter I had growed a little more.

"All us chillun used to pick cotton for Marster, and he bought all our clothes and shoes. One day he told me and Mary dat us could go to de store and git us a pair of shoes apiece. 'Course us knowed what kind of shoes he meant for us to git, but Mary wanted a fine pair of Sunday shoes and dat's what she picked out and tuk home. Me, I got brass-toed brogans lak Marster meant for us to git. 'Bout half way home Mary put on her shoes and walked to de big house in 'em. When Marster seed 'em he was sho' mad as a hornet, but it was too late to take 'em back to de store atter de shoes had done been wore and was all scratched up. Marster fussed: 'Blast your hide, I'm a good mind to thrash you to death.' Mary stood dar shakin' and tremblin', but dat's all Marster ever said to her 'bout it. Us heared him tell Mist'ess dat dat gal Mary was a right smart Nigger.

"Marster had a great big old bull dat was mighty mean. He had real long horns, and he could lift de fence railin's down one by one and turn all de cows out. Evvy time he got out he would fight us chillun, so Marster had to keep him fastened up in de stable. One day when us wanted to play in de stable, us turned Old Camel (dat was de bull) out in de pasture. He tuk down rails enough wid his horns to let de cows in Marster's fine gyarden and dey et it all up. Marster was wuss dan mad dat time, but us hid in de barn under some hay 'til he went to bed. Next mornin' he called us all up to git our whuppin', but us cried and said us wouldn't never do it no more so our good old Marster let us off dat time.

"Lak I done said before, I stayed on dar 'til Marster died, den I married Matthew Hartsfield. Lordy, Chile, us didn't have no weddin'. I had on a new calico dress and Matthew wore some new blue jeans breeches. De Reverend Hargrove, de white folks preacher, married us and nobody didn't know nothin' 'bout it 'til it was all over. Us went to Oglethorpe County and lived dar 19 years 'fore Matthew died. I wuked wid white folks dar 'til I married up wid Ben Larken and us come on here to Athens to live. I have done some wuk for 'most all de white folks 'round here. Ben's grandpappy was a miller on Potts Creek, nigh Stephens, and sometimes Ben used to have to go help him out wid de wuk, atter he got old and feeble.

"Dey's all gone now and 'cept for some nieces, I'm left all alone. I kin still mind de chillun and even do a little wuk. For dat I do give thanks to de Good Lord—dat he keeps me able to do some wuk.

"Goodbye Chile," said Julia, when her visitor arose to leave. "You must be more keerful 'bout walkin' 'round when de sun is too hot. It'll make you sick sho'. Folks jus' don't know how to take de right sort of keer of deyselves dese days."

[HW: Dist. 5
Ex-Slave #67
E.F. Driskell
12/31/36]

[HW: GEORGE LEWIS]
[Date Stamp: MAY 2- --]

GEORGE LEWIS

Mr. George Lewis was born in Pensacola, Florida December 17, 1849. In addition to himself and his parents, Sophie and Charles Lewis, there were thirteen other children; two of whom were girls. Mr. Lewis (Geo.) was the third eldest child.

Although married Mr. Lewis' parents belonged to different owners. However, Dr. Brosenhan often allowed his servant to visit his wife on the plantation of her owner, Mrs. Caroline Bright.

In regard to work all of the members of the Lewis clan fared very well. The father, who belonged to Dr. Brosenhan, was a skilled shipbuilder and he was permitted to hire himself out to those needing his services. He was also allowed to hire [HW: out] those children belonging to him who were old enough to work. He was only required to pay his master and the mistress of his children a certain percent of his earnings. On the Bright plantation Mrs. Lewis served as maid and as part of her duties she had to help with the cooking. Mr. Lewis and his brothers and sisters were never required to do very much work. Most of their time was spent in playing around in the yard of the big house.

In answer to a query concerning the work requirements of the other slaves on this particular plantation Mr. Lewis replied "De sun would never ketch dem at de house. By de time it wus up dey had done got to de fiel'— not jes gwine. I've known men to have to wait till it wus bright enough to see how to plow without "kivering" the plants up. Dey lef' so early in de mornings dat breakfus' had to be sent to dem in de fiel'. De chillun was de ones who carried de meals dere. Dis was de first job dat I had. All de pails wus put on a long stick an' somebody hold to each end of de stick. If de fiel' hands was too far away fum de house at dinner time it was sent to dem de same as de breakfus'".

All of the slaves on the plantation were awakened each morning by a bugle or a horn which was blown by the overseer. The same overseer gave the signal for dinner hour by blowing on the same horn. All were usually given one hour for dinner. None had to do any work after leaving the fields unless it happened to be personal work. No work other than the caring for the stock was required on Sundays.

A few years before the Civil War Mrs. Bright married a Dr. Bennett Ferrel and moved to his home in Georgia (Troupe County).

Mr. Lewis states that he and his fellow slaves always had "pretty fair" food. Before they moved to Georgia the rations were issued daily and for the most part an issue consisted of vegetables, rice, beans, meat (pork), all kinds of fish and grits, etc.

"We got good clothes too says Mr. Lewis. All of 'em was bought. All de chillun wore a long shirt until dey wus too big an' den dey was given pants an' dresses. De shoes wus made out of red leather an' wus called brogans. After we moved to Georgia our new marster bought de cloth an' had all de clothes made on de plantation. De food wus "pretty fair" here too. We got corn bread an' biscuit sometimes—an' it was sometimes too—bacon, milk, all kinds of vegetables an' sicha stuff like dat. De flour dat we made de biscuits out of was de third grade shorts."

The food on Sunday was almost identical with that eaten during the week. However, those who desired to were allowed to hunt as much as they pleased to at night. They were not permitted to carry guns and so when the game was treed the tree had to be cut down in order to get it. It was in this way that the family larder was increased.

"All in all", says Mr. Lewis, "we got everything we wanted excep' dere wus no money comin' for our work an' we couldn't go off de place unless we asked. If you wus caught off your plantation without a permit fum marster de Paddy-Rollers whupped you an' sent you home."

The slaves living quarters were located in the rear of the "big house" (this was true of the plantation located in Pensacola as well as the one in Georgia). All were made of logs and, according to Mr. Lewis, all were substantially built. Wooden pegs were used in the place of nails and the cracks left in the walls were sealed with mud and sticks. These cabins were very comfortable and only one family was allowed to a cabin. All floors were of wood. The only furnishings were the beds and one or two benches or bales which served as chairs. In some respects these beds resembled a scaffold nailed to the side of a house.

Others were made of heavy wood and had four legs to stand upon. For the most part, however, one end of the bed was nailed to the wall. The mattresses were made out of any kind of material that a slave could secure, burlap sacks, ausenberg, etc. After a large bag had been made with this material it was stuffed with straw. Heavy cord running from side to side was used for the bed springs. The end of the cord was tied to a handle at the end of the bed. This pemitted the occupant to tighten the cord when it became loosened. A few cooking utensils completed the furnishings. All illumination was secured by means of the door and the open fire place.

All of the slaves on the plantation were permitted to "frolic" whenever they wanted to and for as long a time as they wanted to. The master gave them all of the whiskey that they desired. One of the main times for a frolic was during a corn shucking. At each frolic there was dancing, fiddling, and eating. The next morning, however all had to be prepared to report as usual to the fields.

All were required to attend church each Sunday. The same church was used by the slave owners and their slaves. The owners attended church in the morning at eleven o'clock and the slaves attended at three o'clock. A white minister did all of the preaching. "De bigges' sermon he preached", says Mr. Lewis, "was to read de Bible an' den tell us to be smart an' not to steal chickens, eggs, an' butter, fum our marsters." All baptising was done by this selfsame minister.

When a couple wished to marry the man secured the permission of his intended wife's owner and if he consented, a broom was placed on the floor and the couple jumped over it and were then pronounced man and wife.

There was not a great deal of whipping on the plantation of Dr. Ferrel but at such times all whippings were administered by one of the overseers employed on the plantation. Mr. Lewis himself was only whipped once and then by the Doctor. This was just a few days before the slaves were freed. Mr. Lewis says that the doctor came to the field one morning and called him. He told him that they were going to be freed but that before he did free him he was going to let him see what it was like to be whipped by a white man, and he proceeded to paddle him with a white oak paddle.

When there was serious illness the slaves had the attention of Dr. Ferrel. On other occasions the old remedy of castor oil and turpentine was administered. There was very little sickness then according to Mr. Lewis. Most every family kept a large pot of "Bitters" (a mixture of whiskey and tree barks) and each morning every member of the family took a drink from this bucket. This supposedly prevented illness.

When the war broke out Mr. Lewis says that he often heard the old folks whispering among themselves at night. Several times he saw the Northern troops as well as the Southern troops but he dos'nt know whether they were going or coming from the scene of the fighting. Doctor Ferrel joined the army but on three different occasions he deserted. Before going to war Dr. Ferrel called Mr. Lewis to him and after giving him his favorite horse gave him the following "charge" "Don't let the Yankees get him". Every morning Mr. Lewis would take the horse to the woods where he hid with him all day. On several occasions Dr. Ferrel slipped back to his home to see if the horse was being properly cared for. All of the other valuables belongings to the Ferrels were hidden also.

All of the slaves on the plantation were glad when they were told that they were free but there was no big demonstration as they were somewhat afraid of what the Master might do. Some of them remained on the plantation while others of them left as soon as they were told that they were free.

Several months after freedom was declared Mr. Lewis' father was able to join his family which he had not seen since they had moved to Georgia.

When asked his opinion of slavery and of freedom Mr. Lewis said that he would rather be free because to a certain degree he is able to do as he pleases, on the other hand he did not have to worry about food and shelter as a slave as he has to do now at times.

INTERVIEW WITH:
MIRRIAM McCOMMONS, Age 76
164 Augusta Avenue
Athens, Georgia

Written by:
Miss Grace McCune
Research Worker
Athens, Georgia

Edited by:
Mrs. Sarah H. Hall
Athens

John N. Booth
District Supervisor
Augusta, Georgia
[Date Stamp: APR 29 1938]

MIRRIAM MCCOMMONS

It was a bright sunny day when the interviewer stopped at the home of Aunt Merry, as she is called, and found her tending her old-fashioned flower garden. The old Negress was tired and while resting she talked of days long passed and of how things have changed since she was "a little gal."

"My pa wuz William Young, and he belonged to old Marse Wylie Young and later to young Marse Mack Young, a son of old marster. Pa wuz born in 1841, and he died in 1918.

"Ma wuz Lula Lumpkin, and she belonged to Marse Jack Lumpkin. I forgits de year, but she wuz jus' 38 years old when she died. Ma's young mistis wuz Miss Mirriam Lumpkin, and she wuz sho' good ter my ma. I 'members, 'cause I seed her lots of times. She married Marse William Nichols, and she ain't been dead many years.

"I wuz born at Steebens (Stephens), Georgia, in 1862 at seben 'clock in de mornin' on de 27th day of April. Yassum, I got here in time for breakfast. Dey named me Mirriam Young. When I wuz 'bout eight years old, us moved on de Bowling Green road dat runs to Lexin'ton, Georgia. Us stayed dar 'til I wuz 'bout 10 years old, den us moved to de old Hutchins place. I wukked in de field wid my pa 'til I wuz 'bout 'leben years old. Den ma put me out to wuk. I wukked for 25 dollars a year and my schoolin'. Den I nussed for Marse George Rice in Hutchins, Georgia. I think Marse George and his twin sister stays in Lexin'ton now. When I wuz twelve, I went to wuk for Marse John I. Callaway. Ma hired me for de same pay, 25 dollars a year and my schoolin'.

"Missus Callaway sho' wuz good to me. Sha larnt me my books—readin' and writin'—and sewin', knittin', and crochetin'. I still got some of de wuk dat she larnt me to do." At this point Aunt Merry proudly displayed a number of articles that she had crocheted and knitted. All were fashioned after old patterns and showed fine workmanship. "Mistis larnt me to be neat and clean in evvything I done, and I would walk 'long de road a-knittin' and nebber miss a stitch. I just bet none of dese young folkses now days could do dat. Dey sho' don't do no wuk, just run 'round all de time, day and night. I don't know what'll 'come of 'em, lessen dey change deir ways.

"Whilst I wuz still nussin' Missis' little gal and baby boy dey went down to Buffalo Crick to stay, and dey give me a pretty gray mare. She wuz all mine and her name wuz Lucy.

"I tuk de chillun to ride evvy day and down at de crick, I pulled off dey clo'es and baptized 'em, in de water. I would wade out in de crick wid 'em, and say: 'I baptizes you in de name of de Fadder and de Son and de Holy Ghost.' Den I would souse 'em under de water. I didn't know nobody wuz seein' me, but one mornin' Missis axed me 'bout it and I thought she mought be mad but she just laughed and said dat hit mought be good for 'em, 'cause she 'spect dey needed baptizin', but to be keerful, for just on t'other side of de rock wuz a hole dat didn't have no bottom.

"Dere wuz just two things on de place dat I wuz 'fraid of, and one wuz de big registered bull dat Marster had paid so much money for. He sho' wuz bad, and when he got out, us all stayed in de house 'til dey cotched 'im. Marster had a big black stallion dat cost lots of money. He wuz bad too, but Marster kept 'im shut up most of de time. De wust I ever wuz skeert wuz de time I wuz takin' de baby to ride horseback. When one of de Nigger boys on de place started off on Marster's horse, my mare started runnin' and I couldn't stop 'er. She runned plumb away wid me, and when de boy cotched us, I wuz holdin' de baby wid one hand and de saddle wid t'other.

"I sho' did have a big time once when us went to Atlanta. De place whar us stayed wuz 'bout four miles out, whar Kirkwood is now, and it belonged to Mrs. Robert A. Austin. She wuz a widder 'oman. She had a gal name' Mary and us chillun used to play together. It wuz a pretty place wid great big yards, and de mostes' flowers. Us used to go into Atlanta on de six 'clock 'commodation, and come home on de two 'clock 'commodation, but evvythings changed now.

"At de Callaway place us colored folks had big suppers and all day dinners, wid plenty to eat—chicken, turkey, and 'possum, and all de hogs us wanted. But dere warnt no dancin' or fightin', 'cause old Missis sho' didn't 'low dat.

"I married when I wuz sebenteen. I didn't have no weddin'. I wuz just married by de preacher to Albert McCommons, at Hutchins. Us stayed at Steebens 'bout one year after us married and den come to Athens, whar I stays now. I ain't never had but two chillun; dey wuz twins, one died, but my boy is wid me now.

"I used to nuss Miss Calline Davis, and she done got married and left here, but I still hears from 'er. She done married one of dem northern mens, Mr. Hope. I 'members one time whilst dey wuz visitin' I stayed wid 'em to nuss deir baby. One of Mr. Hope's friends from New York wuz wid 'em. When dey got to de train to go home, Miss Calline kissed me good-bye and de yankee didn't know what to say. Miss Calline say de yankees 'low dat southern folks air mean to us Niggers and just beat us all de time. Dey just don't know 'cause my white folkses wuz all good to me, and I loves 'em all."

As the interviewer left, Aunt Merry followed her into the yard asking for a return visit and promising to tell more, "bout my good white folkses."

PLANTATION LIFE

As viewed by
ED McCREE, Age 76
543 Reese Street
Athens, Georgia

Written by:
Sadie B. Hornsby [HW: (White)]
Athens

Edited by:
Sarah H. Hall
Athens

Leila Harris
Augusta

and
John N. Booth
District Supervisor
Federal Writers' Project
Residencies 6 & 7

ED MCCREE

E d McCree's home was pointed out by a little albino Negro girl about 10 years old. The small front yard was gay with snapdragons, tiger lilies, dahlias, and other colorful flowers, and the two-story frame house, painted gray with white trimmings seemed to be in far better repair than the average Negro residence.

Chewing on a cud of tobacco, Ed answered the knock on his front door. "Good evenin' Lady," he said. "Have a cheer on de porch whar it's cool." Ed is about five feet, six inches in height, and on this afternoon he was wearing a blue striped shirt, black vest, gray pants and black shoes. His gray hair was topped by a soiled gray hat.

Nett, his wife, came hobbling out on the porch and sat down to listen to the conversation. At first the old man was reluctant to talk of his childhood experiences, but his interest was aroused by questioning and soon he began to eagerly volunteer his memories. He had just had his noon meal and now and then would doze a little, but was easily aroused when questions called him back to the subject.

"I was borned in Oconee County," he said, "jus' below Watkinsville. My Ma and Pa was Louisa and Henry McCree, but Old Marster called Pa 'Sherm' for short. Far as I ever heared, my Ma and Pa was borned and brung up right dar in Oconee County. Dere was six of us chillun: Silas, Lumpkin, Bennie, Lucy, Babe, and me. Babe, she was borned a long time atter de war.

"Little Niggers, what was too young to wuk in de fields, toted water to de field hands and waited on de old 'omans what was too old to wuk in de craps. Dem old 'omans looked atter de babies and piddled 'round de yards.

"Slave quarters was lots of log cabins wid chimlies of criss-crossed sticks and mud. Pore white folks lived in houses lak dat too. Our bed was made wid high posties and had cords, what run evvy which a-way, for springs. 'Course dey had to be wound tight to keep dem beds from fallin' down when you tried to git in 'em. For mattresses, de 'omans put wheat straw in ticks made out of coarse cloth wove right dar on de plantation, and de pillows was made de same way. Ole Miss, she let her special favorite Niggers, what wuked up at de big house, have feather mattresses and pillows. Dem other Niggers shined dey eyes over dat, but dere warn't nothin' dey could do 'bout it 'cept slip 'round and cut dem feather beds and pillows open jus' to see de feathers fly. Kivver was 'lowanced out evvy year to de ones what needed it most. In dat way dere was allus good kivver for evvybody.

"Grandma Liza b'longed to Marse Calvin Johnson long 'fore Marse John McCree buyed her. She was cook at de big house. Grandpa Charlie, he b'longed to Marse Charlie Hardin, but atter him and Grandma married, she still went by de name of McCree.

"Lawdy Miss! Who ever heared of folks payin' slaves to wuk? Leastwise, I never knowed 'bout none of 'em on our place gittin' money for what dey done. 'Course dey give us plenty of somepin' t'eat and clothes to wear, and den dey made us keep a-humpin' it. I does 'member seein' dem paper nickels, dimes, and quarters what us chillun played wid atter de war. Us used to pretend us was rich wid all dat old money what warn't no good den.

"'Bout dem eatments, Miss, it was lek dis, dere warn't no fancy victuals lak us thinks us got to have now, but what dere was, dere was plenty of. Most times dere was poke sallet, turnip greens, old blue head collards, cabbages, peas, and 'taters by de wholesale for de slaves to eat and, onct a week, dey rationed us out wheat bread, syrup, brown sugar, and ginger cakes. What dey give chillun de most of was potlicker poured over cornbread crumbs in a long trough. For fresh meat, outside of killin' a shoat, a lamb, or a kid now and den, slaves was 'lowed to go huntin' a right smart and dey fotch in a good many turkles (turtles), 'possums, rabbits, and fish. Folks didn't know what iron cookstoves was dem days. Leastwise, our white folks didn't have none of 'em. All our cookin' was done in open fireplaces in big old pots and pans. Dey had thick iron skillets wid heavy lids on 'em, and dey could bake and fry too in dem skillets. De meats, cornbread, biscuits, and cakes what was cooked in dem old skillets was sho' mighty good.

"De cotton, flax, and wool what our clothes was made out of was growed, spun, wove, and sewed right dar on our plantation. Marse John had a reg'lar seamster what didn't do nothin' else but sew. Summertime us chillun wore shirts what looked lak nightgowns. You jus' pulled one of dem slips over your haid and went on 'cause you was done dressed for de whole week, day and night. Wintertime our clothes was a heap better. Dey give us thick jeans pants, heavy shirts, and brogan shoes wid brass toes. Summertime us all went bar'foots.

"Old Marster John McCree was sho' a good white man, I jus' tells you de truf, 'cause I ain't in for tellin' nothin' else. I done jus' plum forgot Ole Miss' fust name, and I can't git up de chilluns' names no way. I didn't play 'round wid 'em much nohow. Dey was jus' little young chillun den anyhow. Dey lived in a big old plank house—nothin' fine 'bout it. I 'members de heavy timbers was mortised together and de other lumber was put on wid pegs; dere warn't no nails 'bout it. Dat's all I ricollects 'bout dat dere house right now. It was jus' a common house, I'd say.

"Dere was a thousand or more acres in dat old plantation. It sho' was a big piece of land, and it was plumb full of Niggers—I couldn't say how many, 'cause I done forgot. You could hear dat bugle de overseer blowed to wake up de slaves for miles and miles. He got 'em up long 'fore sunup and wuked 'em in de fields long as dey could see how to wuk. Don't talk 'bout dat overseer whuppin' Niggers. He beat on 'em for most anything. What would dey need no jail for wid dat old overseer a-comin' down on 'em wid dat rawhide bull-whup?

"If dey got any larnin', it was at night. Dere warn't no school 'ouse or no church on dat plantation for Niggers. Slaves had to git a pass when dey wanted to go to church. Sometimes de white preacher preached to de Niggers, but most of de time a Nigger wid a good wit done de preachin'. Dat Nigger, he sho' couldn't read nary a word out of de Bible. At de baptizin's was when de Nigger boys shined up to de gals. Dey dammed up de crick to make de water deep enough to duck 'em under good and, durin' de service, dey sung: _It's de Good Old Time Religion_.

"When folks died den, Niggers for miles and miles around went to de funeral. Now days dey got to know you mighty well if dey bothers to go a t'all. Dem days folks was buried in homemade coffins. Some of dem coffins was painted and lined wid cloth and some warn't. De onliest song I ricollects 'em singin' at buryin's was: _Am I Born to Lay Dis Body Down_? Dey didn't dig graves lak dey does now. Dey jus' dug straight down to 'bout five feet, den dey cut a vault to fit de coffin in de side of de grave. Dey didn't put no boards or nothin' over de coffins to keep de dirt off.

"'Bout dem patterollers! Well, you knowed if dey cotched you out widout no pass, dey was gwine to beat your back most off and send you on home. One night my Pa 'lowed he would go to see his gal. All right, he went.

When he got back, his cabin door was fastened hard and fast. He was a-climbin' in de window when de patterollers got to him. Dey 'lowed: 'Nigger, is you got a pass?' Pa said: 'No Sir.' Den dey said: 'Us can't beat you 'cause you done got home on your marster's place, but us is sho' gwine to tell your Marster to whup your hide off. But Old Marster never tetched him for dat.

"Atter dey come in from de fields, dem Niggers et deir supper, went to deir cabins, sot down and rested a little while, and den dey drapped down on de beds to sleep. Dey didn't wuk none Sadday atter dinner in de fields. Dat was wash day for slave 'omans. De mens done fust one thing and den another. Dey cleant up de yards, chopped wood, mended de harness, sharpened plow points, and things lak dat. Sadday nights, Old Marster give de young folks passes so dey could go from one place to another a-dancin' and a-frolickin' and havin' a big time gen'ally. Dey done most anything dey wanted to on Sundays, so long as dey behaved deyselfs and had deir passes handy to show if de patterollers bothered 'em.

"Yessum, slaves sho' looked forward to Christmas times. Dere was such extra good eatin's dat week and so much of 'em. Old Marster had 'em kill a plenty of shoats, lambs, kids, cows, and turkeys for fresh meat. De 'omans up at de big house was busy for a week ahead cookin' peach puffs, 'tater custards, and plenty of cakes sweetened wid brown sugar and syrup. Dere was plenty of home-made candy for de chilluns' Santa Claus and late apples and peaches had done been saved and banked in wheat straw to keep 'em good 'til Christmas. Watermelons was packed away in cottonseed and when dey cut 'em open on Christmas Dey, dey et lak fresh melons in

July. Us had a high old time for a week, and den on New Year's Day dey started back to wuk.

"Come winter, de mens had big cornshuckin's and dere was quiltin's for de 'omans. Dere was a row of corn to be shucked as long as from here to Milledge Avenue. Old Marster put a gang of Niggers at each end of de row and it was a hot race 'tween dem gangs to see which could git to de middle fust. Dere was allus a big feast waitin' for 'em when de last ear of corn was shucked. 'Bout dem quiltin's!" Now Lady, what would a old Nigger man know 'bout somepin' dat didn't nothin' but 'omans have nothin' to do wid?

"Dem cotton pickin's was grand times. Dey picked cotton in de moonlight and den had a big feast of barbecued beef, mutton, and pork washed down wid plenty of good whiskey. Atter de feast was over, some of dem Niggers played fiddles and picked banjoes for de others to dance down 'til dey was wore out.

"When slaves got sick, our white folks was mighty good 'bout havin' 'em keered for. Dey dosed 'em up wid oil and turpentine and give 'em teas made out of hoarhound for some mis'ries and bone-set for other troubles. Most all the slaves wore a sack of assfiddy (asafetida) 'round deir necks all de time to keep 'em from gittin' sick.

"It was a happy day for us slaves when news come dat de war was over and de white folks had to turn us 'loose. Marster called his Niggers to come up to de big house yard, but I never stayed 'round to see what he had to say. I runned 'round dat place a-shoutin' to de top of my voice. My folks stayed on wid Old Marster for 'bout a year or more. If us had left, it would have been jus' lak swappin' places from de fryin' pan to de fire, 'cause Niggers didn't have no money to buy no land wid for a long time atter de war. Schools was soon scattered 'bout by dem Yankees what had done sot us free. I warn't big enough den to do nothin' much 'cept tote water to de field and chop a little cotton.

"Me and Nettie Freeman married a long time atter de war. At our weddin' I wore a pair of brown jeans pants, white shirt, white vest, and a cutaway coat. Nettie wore a black silk dress what she had done bought from Miss Blanche Rutherford. Pears lak to me it had a overskirt of blue what was scalloped 'round de bottom."

At this point, Nettie, who had been an interested listener, was delighted. She broke into the conversation with: "Ed, you sho' did take in dat dress and you ain't forgot it yit."

"You is right 'bout dat, Honey," he smilingly replied, "I sho' ain't and I never will forgit how you looked dat day."

"Miss Blanche give me a pair of white silk gloves to wear wid dat dress," mused Nettie.

"Us didn't have no sho' 'nough weddin'," continued Ed. "Us jus' went off to de preacher man's house and got married up together. I sho' is glad my Nett is still a-livin', even if she is down wid de rheumatiz."

"I'm glad I'm livin' too," Nettie said with a chuckle.

Ed ignored the question as to the number of their children and Nettie made no attempt to take further part in the conversation. There is a deep seated idea prevalent among old people of this type that if the "giver'ment folks" learn that they have able-bodied children, their pensions and relief allowances will be discontinued.

Soon Ed was willing to talk again. "Yessum," he said. "I sho' had ruther be free. I don't never want to be a slave no more. Now if me and Nett wants to, us can set around and not fix and eat but one meal all day long. If us don't want to do dat, us can do jus' whatsomever us pleases. Den, us had to wuk whether us laked it or not.

"Lordy Miss, I ain't never jined up wid no church. I ain't got no reason why, only I jus' ain't never had no urge from inside of me to jine. 'Course, you know, evvybody ought to lissen to de services in de church and live right and den dey wouldn't be so skeered to die. Miss, ain't you through axin' me questions yit? I is so sleepy, and I don't know no more to tell you. Goodbye."

United States. Work Projects Administration

[HW: Dist. 1
Ex Slave #68]

EX-SLAVE INTERVIEW:
LUCY McCULLOUGH, Age 79

BY: SARAH H. HALL
ATHENS, GA.
[Date Stamp: MAY 8 1937]

[TR: This first half of this interview was edited by hand to change many 'er' sounds to 'uh', for example, 'der' to 'duh', 'ter' to 'tuh'; as a single word, 'er' was also changed to 'a'.]

LUCY MCCULLOUGH,

"Does Ah 'member 'bout war time, en dem days fo' de war? Yassum, Ah sho' does. Ah blong ter Marse Ned Carter in Walton county."

"Whut Ah 'members mos' is duh onliest beatin' Ah ebber got fum de overseer on Marse Ned's place. De hawgs wuz dyin' moughty bad wid cholry, en Marse Ned hed 'is mens drag evvy dead hawg off in de woods 'en bun 'em up ter keep de cholry fum spreadin' mongst de udder hawgs. De mens wuz keerless 'bout de fire, en fo' long de woods wuz on fire, en de way dat fire spread in dem dry grape vines in de woods mek it 'peer lak jedgment day tuh us chilluns. Us run 'bout de woods lookin' at de mens fight de fire, en evvy time we see uh new place a-blaze we run dis way en dat way, twel fus' thing us knows, we is plum off Marse Ned's plantation, en us doan rightly know whar us is. Us play 'roun' in de woods en arter while

Marse Ned's overseer cum fine us, en he druv us back tuh de big house yahd en give evvy one uv us uh good beaten'. Ah sho' wuz black en blue, en Ah nebber did fuhgit en run offen Marse Ned's lan' no mo' lessen I hed uh pass."

"Mah mammy, she wuz cook at duh big house, en Ah wuz raised dah in de kitchen en de back yahd at de big house. Ah wuz tuh be uh maid fer de ladies in de big house. De house servants hold that dey is uh step better den de field niggers. House servants wuz niggah quality folks."

Ah mus' not a been mo' en thee uh fo' yeahs ole when Miss Millie cum out in de kitchen one day, en 'gin tuh scold my mammy 'bout de sorry way mammy done clean de chitlins. Ah ain' nebber heard nobuddy fuss et my mammy befo'. Little ez Ah wuz, Ah swell up en rar' back, en I sez tuh Miss Millie, "Doan you no' Mammy is boss uh dis hyar kitchen. You cyan' cum a fussin' in hyar." "Miss Millie, she jus laff, but Mammy grab a switch en 'gin ticklin' my laigs, but Miss Millie mek her quit it." "Who wuz Miss Millie? Why, she wuz Marse Ned's wife."

"Whilst Marse Ned wuz 'way at de war, bad sojer mens cum thoo de country. Miss Millie done hyar tell dey wuz on de way, an she had de mens haul all Marse Ned's cotton off in de woods en hide it. De waggins wuz piled up high wid cotton, en de groun' wuz soft atter de rain. De waggins leff deep ruts in de groun', but none us folks on de plantation pay no heed ter dem ruts. When de sojer mens cum, dey see dem ruts en trail 'em right out dar in de woods ter de cotton. Den dey sot fire ter de cotton en bun it all up. Dey cum back ter de big house en take all de sweet milk in de dairy house, en help 'emselfs ter evvy thing in de smoke houses. Den dey pick out de stronges' er Marse Ned's slave mens en take 'em 'way wid 'em. Dey take evvy good horse Marse Ned had on de plantation. No Ma'am, dey diden' bun nuffin ceppen' de cotton."

"Us wuz mo' skeered er patter-rollers den any thing else. Patter-rollers diden' bodder folks much, lessen dey caught 'em offen dar marsters plantations en dey diden' hab no pass. One night en durin' de war, de patter-rollers cum ter our cabin, en I scrooge down under de kiver in de bed. De patter-roller man tho' de kiver offen mah face, en he see me blong dar, en he let me be, but Ah wuz skeered plumb ter death. Courtin' folks got ketched en beat up by de patter-rollers mo' den enny buddy else, kazen dey wuz allus slippen' out fer ter meet one er nudder at night."

"When folks dat lived on diffunt plantations, en blonged ter diffunt marsters wanted ter git married, dey hed ter ax both dar marsters fus'. Den effen dar marsters 'gree on it, dey let 'em marry. De mans marster 'ud give de man er pass so he cud go see his wife et night, but he sho' better be back on his own marsters farm when de bell ring evvy morning. De chilluns 'ud blong ter de marster dat own de 'oman."

"Black folks wuz heap smarter den dey is now. Dem days de 'omans knowed how ter cyard, en spin, en weave de cloff, en dey made de close. De mens know how ter mek shoes ter wear den. Black folks diden' hev ter go cole er hongry den, kaze dey marsters made 'em wuk en grow good crops, en den der marsters fed 'em plenty en tuk keer uv 'em."

"Black folks wuz better folks den dey is now. Dey knowed dey hed ter be good er dey got beat. De gals dey diden't sho' dare laigs lak dey do now. Cloff hed ter be made den, en hit wuz er heap mo' trouble ter mek er yahd er cloff, den it is ter buy it now, but 'omans en gals, dey stayed kivvered up better den. Why, Ah 'member one time my mammy seed me cummin' crost de yahd en she say mah dress too short. She tuk it offen me, en rip out de hem, en ravel at de aig' er little, en den fus' thing I knows, she got dat dress tail on ter de loom, en weave more cloff on hit, twel it long enuf, lak she want it."

"Long 'bout dat time dey wuz killin' hawgs on de plantation, en it wuz er moughty cole day. Miss Millie, she tell me fer ter tote dis quart er brandy out dar fer ter warm up de mens dat wuz er wukkin in de cole win'. 'Long de way, Ah keep er sippin' dat brandy, en time Ah got ter de hawg killin' place Ah wuz crazy drunk en tryin' ter sing. Dat time 'twon't no overseer beat me. Dem slave mens beat me den fo' drinkin' dat likker."

"Mah folks stayed on en wukked fo' Marse Ned long atter de war. When Ah wuz mos' grown mah fam'ly moved ter Logansville. No, Ma'am, I ain't nebber been so free en happy es when I diden' hev ter worry 'bout whar de vittles en close gwine cum fum, en all Ah had ter do wuz wuk evvy day lak mah whitefolks tole me."

[HW: Dist. 5 (Driskell)
Ex Slave #69]

AMANDA MCDANIEL, 80 yrs old
Ex-slave
[Date Stamp: MAY 8 1937]

AMANDA MCDANIEL

Among these few remaining persons who have lived long enough to tell of some of their experiences during the reign of "King Slavery" in the United States is one Mrs. Amanda McDaniel.

As she sat on the porch in the glare of the warm October sun she presented a perfect picture of the old Negro Mammy commonly seen during the days of slavery. She smiled as she expectorated a large amount of the snuff she was chewing and began her story in the following manner: "I was born in Watsonville, Georgia in 1850. My mother's name was Matilda Hale and my father was Gilbert Whitlew. My mother and father belonged to different master's, but the plantations that they lived on were near each other and so my father was allowed to visit us often. My mother had two other girls who were my half-sisters. You see—my mother was sold to the speculator in Virginia and brought to Georgia where she was sold to Mr. Hale, who was our master until freedom was declared. When she was sold to the speculator the two girls who were my half-sisters had to be sold with her because they were too young to be separated from their mother. My father, Gilbert Whitlew, was my mother's second husband.

"Mr. Hale, our master, was not rich like some of the other planters in the community. His plantation was a small one and he only had eight servants who were all women. He wasn't able to hire an overseer and all of the heavy work such as the plowing was done by his sons. Mrs. Hale did all of her own cooking and that of the slaves too. In all Mr. Hale had eleven children. I had to nurse three of them before I was old enough to go to the field to work."

When asked to tell about the kind of work the slaves had to do Mrs. McDaniel said: "Our folks had to get up at four o'clock every morning and feed the stock first. By the time it was light enough to see they had to be in the fields where they hoed the cotton and the corn as well as the other crops. Between ten and eleven o'clock everybody left the field and went to the house where they worked until it was too dark to see. My first job was to take breakfast to those working in the fields. I used buckets for this. Besides this I had to drive the cows to and from the pasture. The rest of the day was spent in taking care of Mrs. Hale's young children. After a few years of this I was sent to the fields where I planted peas, corn, etc. I also had to pick cotton when that time came, but I never had to hoe and do the heavy work like my mother and sisters did." According to Mrs. McDaniel they were seldom required to work at night after they had left the fields but when such occasions did arise they were usually in the form of spinning thread and weaving cloth. During the winter months this was the only type of work that they did. On days when the weather was too bad for work out of doors they shelled the corn and peas and did other minor types of work not requiring too much exposure. Nobody had to work on Saturday afternoons or on Sundays. It was on Saturdays or at night that the slaves had the chance to do their own work such as the repairing of clothing, etc.

On the Hale plantation clothing was issued two times each year, once at the beginning of summer and again at the beginning of the winter season. On this first issue all were given striped dresses made of cotton material. These dresses were for wear during the week while dresses made of white muslin were given for Sunday wear. The dye which was necessary in order to color those clothes worn during the week was made by boiling red dirt or the bark of trees in water. Sometimes the indigo berry was also used. The winter issue consisted of dresses made of woolen material. The socks and stockings were all knitted. All of this wearing apparel was made by Mrs. Hale. The shoes that these women slaves wore were made in the nearby town at a place known as the tan yards. These shoes were called "Brogans" and they were very crude in construction having been made of very stiff leather. None of the clothing that was worn on this plantation was bought as everything necessary for the manufacture of clothing was available on the premises.

As has been previously stated, Mrs. Hale did all of the cooking on the plantation with the possible exception of Sundays when the slaves cooked for themselves. During the week their diet usually consisted of corn bread, fat meat, vegetables, milk, and potliquor. The food that they ate on Sunday was practically the same. All the food that they ate was produced in the master's garden and there was a sufficient amount for everyone at all times.

There were two one-room log cabins in the rear of the master's house. These cabins were dedicated to slave use. Mrs. McDaniel says: "The floors were made of heavy wooden planks. At one end of the cabin was the chimney which was made out of dried mud, sticks, and dirt. On the side of the cabin opposite the door there was a window where we got a little air and a little light. Our beds were made out of the same kind of wood that the floors were and we called them "Bed-Stilts." Slats were used for springs while the mattresses were made of large bags stuffed with straw. At night we used tallow candles for light and sometimes fat pine that we called light-wood. As Mrs. Hale did all of our cooking we had very few pots and pans. In the Winter months we used to take mud and close the cracks left in the wall where the logs did not fit close together."

According to Mrs. McDaniel all the serious illnesses were handled by a doctor who was called in at such times. At other times Mr. or Mrs. Hale gave them either castor oil or salts. Sometimes they were given a type of oil called "lobelia oil." At the beginning of the spring season they drank various teas made out of the roots that they gathered in the surrounding woods. The only one that Mrs. McDaniel remembers is that which was made from sassafras roots. "This was good to clean the system," says Mrs. McDaniel. Whenever they were sick they did not have to report to the master's house each day as was the case on some of the other plantations. There were never any pretended illnesses to avoid work as far as Mrs. McDaniel knows.

On Sunday all of the slaves on the Hale plantation were permitted to dress in their Sunday clothes and go to the white church in town. During the morning services they sat in the back of the church where they listened to the white pastor deliver the sermon. In the afternoon they listened to a sermon that was preached by a colored minister. Mrs. McDaniel hasn't the slightest idea of what these sermons were about. She remembers how marriages were performed, however, although the only one that she ever witnessed took place on one of the neighboring plantations. After a broom was placed on the ground a white minister read the scriptures and then the couple in the process of being married jumped over this broom. They were then considered as man and wife.

Whippings were very uncommon the the Hale plantation. Sometimes Mr. Hale had to resort to this form of punishment for disobedience on the part of some of the servants. Mrs. McDaniel says that she was whipped many times but only once with the cowhide. Nearly every time that she was whipped a switch was used. She has seen her mother as well as some of the others punished but they were never beaten unmercifully. Neither she or any of the other slaves on the Hale plantation ever came in contact with the "Paddie-Rollers," whom they knew as a group of white men who went around whipping slaves who were caught away from their respective homes without passes from their masters. When asked about the buying and the selling of slaves Mrs. McDaniel said that she had never witnessed an auction at which slaves were being sold and that the only thing she knew about this was what she had been told by her mother who had been separated from her husband and sold in Georgia. Mr. Hale never had the occasion to sell any of those slaves that he held.

Mrs. McDaniel remembers nothing of the talk that

transpired between the slaves or her owners at the beginning of the war. She says: "I was a little girl, and like the other children then, I didn't have as much sense as the children of today who are of the age that I was then. I do remember that my master moved somewhere near Macon, Georgia after General Wheeler marched through. I believe that he did more damage than the Yanks did when they came through. When my master moved us along with his family we had to go out of the way a great deal because General Wheeler had destroyed all of the bridges. Besides this he damaged a great deal of the property that he passed." Continuing, Mrs. McDaniel said: "I didn't see any of the fighting but I did hear the firing of the cannons. I also saw any number of Confederate soldiers pass by our place." Mr. Hale didn't join the army although his oldest son did.

At the time that the slaves were freed it meant nothing in particular to Mrs. McDaniel, who says that she was too young to pay much attention to what was happening. She never saw her father after they moved away from Watsonville. At any rate she and her mother remained in the service of Mr. Hale for a number of years after the war. In the course of this time Mr. Hale grew to be a wealthy man. He continued to be good to those servants who remained with him. After she was a grown woman Mrs. McDaniel left Mr. Hale as she was then married.

Mrs. McDaniel says that she has reached such an old age because she has always taken care of herself, which is more than the young people of today are doing, she added as an after thought.

Dist. 7
Ex. Slave #74

TOM McGRUDER, 102 years old
Ex-Slave

By Elizabeth Watson, Hawkinsville, Georgia
[Date Stamp: MAY 8 1937]

TOM MCGRUDER

Tom McGruder, one of the oldest living ex-slaves in Pulaski County, was sitting on the porch of his son's home when we went in to see him. His grizzled old head began to nod a "Good morning" and his brown face became wreathed in smiles when he saw us.

He looked very small as he sat in a low straight chair by the door. His shirt and overalls were ragged but spotlessly clean. On his feet were heavy shoes that were kept free from dirt. His complexion was not black as some of the other members of his race but was a light brown. There were very few wrinkles in his face considering the fact that he was one hundred and two years old in June. He spoke in a quiet voice though somewhat falteringly as he suffers greatly from asthma.

"Were you born in this county, Uncle Tom?" we asked.

"No mam, Missus," he replied. "Me and my mother and sister wuz brought from Virginia to this state by the speculators and sold here. I was only about eighteen or twenty and I was sold for $1250. My mother was given to one of Old Marster's married chillun.

"You see, Missus," he spoke again after a long pause. "We wuz put on the block just like cattle and sold to one man today and another tomorrow. I wuz sold three times after coming to this state."

Tom could tell us very little about his life on the large plantations because his feeble old mind would only be clear at intervals. He would begin relating some incident but would suddenly break off with, "I'd better leave that alone 'cause I done forgot." He remembered, however, that he trained dogs for his "whie folks," trained them to be good hunters as that was one of the favorite sports of the day.

The last man to whom Tom was sold was Mr. Jim McGruder, of Emanuel County. He was living in a small cabin belonging to Mr. McGruder, when he married. "I 'members", said Tom, "That Old Marster and Missus fixed up a lunch and they and their chillun brought it to my cabin. Then they said, 'Nigger, jump the broom' and we wuz married, 'cause you see we didn't know nothing 'bout no cer'mony."

It was with Mr. McGruder that Tom entered the army, working for him as his valet.

"I wuz in the army for 'bout four years," Tom said. "I fought in the battles at Petersburg, Virginia and Chattanooga, Tennessee. I looked after Old Marster's shoes and clothes. Old Marster, what he done he done well. He was kind to me and I guess better to me sometimes than I deserved but I had to do what he told me."

"Do you remember any of the old songs you used to sing?" we asked. "Missus, I can't sing no mo'," he replied. But pausing for a few minutes he raised his head and sang in a quiet voice, the words and melody perfectly clear;

> "Why do you wait, dear brother,
>
> Oh, why do you tarry so long?
>
> Your Saviour is waiting to give you
>
> A place in His sanctified throng."

United States. Work Projects Administration

PLANTATION LIFE as viewed by ex-slave

SUSAN McINTOSH, Age 87
1203 W. Hancook Avenue
Athens, Georgia

Written by:
Sadie B. Hornsby
Federal Writers' Project
Athens, Ga.

Edited by:
Sarah H. Hall
Athens

John N. Booth
Augusta

Leila Harris
Augusta

April 28, 1938
[Date Stamp: MAY 6 1938]

SUSAN MCINTOSH

A driving rain sent the interviewer scurrying into the house of Susan McIntosh who lives with her son, Dr. Andrew Jones, at the corner of Hancock Avenue and Billups Street.

Susan readily gave her story: "They tell me I was born in November 1851," she said, "and I know I've been here a long time 'cause I've seen so many come and go. I've outlived 'most all of my folks 'cept my son that I live with now. Honey, I've 'most forgot about slavery days. I don't read, and anyway there ain't no need to think of them times now. I was born in Oconee County on Judge William Stroud's plantation. We called him Marse Billy. That was a long time before Athens was the county seat. Ma's name was Mary Jen, and Pa was Christopher Harris. They called him Chris for short. Marster Young L.G. Harris bought him from Marster Hudson of Elbert County and turned him over to his niece, Miss Lula Harris, when she married Marster Robert Taylor. Marse Robert was a son of General Taylor what lived in the Grady house before it belonged to Mr. Henry Grady's mother. Pa was coachman and house boy for Miss Lula.

"Marse Billy owned Ma, and Marse Robert owned Pa, and Pa, he come to see Ma about once or twice a month. The Taylor's, they done a heap of travellin' and always took my Pa with 'em. Oh! there was thirteen of us chillun, seven died soon after they was born, and none of 'em lived to git grown 'cept me. Their names was Nanette and Ella, what was next to me; Susan—thats me; Isabelle, Martha, Mary, Diana, Lila, William, Gus, and the twins what was born dead; and Harden. He was named for a Dr. Harden what lived here then.

"Marse Billy bought my gran'ma in Virginia. She was part Injun. I can see her long, straight, black hair now, and when she died she didn't have gray hair like mine. They say Injuns don't turn gray like other folks. Gran'ma made cloth for the white folks and slaves on the plantation. I used to hand her thread while she was weavin'. The lady what taught Gran'ma to weave cloth, was Mist'ess Gowel, and she was a foreigner, 'cause she warn't born in Georgia. She had two sons what run the factory between Watkinsville and Athens. My aunt, Mila

Jackson, made all the thread what they done the weavin' with. Gran'pa worked for a widow lady what was a simster (seamstress) and she just had a little plantation. She was Mist'ess Doolittle. All Gran'pa done was cut wood, 'tend the yard and gyarden. He had rheumatism and couldn't do much.

"There ain't much to tell about what we done in the slave quarters, 'cause when we got big enough, we had to work: nussin' the babies, totin' water, and helpin' Gran'ma with the weavin', and such like. Beds was driv to the walls of the cabin; foot and headboard put together with rails, what run from head to foot. Planks was laid crossways and straw put on them and the beds was kivvered with the whitest sheets you ever seen. Some made pallets on the floor.

"No, Ma'am, I didn't make no money 'til after freedom. I heard tell of ten and fifteen cents, but I didn't know nothing 'bout no figgers. I didn't know a nickel from a dime them days.

"Yes, Ma'am, Marse Billy 'lowed his slaves to have their own gyardens, and 'sides plenty of good gyarden sass, we had milk and butter, bread and meat, chickens, greens, peas, and just everything that growed on the farm. Winter and summer, all the food was cooked in a great big fireplace, about four feet wide, and you could put on a whole stick of cord wood at a time. When they wanted plenty of hot ashes to bake with, they burnt wood from ash trees. Sweet potatoes and bread was baked in the ashes. Seems like vittuls don't taste as good as they used to, when we cooked like that. 'Possums, Oh! I dearly love 'possums. My cousins used to catch 'em and when they was fixed up and cooked with sweet potatoes, 'possum meat was fit for a king. Marse Billy had a son named Mark, what was a little bitty man. They said he was a dwarf. He never done nothing but play with the children on the plantation. He would take the children down to the crick what run through the plantation and fish all day. We had rabbits, but they was most generally caught in a box trap, so there warn't no time wasted a-huntin' for 'em.

"In summer, the slave women wore white homespun and the men wore pants and shirts made out of cloth what looked like overall cloth does now. In winter, we wore the same things, 'cept Marse Billy give the men woolen coats what come down to their knees, and the women wore warm wraps what they called sacks. On Sunday we had dresses dyed different colors. The dyes were made from red clay and barks. Bark from pines, sweetgums, and blackjacks was boiled, and each one made a different color dye. The cloth made at home was coarse and was called 'gusta cloth. Marse Billy let the slaves raise chickens, and cows, and have cotton patches too. They would sell butter, eggs, chickens, brooms, made out of wheat straw and such like. They took the money and bought calico, muslin and good shoes, pants, coats and other nice things for their Sunday clothes. Marse Billy bought leather from Marster Brumby's tanyard and had shoes made for us. They was coarse and rough, but they lasted a long time.

"My Marster was father-in-law of Dr. Jones Long. Marse Billy's wife, Miss Rena, died long before I was born. Their six children was all grown when I first knowed 'em. The gals was: Miss Rena, Miss Selena, Miss Liza, and Miss Susan. Miss Susan was Dr. Long's wife. I was named for her. There was two boys; Marse John and

Marse Mark. I done told you 'bout Marse Mark bein' a dwarf. They lived in a big old eight room house, on a high hill in sight of Mars Hill Baptist Church. Marse Billy was a great deacon in that church. Yes, Ma'am, he sho' was good to his Negroes. I heard 'em say that after he had done bought his slaves by working in a blacksmith shop, and wearin' cheap clothes, like mulberry suspenders, he warn't goin' to slash his Negroes up. The older folks admired Mist'ess and spoke well of her. They said she had lots more property than Marse Billy. She said she wanted Marse Billy to see that her slaves was give to her children. I 'spose there was about a hundred acres on that plantation and Marse Billy owned more property besides. There was about fifty grown folks and as to the children, I just don't know how many there was. Around the quarters looked like a little town.

"Marse Billy had a overseer up to the time War broke out, then he picked out a reliable colored man to carry out his orders. Sometimes the overseer got rough, then Marse Billy let him go and got another one. The overseer got us up about four or five o'clock in the morning, and dark brought us in at night.

"Jails! Yes, Ma'am, I ricollect one was in Watkinsville. No, Ma'am, I never saw nobody auctioned off, but I heard about it. Men used to come through an buy up slaves for foreign states where there warn't so many.

"Well, I didn't have no privilege to learn to read and write, but the white lady what taught my gran'ma to weave, had two sons what run the factory, and they taught my uncles to read and write.

"There warn't no church on the plantation, so we went

to Mars Hill Church. The white folks went in the mornings from nine 'til twelve and the slaves went in the evenings from three 'till about five. The white folks went in the front door and slaves used the back door. Rev. Bedford Lankford, what preached to the white folks helped a Negro, named Cy Stroud, to preach to the Negroes. Oh! Yes, Ma'am, I well remembers them baptizings. I believe in church and baptizing.

"They buried the slaves on the plantation, in coffins made out of pine boards. Didn't put them in two boxes lak dey does now, and dey warn't painted needer.

"Did you say patterollers? Sho' I seen 'em, but they didn't come on our plantation, 'cause Marse Billy was good to his Negroes and when they wanted a pass, if it was for a good reason, he give 'em one. Didn't none of Marse Billy's slaves run off to no North. When Marse Billy had need to send news somewhere, he put a reliable Negro on a mule and sent him. I sho' didn't hear about no trouble twixt white folks and Negroes.

"I tell you, Honey, when the days work was over them slaves went to bed, 'cep' when the moon was out and they worked in their own cotton patches. On dark nights, the women mended and quilted sometimes. Not many worked in the fields on Saturday evenin's. They caught up on little jobs aroun' the lot; a mending harness and such like. On Saturday nights the young folks got together and had little frolics and feasts, but the older folks was gettin' things ready for Sunday, 'cause Marse Billy was a mighty religious man: we had to go to church, and every last one of the children was dragged along too.

"We always had one week for Christmas. They

brought us as much of good things to eat as we could destroy in one week, but on New Year's Day we went back to work. No, Ma'am, as I ricollect, we didn't have no corn shuckings or cotton pickings only what we had to do as part of our regular work.

"The white folks mostly got married on Wednesday or Thursday evenin's. Oh! they had fine times, with everything good to eat, and lots of dancing too. Then they took a trip. Some went to Texas and some to Chicago. They call Chicago, the colored folks' New York now. I don't remember no weddings 'mongst the slaves. My cousin married on another plantation, but I warn't there.

"Where I was, there warn't no playing done, only 'mongst the little chillun, and I can't remember much that far back. I recall that we sung a little song, about:

> 'Little drops of water
>
> Little grains of sand,
>
> Make the mighty ocean
>
> And the pleasant land.'

"Oh! Yes, Ma'am, Marse Billy was good to his slaves, when they got sick. He called in Dr. Jones Long, Dr. Harden, and Dr. Lumpkin when they was real sick. There was lots of typhoid fever then. I don't know nothing about no herbs, they used for diseases; only boneset and hoarhound tea for colds and croup. They put penrile (pennyroyal) in the house to keep out flies and fleas, and if there was a flea in the house he would shoo from that place right then and there.

"The old folks put little bags of assfiddy (assafoetida) around their chillun's necks to keep off measles and chickenpox, and they used turpentine and castor oil on chillun's gums to make 'em teethe easy. When I was living on Milledge Avenue, I had Dr. Crawford W. Long to see about one of my babies, and he slit that baby's gums so the teeth could come through. That looked might bad to me, but they don't believe in old ways no more."

She laughed and said: "No, Ma'am, I don't know nothing about such low down things as hants and ghosts! Rawhead and Bloody Bones, I just thought he was a skelerpin, with no meat on him. Course lots of Negroes believe in ghosts and hants. Us chillun done lots of flightin' like chillun will do. I remember how little Marse Mark Stroud used to take all the little boys on the plantation and teach 'em to play Dixie on reeds what they called quills. That was good music, but the radio has done away with all that now.

"I knowed I was a slave and that it was the War that sot me free. It was 'bout dinner time when Marse Billy come to the door and called us to the house. He pulled out a paper and read it to us, and then he said: 'You all are free, as I am.' We couldn't help thinking about what a good marster he always had been, and how old, and feeble, and gray headed he looked as he kept on a-talkin' that day. 'You all can stay on here with me if you want to,' he 'lowed, 'but if you do, I will have to pay you wages for your work.'

"I never saw no Yankees in Athens, but I was in Atlanta at Mrs. Winship's on Peachtree Street, when General Sherman come to that town 'parin' his men for to go home. There was about two thousand in all, white and black. They marched up and down Marietta Street from three o'clock in the evening 'til seven o'clock next morning. Then they left. I remember well that there warn't a house left standing in Atlanta, what warn't riddled with shell holes. I was scared pretty nigh to death and I never want to leave home at no time like that again. But Pa saw 'em soon after that in Athens. They was a marching down Broad Street on their way to Macon, and Pa said it looked like a blue cloud going through.

"Ma and me stayed on with Marse Billy 'bout six months after the War ended before we come to town to live with Pa. We lived right back of Rock College and Ma took in washin' for the folks what went to school there. No, Ma'am I never saw no Ku Kluxers. Me and Ma didn't leave home at night and the white folks wouldn't let 'em git Pa.

"Major Knox brought three or four teachers to teach in a school for Negroes that was started up here the first year after the War. Major Knox, he was left like a sort of Justice of Peace to get things to going smooth after the War. I went to school there about three months, then Ma took sick, and I didn't go no more. My white teacher was Miss Sarah, and she was from Chicago.

"Now and then the Negroes bought a little land, and white folks gave little places to some Negroes what had been good slaves for 'em.

"I didn't take in about Mr. Abraham Lincoln. A long time after the War, I heard 'em say he got killed. I knowed Mr. Jeff. Davis was President of the Confederacy. As for Booker Washington, I never saw him, but I heard his son whan he was here once and gave a musical of some sort at the Congregational Church.

"I was a old gal when I married 'bout thirty or forty years after the War. I married George McIntosh. Wedding clothes!" she chuckled, and said: "I didn't have many. I bought 'em second hand from Mrs. Ed. Bond. They was nice though. The dress I married in was red silk. We had a little cake and wine; no big to do, just a little fambly affair. Of our four chillun, two died young, and two lived to git grown. My daughter was a school teacher and she has been dead sometime. I stays wid my only living child. My husban' died a long time ago.

"I cooked and washed for Mr. Prince Hodgson for thirty years. Miss Mary Franklin used to tell me 'bout all them strange places she had been to while she was paintin'. There never was nobody in this town could paint prettier pictures than Miss Mary's.

"I'm glad slavery is over. I'm too old to really work anymore, but I'm like a fish going down the crick and if he sees a bug he will catch him if he can.

"I joined the church 'cause I believe in the Son of God. I know he is a forgiving God, and will give me a place to rest after I am gone from the earth. Everybody ought to 'pare for the promised land, where they can live always after they are done with this world."

After the interview, she said: "Honey, this is the most I have talked about slavery days in twelve years; and I believe what I told you is right. Of course, lots has faded from my mind about it now."

District #7
Adella S. Dixon, Macon, Georgia

MATILDA McKINNEY
100 Empire Avenue, Macon, Georgia
[Date Stamp: JUL 28 1937]

MATILDA MCKINNEY

Matilda McKinney was born in Texas but was brought to southwest Georgia, near Albany, at an early age. Her mother, Amy Dean, had eight children, of which Aunt Matilda is the eldest. The plantation on which they lived was owned by Mr. Milton Ball, and it varied little in size or arrangement from the average one of that time. Here was found the usual two-story white house finished with high columns and surrounded by trees.

Most of the Negro mothers did field work, so it was necessary for others to care for the children. Mr. Ball handled this problem in the usual way. He established what would today be called a day nursery. Each mother brought her offspring to the home of an elderly woman before leaving for her day's work. Here, they were safely kept until their parents returned. The midday meal for everyone was prepared at the Big House and the slaves were served from huge tubs of vegetables and pots of meat. "Aunt" Julia was responsible for the children's noon meal.

When "Aunt" Matilda was old enough to do a little work, she was moved into the house where she swept floors, waited on the table, and fanned flies while a meal was being served. The adult females who lived in the house did most of the weaving and sewing. All the summer, garments were made and put away for winter use. Two dresses of osnaburg were then given each person.

The field hands, always considered an inferior group by the house servants, worked from sunup to sundown. When they returned from the fields they prepared supper for their families and many times had to feed the children in the dark, for a curfew horn was blown and no lights could be lighted after its warning note had sounded. There was very little visiting to or from the group which dwelt here, as the curfew hour was early.

Saturday varied a little from the other week days. The field work was suspended in the afternoon to allow the mothers time to wash their clothing. With sunset came the preparations for the weekly frolic. A fiddler furnished music while the dancers danced numerous square dances until a late hour.

Home remedies for illness were used much more extensively than any doctor's medicine. Teas, compounded from sage, boneset, tansy, and mullen, usually sufficed for any minor sickness, and serious illness was rare.

Food was distributed on Sunday morning. Two-and-a-half pounds of meat, a quantity of syrup, and a peck of meal were given each adult for the week. A special ration for Sunday alone was potatoes, buttermilk, and material for biscuits. Each family had its own garden from which a supply of vegetables could always be obtained in season. The smaller children had additional delicacies, for they early learned that the house where produce was kept had holes in the floor which yielded peanuts, etc, when punched with a stick.

"Aunt" Matilda was unable to give any information regarding the war, but remembers that her family remained at her former owner's plantation for some time after they were freed. She now lives with her granddaughter who takes excellent care of her. Her long life is attributed to her habit of going to bed early and otherwise caring for herself properly.

United States. Work Projects Administration

PLANTATION LIFE AS VIEWED BY EX-SLAVE

WILLIAM McWHORTER, Age 78
383 W. Broad Street
Athens, Georgia

Written by:
Mrs. Sadie B. Hornsby
Athens

Edited by:
Mrs. Sarah H. Hall
Athens

and
John N. Booth
District Supervisor
Federal Writers' Project
Residencies 6 & 7
Augusta, Ga.

Sept. 30, 1938

WILLIAM MCWHORTER

The rambling, one-story frame building where William McWhorter makes his home with his cousin, Sarah Craddock, houses several families and is proudly referred to by the neighbors as "de 'partment house."

William, better known as "Shug," is a very black man of medium build. He wore a black slouch hat pulled well down over tangled gray hair, a dingy blue shirt, soiled gray pants, and black shoes. The smile faded from his face when he learned the nature of the visit. "I thought you was de pension lady 'comin' to fetch me some money," he said, "and 'stid of dat you wants to know 'bout slavery days. I'se disapp'inted.

"Mistess, it's been a long time since I was born on Marse Joe McWhorter's plantation down in Greene County and I was jus' a little fellow when slavery was done over wid. Allen and Martha McWhorter was my ma and pa. Pa, he was de carriage driver, and ma, she was a field hand. Dey brought her here from Oingebug (Orangeburg), South Carolina, and sold her to Marse Joe when she was jus' a little gal. Me and Annie, Ella, Jim, and Tom was all de chillun in our fambly, and none of us warn't big enough to do no wuk to speak of 'fore de end of de big war. You see, Mistess, it was lak dis; Marse Joe, he owned a old 'oman what didn't do nothin' 'cept stay at de house and look atter us chillun, and dat was one of dem plantations whar dere was sho a heap of slave chillun.

"'Bout our houses? Mistess, I'se gwine to tell you de trufe, dem houses slaves had to live in, dey warn't much, but us didn't know no better den. Dey was jus' one-room log cabins wid stick and dirt chimblies. De beds for slaves was home-made and was held together wid cords wove evvy which away. If you didn't tighten dem cords up pretty offen your bed was apt to fall down wid you. Suggin sacks was sewed together to make our mattress ticks and dem ticks was filled wid straw. Now, don't tell me you ain't heared of suggin sacks a-fore! Dem was coarse sacks sort of lak de guano sacks us uses now. Dey crowded jus' as many Niggers into each cabin as could sleep in one room, and marriage never meant a thing in dem days when dey was 'rangin' sleepin' quarters for slaves. Why, I knowed a man what had two wives livin' in de same cabin; one of dem 'omans had all boys and t'other one didn't have nothin' but gals. It's nigh de same way now, but dey don't live in de same house if a man's got two famblies.

"I 'members dat my pa's ma, Grandma Cindy, was a field hand, but by de time I was old 'nough to take things in she was too old for dat sort of wuk and Marster let her do odd jobs 'round de big house. De most I seed her doin' was settin' 'round smokin' her old corncob pipe. I was named for Grandpa Billy, but I never seed him.

"Mistess, does you know what you'se axin'? Whar was slaves to git money whilst dey was still slaves? Dere warn't but a few of 'em dat knowed what money even looked lak 'til atter dey was made free.

"Now, you is talkin' 'bout somepin sho 'nough when you starts 'bout dem victuals. Marse Joe, he give us plenty of sich as collards, turnips and greens, peas, 'taters, meat, and cornbread. Lots of de cornbread was baked in pones on spiders, but ashcakes was a mighty go in dem days. Marster raised lots of cane so as to have plenty of good syrup. My pa used to 'possum hunt lots and he was 'lowed to keep a good 'possum hound to trail 'em wid. Rabbits and squirrels was plentiful and dey made mighty good eatin'. You ain't never seed sich heaps of fish as slaves used to fetch back atter a little time spent fishin' in de cricks and de river.

"De kitchen was sot off from de big house a little piece, but Old Marster had a roof built over de walkway so fallin' weather wouldn't spile de victuals whilst dey was bein' toted from de kitchen in de yard to de dinin' room in de big house. I don't reckon you ever seed as big a fireplace as de one dey cooked on in dat old kitchen. It had plenty of room for enough pots, skillets, spiders, and ovens to cook for all de folks on dat plantation. No, mam, slaves never had no gardens of deir own; dey never had no time of deir own to wuk no garden, but Old Marster fed 'em from his garden and dat was big enough to raise plenty for all.

"De one little cotton shirt dat was all chillun wore in summertime den warn't worth talkin' 'bout; dey called it a shirt but it looked more lak a long-tailed nightgown to me. For winter, our clothes was made of wool cloth and dey was nice and warm. Mistess, slaves never knowed what Sunday clothes was, 'cept dey did know dey had to be clean on Sunday. No matter how dirty you went in de week-a-days, you had to put on clean clothes Sunday mornin'. Uncle John Craddock made shoes for all de grown folks on our plantation, but chillun went barfoots and it never seemed to make 'em sick; for a fact, I b'lieves dey was stouter den dan dey is now.

"Marse Joe McWhorter and his wife, Miss Emily Key, owned us, and dey was jus' as good to us as dey could be. Mistess, you knows white folks had to make slaves what b'longed to 'em mind and be-have deyselfs in dem days or else dere woulda been a heap of trouble. De big fine house what Marse Joe and his fambly lived in sot in a cedar grove and Woodville was de town nighest de place. Oh! Yes, mam, dey had a overseer all right, but I'se done forgot his name, and somehow I can't git up de names of Marse Joe's chillun. I'se been sick so long my mem'ry ain't as good as it used to be, and since I lost my old 'oman 'bout 2 months ago, I don't 'spect I ever kin reckomember much no more. It seems lak I'se done told you my pa was Marse Joe's carriage driver. He driv de fambly whar-some-ever dey wanted to go.

"I ain't got no idee how many acres was in dat great big old plantation, but I'se heared 'em say Marse Joe had to keep from 30 to 40 slaves, not countin' chillun, to wuk dat part of it dat was cleared land. Dey told me, atter I was old enough to take it in, dat de overseer sho did drive dem slaves; dey had to be up and in de field 'fore sunup and he wuked 'em 'til slap, black dark. When dey got back to de big house, 'fore dey et supper, de overseer got out his big bull whip and beat de ones dat hadn't done to suit him durin' de day. He made 'em strip off deir clothes down to de waist, and evvywhar dat old bull whip struck it split de skin. Dat was awful, awful! Sometimes slaves dat had been beat and butchered up so bad by dat overseer man would run away, and next day Aunt Suke would be sho to go down to de spring to wash so she could leave some old clothes dar for 'em to git at night. I'se tellin' you, slaves sho did fare common in dem days.

"My Aunt Mary b'longed to Marse John Craddock and when his wife died and left a little baby—dat was little Miss Lucy—Aunt Mary was nussin' a new baby of her own, so Marse John made her let his baby suck too. If Aunt Mary was feedin' her own baby and Miss Lucy started cryin' Marse John would snatch her baby up by the legs and spank him, and tell Aunt Mary to go on and nuss his baby fust. Aunt Mary couldn't answer him a word, but my ma said she offen seed Aunt Mary cry 'til de tears met under her chin.

"I ain't never heared nothin' 'bout no jails in slavery time. What dey done den was 'most beat de life out of de Niggers to make 'em be-have. Ma was brung to Bairdstown and sold on de block to Marse Joe long 'fore I was borned, but I ain't never seed no slaves sold. Lordy, Mistess, ain't nobody never told you it was agin de law to larn a Nigger to read and write in slavery time? White folks would chop your hands off for dat quicker dan dey would for 'most anything else. Dat's jus' a sayin', 'chop your hands off.' Why, Mistess, a Nigger widout no hands wouldn't be able to wuk much, and his owner couldn't sell him for nigh as much as he could git for a slave wid good hands. Dey jus' beat 'em up bad when dey cotched 'em studyin' readin' and writin', but folks did tell 'bout some of de owners dat cut off one finger evvy time dey cotch a slave tryin' to git larnin'. How-some-ever, dere was some Niggers dat wanted larnin' so bad dey would slip out at night and meet in a deep gully whar dey would study by de light of light'ood torches; but one thing sho, dey better not let no white folks find out 'bout it, and if dey was lucky 'nough to be able to keep it up 'til dey larned to read de Bible, dey kept it a close secret.

"Slaves warn't 'lowed to have no churches of dey own and dey had to go to church wid de white folks. Dere warn't no room for chillun in de Baptist church at Bairdstown whar Marse Joe tuk his grown-up slaves to meetin', so I never did git to go to none, but he used to take my ma along, but she was baptized by a white preacher when she jined up wid dat church. De crick was nigh de church and dat was whar dey done de baptizin'.

"None of our Niggers never knowed enough 'bout de North to run off up dar. Lak I done told you, some of 'em did run off atter a bad beatin', but dey jus' went to de woods. Some of 'em come right on back, but some didn't; Us never knowed whar dem what didn't come back went. Show me a slavery-time Nigger dat ain't heared 'bout paterollers! Mistess, I 'clar to goodness, paterollers was de devil's own hosses. If dey cotched a Nigger out and his Marster hadn't fixed him up wid a pass, it was jus' too bad; dey most kilt him. You couldn't even go to de Lord's house on Sunday 'less you had a ticket sayin': 'Dis Nigger is de propity of Marse Joe McWhorter. Let him go.'

"Dere warn't never no let-up when it come to wuk. When slaves come in from de fields atter sundown and tended de stock and et supper, de mens still had to shuck corn, mend hoss collars, cut wood, and sich lak; de 'omans mended clothes, spun thread, wove cloth, and some of 'em had to go up to de big house and nuss de white folks' babies. One night my ma had been nussin' one of dem white babies, and atter it dozed off to sleep she went to lay it in its little bed. De child's foot cotch itself in Marse Joe's galluses dat he had done hung on de foot of de bed, and when he heared his baby cry Marse Joe woke up and grabbed up a stick of wood and beat ma over de head 'til he 'most kilt her. Ma never did seem right atter dat and when she died she still had a big old knot on her head.

"Dey said on some plantations slaves was let off from wuk when de dinner bell rung on Saddays, but not on our'n; dere warn't never no let-up 'til sundown on Sadday nights atter dey had tended to de stock and et supper. On Sundays dey was 'lowed to visit 'round a little atter dey had 'tended church, but dey still had to be keerful to have a pass wid 'em. Marse Joe let his slaves have one day for holiday at Christmas and he give 'em plenty of extra good somepin t'eat and drink on dat special day. New Year's Day was de hardest day of de whole year, for de overseer jus' tried hisself to see how hard he could drive de Niggers dat day, and when de wuk was all done de day ended off wid a big pot of cornfield peas and hog jowl to eat for luck. Dat was s'posed to be a sign of plenty too.

"Cornshuckin's was a mighty go dem days, and folks from miles and miles around was axed. When de wuk was done dey had a big time eatin', drinkin', wrestlin', dancin', and all sorts of frolickin'. Even wid all dat liquor flowin' so free at cornshuckin's I never heared of nobody gittin' mad, and Marse Joe never said a cross word at his cornshuckin's. He allus picked bright moonshiny nights for dem big cotton pickin's, and dere warn't nothin' short 'bout de big eats dat was waitin' for dem Niggers when de cotton was all picked out. De young folks danced and cut up evvy chanct dey got and called deyselfs havin' a big time.

"Games? Well, 'bout de biggest things us played when I was a chap was baseball, softball, and marbles. Us made our own marbles out of clay and baked 'em in de sun, and our baseballs and softballs was made out of rags.

"Does I know anything 'bout ghosties? Yes, mam, I sees ha'nts and ghosties any time. Jus' t'other night I seed a man widout no head, and de old witches 'most nigh rides me to death. One of 'em got holt of me night 'fore last and 'most choked me to death; she was in de form of a black cat. Mistess, some folks say dat to see things lak dat is a sign your blood is out of order. Now, me, I don't know what makes me see 'em.

"Marse Joe tuk mighty good keer of sick slaves. He allus called in a doctor for 'em, and kept plenty of castor ile, turpentine, and de lak on hand to dose 'em wid. Miss Emily made teas out of a heap of sorts of leaves, barks, and roots, sich as butterfly root, pine tops, mullein, catnip and mint leaves, feverfew grass, red oak bark, slippery ellum bark, and black gum chips. Most evvybody had to wear little sacks of papaw seeds or of assyfizzy (asafetida) 'round deir necks to keep off diseases.

"Dey used to say dat a free Nigger from de North come through de South and seed how de white folks was treatin' his race, den he went back up der and told folks 'bout it and axed 'em to holp do somepin' 'bout it. Dat's what I heared tell was de way de big war got started dat ended in settin' slaves free. My folks said dat when de Yankee sojers come through, Miss Emily was cryin' and takin' on to beat de band. She had all her silver in her apron and didn't know whar to hide it, so atter awhile she handed it to her cook and told her to hide it. De cook put it in de woodpile. De Yankee mens broke in de smokehouse, brought out meat and lard, kilt chickens, driv off cows and hosses, but dey never found Miss Emily's silver. It was a long time 'fore our fambly left Marse Joe's place.

"Marse Joe never did tell his Niggers dey was free. One day one of dem Yankee sojers rid through de fields whar dey was wukin' and he axed 'em if dey didn't know dey was as free as deir Marster. Dat Yankee kept on talkin' and told em dey didn't have to stay on wid Marse Joe 'less dey wanted to, end dey didn't have to do nothin' nobody told 'em to if dey didn't want to do it. He said dey was deir own bosses and was to do as dey pleased from de time of de surrender.

"Schools was sot up for slaves not long atter dey was sot free, and a few of de old Marsters give deir Niggers a little land, but not many of 'em done dat. Jus' as de Niggers was branchin' out and startin' to live lak free folks, dem nightriders come 'long beatin', cuttin', and slashin' 'em up, but I 'spects some of dem Niggers needed evvy lick dey got.

"Now, Mistess, you knows all Niggers would ruther be free, and I ain't no diffunt from nobody else 'bout dat. Yes, mam, I'se mighty glad Mr. Abraham Lincoln and Jeff Davis fit 'til dey sot us free. Dat Jeff Davis ought to be 'shamed of hisself to want Niggers kept in bondage; dey says dough, dat he was a mighty good man, and Miss Millie Rutherford said some fine things 'bout him in her book what Sarah read to me, but you can't 'spect us Niggers to b'lieve he was so awful good.

"Me and Rosa Barrow had a pretty fair weddin' and a mighty fine supper. I don't ricollect what she had on, but I'se tellin' you she looked pretty and sweet to me. Our two boys and three gals is done growed up and I'se got three grandchillun now. Rosa, she died out 'bout 2 months ago and I'se gwine to marry agin soon as I finds somebody to take keer of me.

"I was happier de day I jined de church at Sander's Chapel, dan I'se been since. It was de joyfullest day of all my life, so far. Folks ought to git ready for a better world dan dis to live in when dey is finished on dis earth, and I'se sho glad our Good Lord saw fit to set us free from sin end slavery. If he hadn't done it, I sho would have been dead long ago. Yistidday I picked a little cotton to git me some bread, and it laid me out. I can't wuk no more. I don't know how de Blessed Lord means to provide for me but I feels sho He ain't gwine to let me perish."

United States. Work Projects Administration

[HW: Dist. 6:
Ex-Slave #72]

Henrietta Carlisle
Alberta Minor
Re-search Workers

MOLLIE MALONE—EX-SLAVE
Route B, Griffin, Georgia
Interviewed

September 16, 1936
[Date Stamp: MAY 8 1937]

MOLLIE MALONE

Mollie was born on a plantation owned by Mr Valentine Brook, near Locust Grove, Georgia. Mr. Brook died before the War and his wife, "the widder Brock", ran the plantation.

Slaves not needed on the home plantation were "hired out" to other land owners for from $200.00 to $300.00 a year. This was done the first of each year by an auction from a "horse block". When Mollie was seven months old her mother, Clacy Brock, was "hired out" and she was taken care of by two old Negroes, too old to work, and who did nothing but care for the little "Niggers". Mollie grew up with these children between the "big house" and the kitchen. When she was old enough she was "put to mind" the smaller children and if they did'nt behave she pinched them, but "when the 'ole Miss found it out, she'd sure 'whup me'", she said. These children were fed cornbread and milk for breakfast and supper, and "pot licker" with cornbread for dinner. They slept in a large room on quilts or pallets. Each night the larger children were given so many "cuts" to spin, and were punished if all weren't finished. The thread was woven into cloth on the loom and made into clothes by the slaves who did the sewing. There were no "store bought" clothes, and Mollie was free before she ever owned a pair of shoes. Clothes had to be furnished by the owner for the slaves he "hired out".

Mr. and Mrs. Brock had two daughters, Margaret and Mary Anne, who led very quiet secluded lives. Mollie remembers visits of the traveling preacher, who conducted services in a nearby church once a month. The slaves walked behind the White folks' carriages to and from the church, where they were seated in the rear during the services. If there were baptisms, the Whites were baptized first, then the Darkies.

On this plantation the Negroes were not allowed to engage in any frolics or attend social gatherings. They only knew Christmas by the return of the hired out slaves, who came home for a week before the next auction.

The young lady daughters of Mr. and Mrs. Brock wore "drag tail" dresses, and Mollie says the little Negroes had to hold these long skirts off the ground whenever they were out doors, then spread them as they went into the house so they could "strut."

The children were not allowed any education other than the "old Miss" reading them the Bible on Sunday afternoons.

The older Negroes were not allowed to visit on other plantations often, but when they did go they had to have passes from their masters or the "patarolers" would whip them—if they were caught.

Hoar-hound and penny-royal were used for minor ailments, and "varnish" was put on cuts by the "ole Miss". Mollie doesn't remember ever seeing a doctor, other than a mid-wife, on the plantation. Home made remedies for "palpitation of the heart" was to wear tied around the neck a piece of lead, pounded into the shape of the heart, and punched with nine holes, or to get some one "not kin to you", to tie some salt in a small bag and wear it over your heart. Toothache was cured by smoking a pipe of "life everlasting", commonly called "rabbit tobacco". Headaches were stopped by beating the whites of an egg stiff, adding soda and putting on a cloth, then tying around the head.

Mr. Brock died before the War, consequently not having any men to go from the plantation, Mollie knew very little about it. She remembers Confederate soldiers "practicin" at Locust Grove, the nearest town, and one time the Yankees came to the plantation and "took off" a horse Mrs. Brock had hidden in the swamp, also all the silver found buried.

Mollie knew nothing of the freedom of the slaves until her mother came to get her. For two years they "hired out" on a farm in Butts County, where they worked in the fields. Several times in later years Mollie returned to the Brock plantation to see "the ole Miss" and the young Misses. Mrs. Brock and her daughters, who had never married, died on the plantation where they had always lived.

Mollie's family "knocked around awhile", and then came to Griffin where they have since made their home. She became a familiar figure driving an ox-cart on the streets and doing odd jobs for White families and leading a useful life in the community. Besides her own family, Mollie has raised fifteen orphaned Negro children. She is approximately ninety years old, being "about growd" when the War ended.

District Two
EX-SLAVE INTERVIEW

AUNT CARRIE MASON
Milledgeville, Georgia
(Baldwin County)

Written By:
Mrs. Estelle G. Burke
Research Worker
Federal Writers' Project
Milledgeville, Georgia

Edited By:
John N. Booth
Asst. District Supervisor
Federal Writers' Project
Athens, Georgia

July 7, 1937
[Date Stamp: JUL 20 1937]

CARRIE MASON

"Howdy, Miss, Howdy. Come on in. George is poly today. My grandchillun is doin' a little cleanin' up fer me 'cause us thinks George ain't got long on this earth an' us don' want de place ter be dirty an' all when he's gone."

The home of Aunt Carrie and Uncle George Mason, a two-room cabin surrounded by a dirty yard, stands in a clearing. Old tin cans, bottles, dusty fruit jars, and piles of rat-tail cotton from gutted mattresses littered the place. An immense sugarberry tree, beautifully proportioned, casts inviting shade directly in front of the stoop. It is the only redeeming feature about the premises. Aunt Carrie, feeble and gray haired, hobbled out in the yard with the aid of a stick.

"Have a seat, Miss. Dat cheer is all right. It won't fall down. Don't git yo' feet wet in dat dirty water. My grandchillun is scourin' terday. Effen yer want to, us'll set under de tree. Dey's a cool breeze dar all de time.

"You wants to fin' out my age an' all? Law Miss, I don' know how ole I is. George is nigh 'bout 90. I 'members my mammy said I wuz bawn a mont' or two 'fore freedom wuz 'clared. Yas'um I rekymembers all 'bout de Yankees. How cum I 'members 'bout dem an' de war wuz over den? I cain't tell yer dat, but I knows I 'members seein' 'em in de big road. It mought not uv been Mister Sherman's mens but mammy said de Yankees wuz in de big road long after freedom wuz 'clared, and dey wuz down here gettin' things straight. Dey wuz sho' in er mess atter de war! Evvythin' wuz tore up an' de po' niggers didn't know which away to turn.

"My mammy's name wuz Catherine Bass an' my pappy wuz Ephriam Butts. Us b'longed ter Mars' Ben Bass an' my mammy had de same name ez marster twell she ma'ied pappy. He b'longed ter somebody else 'til marster bought him. Dey had ten chillun. No, mam, Mammy didn't have no doctor," Aunt Carrie chuckled, "Didn't nobody hardly have a doctor in dem days. De white folks used yarbs an' ole 'omans to he'p 'em at dat time. Mammy had er ole 'oman whut lived on de place evvy time she had a little 'un. She had one evvy year too. She lost one. Dat chile run aroun' 'til she wuz one year ole an' den died wid de disentery.

"Us had er right hard time in dem days. De beds us used den warn't like dese here nice beds us has nowadays. Don't you laugh, Berry, I knows dese beds us got now is 'bout to fall down," Aunt Carrie admonished her grandson when he guffawed at her statement, "You chilluns run erlong now an' git thoo' wid dat cleanin'." Aunt Carrie's spirits seemed dampened by Berry's rude laugh and it was several minutes before she started talking again. "Dese young folks don't know nuthin' 'bout hard times. Us wukked in de ole days frum before sunup 'til black night an' us knowed whut wuk wuz. De beds us slep' on had roun' postes made outen saplins of hickory or little pine trees. De bark wuz tuk off an' dey wuz rubbed slick an' shiny. De sprangs wuz rope crossed frum one side uv de bed to de udder. De mattress wuz straw or cotton in big sacks made outen osnaberg or big salt sacks pieced tergether. Mammy didn't have much soap an' she uster scrub de flo' wid sand an' it wuz jes ez white. Yas mam, she made all de soap us used, but it tuk a heap. We'uns cooked in de ashes an' on hot coals, but de vittals tasted a heap better'n dey does nowadays. Mammy had to wuk in de fiel' an' den cum home an' cook fer marster an' his fambly. I didn' know nuthin' 'bout it 'till atter freedom but I hyearn 'em tell 'bout it.

"Mammy an' pappy stayed on Marster's plantation 'til a year or mo' atter dey had dey freedom. Marster paid 'em wages an' a house ter stay in. He didn't hav' many slaves, 'bout 20, I reckon. My brothers wuz Berry, Dani'l, Ephriam, Tully, Bob, Lin, an' George. De yuthers I disremembers, caze dey lef' home when dey wuz big enough to earn dey livin' an' I jes don't recollec'.

"Conjur' woman! Law miss, I aims ter git ter Hebem

when I dies an' I show don't know how ter conjur' nobody. No mam, I ain't never seed no ghost. I allus pray to de Lord dat He spar' me dat trouble an' not let me see nary one. No good in folks plunderin' on dis earth atter dey leave here de fus time. Go 'way, dog."

A spotted hound, lean and flop-eared was scratching industriously under Aunt Carrie's chair. It was a still summer day and the flies droned ceaselessly. A well nearby creaked as the dripping bucket was drawn to the top by a granddaughter who had come in from the field to get a cool drink. Aunt Carrie watched the girl for a moment and then went back to her story.

"Effen my mammy or pappy ever runned away from Marster, I ain't heered tell uv it, but Mammy said dat when slaves did run away, dey wuz cotched an' whupped by de overseer. Effen a man or a 'oman kilt another one den dey wuz branded wid er hot i'on. Er big S wuz put on dey face somewhars. S stood fer 'slave, 'an' evvybody knowed dey wuz er mudderer. Marster din't have no overseer; he overseed hisself.

"Why is George so white? 'Cause his marster wuz er white genemun named Mister Jimmie Dunn. His mammy wuz er cullud 'oman name' Frances Mason an' his marster wuz his paw. Yas mam, I see you is s'prised, but dat happ'ned a lots in dem days. I hyeared tell of er white man what would tell his sons ter 'go down ter dem nigger quarters an' git me mo' slaves.' Yas mam, when George wuz borned ter his mamny, his pappy wuz er white man an' he made George his overseer ez soon ez he wuz big e'nuf ter boss de yuther slaves. I wish he wuz able to tell yer 'bout it, but since he had dat las' stroke he ain't been able ter talk none."

Aunt Carrie took an old clay pipe from her apron pocket and filled it with dry scraps of chewing tobacco. After lighting it she puffed quietly and seemed to be meditating. Finally she took it from her mouth and continued.

"I ain't had no eddication. I 'tended school part of one term but I wuz so skairt of my teacher that I couldn't larn nuthin'. He wuz a ole white man. He had been teachin' fer years an' years, but he had a cancer an' dey had done stopped him frum teachin' white chillun'. His name wuz Mister Bill Greer. I wuz skairt 'cause he was a white man. No mam, no white man ain't never harmed me, but I wuz skairt of him enyhow. One day he says to me, 'chile I ain't goin to hurt yer none 'cause I'm white.' He wuz a mighty good ole man. He would have larned us mo' but he died de nex' year. Mammy paid him ten cents a mont' a piece fer all us chillun. De boys would wuk fer dey money but I wuz the onliest gal an' Mammy wouldn't let me go off de plantation to make none. Whut I made dar I got, but I didn't make much 'til atter I ma'ied.

"Law honey, does yer want to know 'bout my ma'ige? Well, I wuz 15 years ole an' I had a preacher to ma'y me. His name wuz Andrew Brown. In dem days us allus waited 'til de time of year when us had a big meetin' or at Christmus time. Den effen one of us wanted ter git mai'ed, he would perform de weddin' atter de meetin' or atter Chris'mus celebratin'. I had er bluish worsted dress. I mai'ed in Jannywerry, right atter Chris'mus. At my mai'ge us had barbecue, brunswick stew, an' cake. De whole yard wuz full uv folks.

"Mammy wuz a 'ligous 'oman an' de fust day of Chris'mus she allus fasted ha'f a day an' den she would pray. Atter dat evvybody would hav' eggnog an' barbecue an' cake effen dey had de money to buy it. Mammy said dat when dey wuz still slaves Marster allus gived 'em Chris'mus, but atter dey had freedom den dey had ter buy dey own rations. Us would have banjer playin' an' dance de pijen-wing and de shuffle-toe.

"No mam, George's pa didn' leave him no lan' when he died. Us went ter another farm an' rented when de mai'ge wuz over. George's pa warn't dead, but he didn't offer to do nuthin' fer us.

"Yas'um, I'se had eight chilluns of my own. Us ain' never had no lan' us could call our'n. Us jes moved from one farm ter another all our days. This here lan' us is on now 'longs ter Mr. Cline. My son an' his chillun wuks it an' dey give us whut dey kin spare. De Red Cross lady he'ps us an' us gits along somehow or nother."

Works Progress Administration
Harry L. Hopkins, Administrator
Ellen S. Woodward, Assistant Administrator
Henry S. Alsberg, Director of the Federal Writers' Project

PLANTATION LIFE

Interview with:
SUSAN MATTHEWS, Age 84
Madison Street,
Macon, Georgia

Written by:
Ruth H. Sanford,
Macon, Georgia

Edited by:
Annie A. Rose,
Macon, Georgia

SUSAN MATTHEWS

Susan Matthews is an intelligent old negress, very tall and weighing close to two hundred pounds. Her eyes were bright, her "store-bought" teeth flashed in a smile as she expressed her willingness to tell us all she remembered "'bout ole times." In a tattered, faded print dress, a misshapen hat and ragged shoes, she sat enjoying the sunshine on the porch while she sewed on an underskirt she was making for herself from old sugar sacks. Her manner was cheerful; she seemed to get genuine enjoyment from the interview and gave us a hearty invitation to come to see her again.

"I was jes a chile" she began, "when de white folks had slaves. My ma an her chillen wuz the onliest slaves my marster and mistis had. My pa belonged to some mo white folks that lived 'bout five miles from us. My marster and mistis were poor folks. They lived in a white frame house; it wuz jes a little house that had 'bout five rooms, I reckon. The house had a kitchen in the backyard and the house my ma lived wuz in the back yard too, but I wuz raised in my mistis' house. I slept in her room; slep' on the foot of her bed to keep her feets warm and everwhere my mistis went I went to. My marster and mistis wuz sho good to us an we loved 'em. My ma, she done the cooking and the washing fer the family and she could work in the fields jes lak a man. She could pick her three hundred pounds of cotton or pull as much fodder as any man. She wuz strong an she had a new baby mos' ev'y year. My marster and Mistis liked for to have a lot of chillen 'cause that helped ter make 'em richer."

I didn't have much time fer playin' when I wus little cause I wuz allus busy waitin' on my mistis er taking care of my little brothers and sisters. But I did have a doll to play with. It wuz a rag doll an my mistis made it fer me. I wuz jes crazy 'bout that doll and I learned how to sew making clothes fer it. I'd make clothes fer it an wash an iron 'em, and it wasn't long 'fo I knowed how to sew real good, an I been sewing ever since.

My white folks wern't rich er tall but we always had plenty of somep'n to eat, and we had fire wood to keep us warm in winter too. We had plenty of syrup and corn bread, and when dey killed a hog we had fine sausage an chitlin's, an all sorts of good eating. My marster and the white an collored boys would go hunting, and we had squirrels an rabbits an possums jes lots of time. Yessum, we had plenty; we never did go hongry.

"Does I remember 'bout the Yankees coming?, Yes ma'am, I sho does. The white chillen an us had been looking fer 'em and looking fer 'em. We wanted 'em to come. We knowed 'twould be fun to see 'em. And sho 'nuf one day I was out in de front yard to see and I seed a whole passel of men in blue coats coming down de road. I hollered "Here come de Yankees". I knowed 'twuz dem an my mistis an my ma an ev'y body come out in the front yard to see 'em. The Yankees stopped an the leading man with the straps on his shoulders talked to us an de men got water outen de well. No'm, they didn't take nothing an they hurt nothing. After a while they jes went on down the road; they sho looked hot an dusty an tired.

"After de war wuz over my pa, he comed up to our house an got my ma an all us chillen an carries us down to his marster's place. I didn't want ter go cause I loved my mistis an she cried when we left. My pa's ole marster let him have some land to work on shares. My pa wuz a hard worker an we helped him an in a few years he bought a little piece of land an he owned it till he died. 'Bout once er twice a year we'd all go back ter see our mistis. She wuz always glad to see us an treated us fine.

"After de war a white woman started a school fer nigger chillen an my pa sent us. This white lady wuz a ole maid an wuz mighty poor. She an her ma lived by dereselves, I reckon her pa had done got kilt in de war. I don't know 'bout that but I knows they wuz mighty poor an my pa paid her fer teaching us in things to eat from his farm. We didn't never have no money. I loved to go to school; I had a blue back speller an I learned real quick but we didn't get ter go all the time. When there wuz work ter do on the farm we had ter stop an do it.

"Times warn't no better after de war wuz over an dey warnt no wuss. We wuz po before de war an we wuz po after de war. But we allus had somep'n to wear and plenty to eat an we never had no kick coming.

"I never did get married. I'se a old maid nigger, an they tells me you don't see old maid niggers. How come I ain't married I don't know. Seems like when I was young I seed somep'n wrong with all de mens that would come around. Then atter while I wuz kinder ole an they didn't come around no mo. Jes' last week a man come by here what used to co't me. He seed me settin here on the porch an I says 'Come on in an set a while', an he did. So maybe, I ain't through co'tin, maybe I'll get married yet." Here she laughed gleefully.

When asked which she preferred freedom or slavery she replied, "Well, being free wuz all right while I wuz young but now I'm old an I wish I b'longed to somebody cause they would take keer of me an now I ain't got nobody to take keer of me. The government gives me eight dollars a month but that don't go fer enough. I has er hard time cause I can't git around an work like I used to."

[HW: DIST. 6
Ex-slave #77]

Alberta Minor
Re-search Worker

EMILY MAYS
East Solomon Street,
Griffin, Georgia
Interviewed
[Date Stamp: MAY 8 1937]

EMILY MAYS

Emily was born in 1861 on the Billy Stevens plantation in Upson County. Her mother, Betsy Wych, was born at Hawkinsville, Georgia, and sold to Mr. Billy Stevens. The father, Peter Wych, was born in West Virginia. A free man, he was part Indian and when driving a team of oxen into Virginia for lime, got into the slave territory, was overtaken by a "speculator" and brought to Georgia where he was sold to the Wyches of Macon. He cooked for them at their Hotel, "The Brown House" for a number of years, then was sold "on the block" to Mr. Stevens of Upson County. Betsy was sold at this same auction. Betsy and Peter were married by "jumping the broomstick" after Mr. Stevens bought them. They had sixteen children, of which Emily is the next to the last. She was always a "puny", delicate child and her mother died when she was about seven years old. She heard people tell her father that she "wasn't intented to be raised" 'cause she was so little and her mother was "acomin' to get her soon." Hearing this kind of remarks often had a depressing effect upon the child, and she "watched the clouds" all the time expecting her mother and was "bathed in tears" most of the time.

After the war, Peter rented a "patch" from Mr. Kit Parker and the whole family worked in the fields except Emily. She was not big enough so they let her work in the "big house" until Mrs. Parker's death. She helped "'tend" the daughter's babies, washed and ironed table napkins and waited on them "generally" for which she can't remember any "pay", but they fed and clothed her.

Her older sister learned to weave when she was a slave, and helped sew for the soldiers; so after freedom she continued making cloth and sewing for the family while the others worked in the fields. [Buttons were made from dried gourds.] They lived well, raising more on their patch than they could possibly use and selling the surplus. For coffee they split and dried sweet potatoes, ground and parched them.

The only education Emily received was at the "Sugar Hill" Sunday School. They were too busy in the spring for social gatherings, but after the crops were harvested, they would have "corn shuckings" where the Negroes gathered from neighboring farms and in three or four days time would finish at one place then move on to the next farm. It was quite a social gathering and the farm fed all the guests with the best they had.

The Prayer Meetings and "singings" were other pleasant diversions from the daily toil.

After Mrs. Parker's death Emily worked in her father's

fields until she was married to Aaron Mays, then she came to Griffin where she has lived ever since. She is 75 years old and has cooked for "White folks" until she was just too old to "see good", so she now lives with her daughter.

United States. Work Projects Administration

INTERVIEW WITH LIZA MENTION
BEECH ISLAND, S.C.

Written and Edited By:
Leila Harris
and
John N. Booth

Federal Writers' Project
Augusta, Georgia

March 25, 1938

LIZA MENTION

"Come right in. Have a seat. I'll be glad to tell you anything I can 'bout dem early days", said Liza Mention. "Course I warn't born till de second year atter freedom, so I don't 'member nothin' 'bout all dat fightin' durin' de war. I'se sho' glad I warn't born in slavery from what I heared 'em tell 'bout dem patterollers ketchin' and beatin' up folks." Liza's house, a 2-room hut with a narrow front porch, stands in a peaceful spot on the edge of the Wilson plantation at Beech Island, South Carolina. A metal sign on the door which revealed that the property is protected by a theft insurance service aroused wonder as to what Liza had that could attract a burglar. The bedroom was in extreme disorder with clothing, shoes, bric-a-brac, and just plain junk scattered about. The old Negress had been walking about the sunshiny yard and apologized for the mess by saying that she lived alone and did as she pleased. "Folks says I oughtn't to stay here by myself," she remarked, "but I laks to be independent. I cooked 25 years for de Wilson fambly and dey is gonna let me have dis house free 'til I die 'cause I ain't able to do no work."

Liza's close-fitting hat pinned her ears to her head. She wore a dress that was soiled and copiously patched and her worn out brogans were several sizes too large. Ill health probably accounts for this untidiness for, as she expressed it, "when I gits up I hate to set down and when I sets down, I hates to git up, my knees hurts me so," however, her face broke into a toothless grin on the slightest provocation.

"I wuz born up on de Reese's place in McDuffie County near Thomson, Georgia. When I wuz chillun us didn't know nothin' 'bout no wuk," she volunteered. "My ma wuz a invalis (invalid) so when I wuz 6 years old she give me to her sister over here at Mr. Ed McElmurray's place to raise. I ain't never knowed who my pa wuz. Us chaps played all de time wid white chillun jus' lak dey had all been Niggers. Chillun den didn't have sense lak dey got now; us wuz satisfied jus' to play all de time. I 'members on Sundays us used to take leaves and pin 'em together wid thorns to make usselves dresses and hats to play in. I never did go to school none so I don't know nothin' 'bout readin' and writin' and spellin'. I can't spell my own name, but I think it begins wid a M. Hit's too late to study 'bout all dat now 'cause my old brain couldn't learn nothin'. Hit's done lost most all of what little I did know.

"Back in dem times, folkses cooked on open fireplaces in winter time and in summer dey built cook stands out in de yard to set de spiders on, so us could cook and eat outdoors. Dere warn't no stoves nowhar. When us wuz hard up for sompin' green to bile 'fore de gyardens got goin' good, us used to go out and git wild mustard, poke salad, or pepper grass. Us et 'em satisfactory and dey never kilt us. I have et heaps of kinds of diffunt weeds and I still eats a mess of poke salad once or twice a year 'cause it's good for you. Us cooked a naked hunk of fat meat in a pot wid some corn dumplin's. De grown folks would eat de meat and de chilluns would sit around on de floor and eat de potlikker and dumplin's out of tin pans. Us enjoyed dat stuff jus' lak it had been pound cake.

"Dances in dem days warn't dese here huggin' kind of dances lak dey has now. Dere warn't no Big Apple nor no Little Apple neither. Us had a house wid a raised flatform (platform) at one end whar de music-makers sot. Dey had a string band wid a fiddle, a trumpet, and a banjo, but dere warn't no guitars lak dey has in dis day. One man called de sets and us danced de cardrille (quadrille) de virginia reel, and de 16-hand cortillion. When us made syrup on de farm dere would always be a candy pullin'. Dat homemade syrup made real good candy. Den us would have a big time at corn shuckin's too.

"I don't believe in no conjuration. Ain't nobody never done nothin' to me but I have seed people dat other folks said had been hurt. If somebody done somethin' to me I wouldn't know whar to find a root-worker to take it off and anyways I wouldn't trust dem sort of folks 'cause if dey can cyore you dey can kill you too.

"I'se a member of de Silver Bluff Baptist Church, and I been goin' to Sunday School dar nearly ever since I can 'member. You know dey say dat's de oldest Nigger church in de country. At fust a white man come from Savannah and de church wuz built for his family and dey slaves. Later dere wuz so many colored members de white folks come out and built another house so de niggers could have de old one. When dat ole church wuz tore down, de colored folks worshipped for a long time in a goat house and den in a brush arbor. "Some folks calls it de Dead River Church 'cause it used to be near Dead River and de baptisin' wuz done dar for a long time. I wuz baptised dar myself and I loves de old spot of ground. I has tried to be a good church member all my life but it's hard fer me to get a nickel or a dime for preacher money now."

When asked if people in the old days got married by jumping over a broom she made a chuckling sound and replied: "No, us had de preacher but us didn't have to buy no license and I can't see no sense in buyin' a license nohow, 'cause when dey gits ready to quit, dey just quits."

Liza brought an old Bible from the other room in which she said she kept the history of the old church. There were also pictures from some of her "white folks" who had moved to North Carolina. "My husband has been daid for 40 years," she asserted, "and I hasn't a chile to my name, nobody to move nothin' when I lays it down and nobody to pick nothin' up. I gets along pretty well most of de time though, but I wishes I could work so I would feel more independent."

District Two
EX-SLAVE INTERVIEW

AUNT HARRIET MILLER
Toccoa, Georgia
(Stephens County)

Written By:
Mrs. Annie Lee Newton
Research Worker
Federal Writers' Project
Athens, Georgia

Edited By:
John N. Booth
Asst. District Supervisor
Federal Writers' Project
Athens, Georgia

July 15, 1937

HARRIET MILLER

Aunt Harriet Miller, a chipper and spry Indian Half-breed, thinks she is about 100 years old. It is remarkable that one so old should possess so much energy and animation. She is tall and spare, with wrinkled face, bright eyes, a kindly expression, and she wears her iron grey hair wound in a knob in the manner of a past generation. Aunt Harriet was neatly dressed as she had just returned from a trip to Cornelia to see some of her folks. She did not appear at all tired from the trip, and seemed glad to discuss the old days.

"My father," said Aunt Harriet, "was a Cherokee

Indian named Green Norris, and my mother was a white woman named Betsy Richards. You see, I am mixed. My mother give me to Mr. George Naves when I was three years old. He lived in de mountains of South Carolina, just across de river. He didn't own his home. He was overseer for de Jarretts, old man Kennedy Jarrett. Honey, people was just like dey is now, some good and some bad. Mr. Naves was a good man. Dese here Jarretts was good to deir slaves but de ——s was mean to deirs. My whitefolks tried to send me to school but de whitefolks wouldn't receive me in deir school on account of I was mixed, and dere warn't no colored school a t'all, nowhere. Some of de white ladies taught deir slaves. Yes'm, some of 'em did. Now, Miss Sallie Jarrett, dat was Mrs. Bob Jarrett's daughter, used to teach 'em some.

"Slaves had half a day off on Saturday. Dey had frolics at night, quiltings, dances, corn-shuckings, and played de fiddle. Dey stayed in de quarters Sunday or went to church. Dey belonged to de same church wid de whitefolks. I belonged to Old Liberty Baptist Church. De back seats was whar de slaves set. Dey belonged to de same church just like de whitefolks, but I wasn't with 'em much." As a child, Aunt Harriet associated with white people, and played with white children, but when she grew up, had to turn to negroes for companionship.

"If slaves stayed in deir places dey warn't never whipped or put in chains. When company come I knowed to get out doors. I went on to my work. I was treated all right. I don't remember getting but three whippings in my life. Old Mistis had brown sugar, a barrel of sugar setting in de dinin' room. She'd go off and she'd come back and ask me 'bout de sugar. She'd get after me 'bout it and I'd say I hadn't took it, and den when she turned my dress back and whipped me I couldn't hardly set down. She whipped me twice 'bout the sugar and den she let me alone. 'Twasn't de sugar she whipped me 'bout, but she was trying to get me to tell de truth. Yes'm, dat was de best lesson dat ever I learned, to tell de truth, like David.

"I had a large fambly. Lets see, I had ten chillun, two of 'em dead, and I believes 'bout 40 grand-chillun. I could count 'em. Last time I was counting de great-grand-chillun dere was 37 but some have come in since den. Maggie has 11 chillun. Maggie's husband is a farmer and dey lives near Eastonallee. Lizzie, her husband is dead and she lives wid a daughter in Chicago, has 5 chillun. Den Media has two. Her husband, Hillary Campbell, works for de Govemint, in Washington. Lieutenant has six; he farms. Robert has six; Robert is a regular old farmer and Sunday School teacher. Davey has four, den Luther has seven, and dat leaves Jim, my baby boy. He railroads and I lives wid him. Jim is 37. He ain't got no chillun. My husband, Judge Miller, been dead 37 years. He's buried at Tugalo. Dis old lady been swinging on a limb a long time and she going to swing off from here some time. I'm near about a hundred and I won't be here long, but when I go, I wants to go in peace wid everybody.

"I don't know. I'd be 'feard to say dere ain't nothing in voo-doo. Some puts a dime in de shoe to keep de voo-doo away, and some carries a buckeye in de pocket to keep off cramp and colic. Dey say a bone dey finds in de jawbone of a hog will make chillun teethe easy. When de slaves got sick, de whitefolks looked after 'em. De medicines for sickness was nearly all yerbs. Dey give boneset for colds, made tea out of it, and acheing joints. Butterfly root and slippery elm bark was to cool fever. Willow ashes is good for a corn, poke root for rheumatism, and a syrup made of mullein, honey, and alum for colds. Dey use barks from dogwood, wild cherry, and clack haws, for one thing and another. I'll tell you what's good for pizen-oak, powdered alum and sweet cream. Beat it if it's lump alum, and put it in sweet cream, not milk, it has to be cream. Dere's lots of other remedies and things, but I'm getting so sap-skulled and I'm so old I can't remember. Yes'm, I've got mighty trifling 'bout my remembrance.

"Once some Indians camped on de river bottoms for three or four years, and we'd go down; me, and Anne, and Genia, nearly every Saturday, to hear 'em preach. We couldn't understand it. Dey didn't have no racket or nothing like colored folks. Dey would sing, and it sounded all right. We couldn't understand it, but dey enjoyed it. Dey worked and had crops. Dey had ponies, pretty ponies. Nobody never did bother 'em. Dey made baskets out of canes, de beautifulest baskets, and dey colored 'em wid dyes, natchel dyes.

"Indian woman wore long dresses and beads. Deir hair was plaited and hanging down de back, and deir babyes was tied on a blanket on de back. Mens wore just breeches and feathers in deir hats. I wish you could have seen 'em a cooking. Dey would take corn dough, and den dey'd boil birds, make sort of long, not round dumplings, and drop 'em in a pot of hot soup. We thought dat was terrible, putting dat in de pot wid de birds. Dey had blow-guns and dey'd slip around, and first thing dey'd blow, and down come a bird. Dey'd kill a squirrel and ketch fish wid deir blow guns. Dem guns was made out of canes 'bout eight feet long, burned out at de j'ints for de barrel. Dey put in a arrow what had thistles on one end to make it go through quick and de other end sharp.

"Yes honey, I believes in hants. I was going 'long, at nine o'clock one night 'bout the Denham fill and I heard a chain a rattling 'long de cross-ties. I couldn't see a thing and dat chain just a rattling as plain as if it was on dis floor. Back, since the war, dere was a railroad gang working 'long by dis fill, and de boss, Captain Wing, whipped a convict. It killed him, and de boss throwed him in de fill. I couldn't see a thing, and dat chain was just rattling right agai' de fill where dat convict had been buried. I believes de Lord took keer of me dat night and I hope he keeps on doing so."

United States. Work Projects Administration

[HW: Dist. 6
Ex-Slave #75]

Folklore
Alberta Minor
Re-search Worker

MOLLIE MITCHELL, Ex Negro Slave
507 East Chappell Street
Griffin, Georgia

August 31, 1936
[Date Stamp: MAY 8 1937]

MOLLIE MITCHELL

Mollie Mitchell, a white haired old darkey, 85 years old was born on the Newt Woodard plantation. It is the old Jackson Road near Beulah Church. Until she was 7 years old she helped about the house running errands for her "Missus", "tendin' babies", "sweeping the yard", and "sich." At 7 she was put in the fields. The first day at work she was given certain rows to hoe but she could not keep in the row. The Master came around twice a day to look at what they had done and when it was not done right, he whipped them. "Seems like I got whipped all day long," she said. One time when Mollie was about 13 years old, she was real sick, the master and missus took her to the bathing house where there was "plenty of hot water." They put her in a tub of hot water then took her out, wrapped her in blankets and sheets and put her in cold water. They kept her there 4 or 5 days doing that until they broke her fever. Whenever the negroes were sick, they always looked after them and had a doctor if necessary. At Christmas they had a whole week holiday and everything they wanted to eat. The negroes lived a happy carefree life unless they "broke the rules." If one lied or stole or did not work or did not do his work right or stayed out over the time of their pass, they were whipped. The "pass" was given them to go off on Saturday. It told whose "nigger" they were and when they were due back, usually by 4 o'clock Sunday afternoon or Monday morning. "The patta-roll" (patrol) came by to see your pass and if you were due back home, they would give you a whippin'!"

Mollie was 15 years old when the master came out in the fields and told them they were as free as he was. Her family stayed with him. He gave them a horse or mule, their groceries and a "patch to work", that they paid for in about three years time. Before the war whenever his slaves reached 70 years, the master set them free and gave them a mule, cow and a "patch". Mollie can remember her grandmother and grandfather getting theirs. When Mollie married (17 years old), she moved to her husband's farm. She had 9 children. She had to "spin the cloth" for their clothes, and did any kind of work, even the men's work too. Out of herbs she made syrup for worms for her children. With the barks of different trees she made the spring tonic and if their "stomachs was wrong", she used red oak bark. When she was younger, she would "dream a dream" and see it "jes' as clear" next morning and it always came true, but now since she's aged her dreams are "gone away" by next morning. When she was a little girl, they made them go to Sunday School and taught them out of a "blue back speller". After freedom, they were sent to day school "some". The "little missus" used to teach her upstairs after they were supposed to be in bed. She's been a member of the Methodist Church since she was 17 years old. Mollie's husband was always a farmer and he always planted by the moon. Potatoes, turnips and things that grow under the ground were planted in the dark of the moon while beans and peas and things that develope on top the ground were planted in the light of the moon.

She said she couldn't remember many superstitions but she knew a rabbit's foot was tied round your neck or waist for luck and a crowing hen was bad luck, so bad that they killed them and "put 'em in the pot" whenever they found one. When you saw a cat washing its face, it was going to rain sure.

Mollie is quite wrinkled, has thinning white hair, very bad teeth but fairly active physically and her mind is moderately clear.

Elizabeth Watson

BOB MOBLEY, Ex-Slave, Aged about 90
Pulaski County, Georgia
(1937)
[Date Stamp: JUL 20 1937]

BOB MOBLEY

When recently interviewed, this aged colored man—the soul of humbleness and politeness—and long a resident of Pulaski County, sketched his life as follows (his language reconstructed):

"I was the seventh child of the eleven children born to Robert and Violet Hammock, slaves of Mr. Henry Mobley of Crawford County. My parents were also born in Crawford County.

My master was well-to-do: he owned a great deal of land and many Negroes.

Macon was our nearest trading town—and Mr. Mobley sold his cotton and did his trading there, though he sent his children to school at Knoxville (Crawford County).

My mother was the family cook, and also superintended the cooking for many of the slaves.

We slaves had a good time, and none of us were abused or mistreated, though young Negroes were sometimes whipped—when they deserved it. Grown Negro men, in those days, wore their hair long and, as a punishment to them for misconduct (etc.), the master cut their hair off.

I was raised in my master's house—slept in his room when I was a small boy, just to be handy to wait on him when he needed anything.

If a slave became sick, a doctor was promptly called to attend him. My mother was also a kind of doctor and often rode all over the plantation to dose ailing Negroes with herb teas and home medicines which she was an adept in compounding. In cases of [HW: minor] illness, she could straighten up the sick in no time.

Before the war started, I took my young master to get married, and we were certainly dressed up. You have never seen a Nigger and a white man as dressed up as we were on that occasion.

An aunt of mine was head weaver on our plantation, and she bossed the other women weavers and spinners. Two or three seamstresses did all the sewing.

In winter time we slaves wore wool, which had been dyed before the cloth was cut. In summer we wore light goods.

We raised nearly every thing that we ate, except sugar and coffee, and made all the shoes and clothes worn on the place, except the white ladies' silks, fine shawls, and slippers, and the men's broadcloths and dress boots.

My young master went to the war, but his father was too old to go. When we heard that the Yankees were coming, old mister refugeed to Dooly County—where he bought a new farm, and took his Negroes with him.

But the new place was so poor that, right after the war closed, he moved back to his old plantation. I stayed with Mr. Henry for a long time after freedom, then came to Hawkinsville to work at the carpenter's trade. And I did pretty well here until I fell off a house several years ago, since which time I haven't been much good—not able to do hardly any work at all."

Now old, feeble, and physically incapacitated, "Uncle" Bob lives with a stepdaughter—a woman of 72—who, herself, is failing fast. Both are supported mainly by Pulaski County and the Federal Government.

United States. Work Projects Administration

[HW: Dist. 6
Ex-Slave #79]

Folklore
Mary A. Crawford
Re-Search Worker

FANNY NIX—Ex-Slave
Interviewed
[Date Stamp: MAY 8 1937]

FANNY NIX

Fanny was born in slavery and was "a great big girl" when the slaves were freed but does not know her exact age, however, she thinks that she was "at least twelve when the War broke out." According to this method of estimating her age, Fanny is about eighty-seven.

The old woman's parents were John Arnold and Rosetta Green, who were married 'away befo de wah' by steppin' over the broom' in the presence of "old Marse," and a lot of colored friends.

Fanny does not know where her parents were born, but thinks that they were born in Upson County near Thomaston, Georgia, and knows that she and her two brothers and other sister were.

Fanny and her family were owned by Judge Jim Green. Judge Green had a hundred or so acres of land Fanny 'reckon', and between twenty-five and seventy-five slaves.

"The Marster was just as good as he could be to all the slaves, and especially to the little chillun." "The Judge did not 'whup' much—and used a peach tree limb and done it hisself. There wuzn't no strop at Marse Green's big house."

Rosetta Green, the mother of Fanny, "cooked and washed for Judge Green for yeahs and yeahs." Fanny "found her mammy a cookin' at the big house the fust thing she knowed."

As Fanny grew up, she was trained by "ole Miss" to be a house girl, and did "sech wuk" as churning, minding the flies "offen de table when de white folks et, gwine backards and forads to de smoke-house for my mammy."

She recalls that when she "minded the flies offen the table she allus got plenty of biscuits and scraps o' fried chicken the white folks left on their plates." "But," Fanny added with a satisfied smile, "Marse Green's darkies never wanted for sumpin t'eat, case he give 'em a plenty, even molasses all dey wanted." Fanny and her mammy always ate in "de Missis kitchen."

"Yes," said Fanny, "I remembers when de Yankees come through, it tickled us chillun and skeered us too! Dey wuz mo'n a hundred, Miss, riding mighty po' ole wore out hosses. All de men wanted wuz sumpin' t'eat and some good hosses. De men poured into de smoke-house and de kitchen (here Fanny had to laugh again) an how dem Yankee mens did cut and hack "Ole Marse's" best hams! After dey et all dey could hol' dey saddled up "ole Marse's" fine hosses an' away dey rid!"

When asked why the white folks did not hide the horses out in the swamps or woods, Fanny replied, "case, dey didn't have time. Dem Yankees pounced down like hawks after chickens!" "Ole Marse jost did have time to 'scape to de woods hisself." The Judge was too old to go to the war.

John Arnold, Fanny's daddy, was owned by Mr. John Arnold on an adjoining plantation to Judge Greene, and when he and Fanny's mother were married, John was allowed to visit Rosetta each week-end. Of course he had to carry a pass from his "Marster."

John and Rosetta "never lived together year in and year out," according to Fanny's statement, "till long after freedom."

Fanny relates that Judge Green's slaves all went to "meetin" every Sunday in the white folks church. The darkies going in the after-noon and the white people going in the forenoon.

The white preacher ministered to both the white and colored people.

If the Negroes were sick and needed mo [HW: den] "old Marse" knowed what to give em, he "sont the white folk's doctor." "You see, Miss," said old Fanny with pride, "I wuz owned by big white folks."

She tells that Judge Green had two young sons (not old enough to fight) and three daughters, 'jest little shavers, so high', (here Fanny indicated from three, to four or five feet at intervals, to indicate small children's height,) then added, "We allus said, 'Little Miss Peggy', 'Little Miss Nancy', and 'Little Missz Jane', and 'Young Marse Jim' and 'Little Marster Bob'". "Did you ever forget to speak to the children in that way?" the interviewer asked. "No, Miss, we sho didn't, we knowed better dan to fergit!"

Fanny is very feeble in every way, voice is weak and her step most uncertain, but she is straight of figure, and was ripping up smoking tobacco sacks with which her daughter is to make 'a purty bed spread'. Fanny and her husband, another ex-slave, live with Fanny's daughter. The daughter supports her mother.

[HW: Dist. 6
Ex-Slave #80]

Mary A. Crawford
Re-Search Worker

HENRY NIX—Ex-Slave
808 E. Slaton Ave.
Griffin, Georgia
Interviewed

September 24, 1936
[Date Stamp: MAY 8 1937]

[TR: Numerous handwritten changes were made in this interview. Where a word appears in brackets after a HW entry, it was replaced by that handwritten entry. All numbers were originally spelled out.]

HENRY NIX

Henry Nix was born March 15, 1848 in Upson County, about 5 miles from Barnesville, Georgia.

[HW: His] [Henry's] parents were John Nix and Catherine Willis, who were not married, because as Henry reports, John Nix was an overseer on the plantation of Mr. Jasper Willis, "and when Marster found out what kind of man John Nix was he (Nix) had to skip out."

When Henry "was a good sized boy, his mother married a darky man", and 3 other children were born, 2 boys and a girl. Henry loved his mother very much and [HW: says] relates that on her death bed she told him who his father was, and [TR: "also told him" crossed out] how to live so as not to get into trouble, and, [HW: due to her advice] that he has never been in jail nor in any meanness of any kind [TR: "due to what she told him" crossed out].

Mr. Jasper Willis, [TR: "who was" crossed out] Henry's owner, lived on a large plantation of about 300 three hundred acres in Upson County, [HW: and] [Mr. Willis] owned only about 50 or 60 slaves as well as Henry can remember. The old man considers Mr. Willis "the best marster that a darky ever had," saying that he "sho" made his darkies work and mind, but he never beat them or let the patter-role do it, though sometimes he did use a switch on 'em". Henry recalls that he received "a sound whuppin onct, 'case he throwed a rock at one o' Marse Jasper's fine cows and broke her laig!"

When asked if Mr. Willis had the slaves taught to read and write, Henry hooted at the idea, saying emphatically, "No, Mam, 'Ole Marse' wuz sho hard about dat. He said 'Niggers' wuz made by de good Lawd to work, and onct when my Uncle stole a book and wuz a trying to learn how to read and write, Marse Jasper had the white doctor take off my Uncle's fo' finger right down to de 'fust jint'. Marstar said he fixed dat darky as a sign fo de res uv 'em! No, Miss, we wuzn't larned!"

Mr. Willis allowed his slaves from Saturday at noon till Monday morning as a holiday, and then they always had a week for Christmas. All of the Negroes went to meeting on Sunday afternoon in the white people's church and were served by the white minister.

Henry says that they had a "circuit doctor" on his Marster's place and the doctor came around regularly at least every two weeks, "case Marster paid him to do so and [HW: he] 'xamined evah darky big and little on dat plantation."

One time Henry recalls that he "had a turrible cowbunkle" on the back of his neck and 'marse' had the doctor to cut it open. Henry knowed better den to holler and cut up, too, when it was done.

The old man remembers going to war with his young master and remaining with him for the two years he was in service. They were in Richmond when the city surrendered to Grant and soon after that the young master was killed in the fight at Tumlin Gap. Henry hardly knows how he got back to "Ole Marster" but is thankful he did.

After freedom, [HW: al]most all of Mr. Willis' darkies stayed on with him but Henry "had to act smart and run away." He went over into Alabama and managed "to keep [TR: "his" crossed out] body and soul together somehow, for several years and then [TR: "he" crossed out] went back to "Ole Marster."

Henry is well and rather active for his 87 or 88 years and likes to work. He has a job now cleaning off the graves at the white cemetery but he and his wife depend mainly [HW: for support] on their son [TR: "for support" crossed out], who lives just across the street from them.

[HW: Dist. 6]

Mary A. Crawford
Re-Search Worker

LEWIS OGLETREE—Ex-Slave
501 E. Tinsley Street
Griffin, Georgia

August 21, 1936
[Date Stamp: MAY 8 1937]

[TR: Numerous handwritten changes were made in this interview. Where a word appears in brackets after a HW entry, it was replaced by that handwritten entry.]

LEWIS OGLETREE

Lewis Ogletree was born on the plantation of Mr. Fred Crowder of Spalding County, Georgia [HW: Ga], near Griffin. [HW: He] [Lewis] does not know exactly when he was born, but says that [TR: "he knows that" crossed out] he was maybe 17 years old at the end of the war in '65. This would make him 88 now.

Mr. Crowder was the owner of a large number of slaves and among them was Lettie Crowder, [TR: "(married an Ogletree) the" crossed out] housekeeper and head servant in the home of Mr. Fred Crowder. Lettie was Lewis' mother.

Lewis remembers standing inside the picket fence with a lot of other little pick-a-ninnies watching for

Sherman's Army, and when the Yankees got close enough to be heard plainly, they hid in the bushes or under the house.

The Yankees poured into the yard and into the house, making Lettie open the smoke-house and get them Mr. Crowder's best whiskey and oftentimes they made her cook them a meal of ham and eggs.

Mr. Crowder, Lettie's master, was ill during the war, having a cancer on his left hand.

Lewis reports that Mr. Crowder was a very hard master but a good one saying, "That it wasn't any use for the "patty-role" (the Patrol) to come to Marse Crowder's, 'cause he would not permit him to "tech one of his darkies."

Mrs. Crowder, the "ole mistis", had died just before the war broke out and Mr. Crowder lived alone with his house servants.

There were two young sons in the war. The oldest son, Col. Crowder, was in Virginia.

Lewis said that his Master whipped him only once and that was for stealing. One day when the old master was taking a nap, Lewis "minding off the flies" and thinking his "marster" asleep slipped over to the big table and snatched some candy. Just as he picked up a lump, (it was "rock candy,") "Wham! Old [HW: Marster] [mastah] had me, and when he got through, well, Lewis, didn't steal anymore candy nor nothin'." "Mastah nevah took no foolishness from his darkies."

Lewis remembers very clearly when Mr. Crowder

gave his darkies their freedom. "Mastah sont me and my mammy out to the cabin to tell all de darkies to come up to de "big house". When they got there, there were so many that [HW: they] [some] were up on the porch, on the steps and all over the yard."

"Mr. Crowder stood up on the porch and said, "You darkies are all free now. You don't belong to me no more. Now pack up your things and go on off." My Lord! How them darkies did bawl! And most of them did not leave ole mastah."

[RICHARD ORFORD, Age around 85]

RICHARD ORFORD

The following version of slavery was told by Mr. Richard Orford of 54 Brown Avenue in South Atlanta. Mr. Orford is large in statue and although 85 years of age he has a very active mind as well as a good sense of humor.

Mr. Orford was born in Pike County, Georgia (near the present site of Griffin) in 1842. His master's name was Jeff Orford. Mr. Orford describes him as follows: "Marster wus a rich man an' he had 'bout 250 slaves—'course dat was'nt so many 'cause some of de folks 'round dere had 400 and 500. He had plenty of land too—I don't know how many acres. He raised everything he needed on de plantation an' never had to buy nothing. I 'members when de Yankees come through—ol' marster had 'bout 200 barrels of whiskey hid in de smokehouse—dat wus de fust time I ever got drunk."

"Besides hisself an' his wife ol' marster had two boys an' nine girls".

Continuing, Mr. Orford said: "My Ma did'nt have many chillun—jus' ten boys an' nine girls. I went to work in marster's house when I wus five years old an' I stayed dere 'till I wus thirty-five. De fust work I had to do wus to pick up chips, feed chickens, an' keep de yard clean. By de time I wus eight years old I wus drivin' my missus in de carriage."

"All de rest of de slaves wus fiel' hands. Dey spent dere time plowing an' takin' care of de plantation in general. Dere wus some who split rails an' others who took care of de stock an' made de harness—de slaves did everything dat needed to be done on de plantation. Everybody had to git up 'fore daybreak an' even 'fore it wus light enuff to see dey wus in de fiel' waitin' to see how to run a furrow. 'Long 'bout nine o'clock breakfus' wus sent to de fiel' in a wagon an' all of 'em stopped to eat. At twelve o'clock dey stopped again to eat dinner. After dat dey worked 'till it wus to dark to see. Women in dem days could pick five-hundred pounds of cotton a day wid a child in a sack on dere backs."

"When de weather wus too bad to work in de fiel' de hands cribed an' shucked corn. If dey had any work of dere own to do dey had to do it at night".

According to Mr. Orford there was always sufficient food on the Orford plantation for the slaves. All cooking was done by one cook at the cook house. In front of the cook house were a number of long tables where the slaves ate their meals when they came in from the fields. Those children who were too young to work in the fields were also fed at this house but instead of eating from the tables as did the grown-ups they were fed from long troughs much the same as little pigs. Each was given a spoon at meal time and then all of the food was dumped into the trough at the same time.

The week day diet for the most part consisted of meats and vegetables—"sometimes we even got chicken an' turkey"—says Mr. Orford. Coffee was made by parching meal or corn and then boiling it in water. None of the slaves ever had to steal anything to eat on the Orford plantation.

All of the clothing worn on this plantation was made there. Some of the women who were too old to work in the fields did the spinning and the weaving as well as the sewing of the garments. Indigo was used to dye the cloth. The women wore callico dresses and the men wore ansenberg pants and shirts. The children wore a one piece garment not unlike a slightly lengthened dress. This was kept in place by a string tied around their waists. There were at least ten shoemakers on the plantation and they were always kept bust [TR: busy?] making shoes although no slave ever got but one pair of shoes a year. These shoes were made of very hard leather and were called brogans.

In the rear of the master's house was located the slave's quarters. Each house was made of logs and was of the double type so that two families could be accommodated. The holes and chinks in the walls were daubed with mud to keep the weather out. At one end of the structure was a large fireplace about six feet in width. The chimney was made of dirt.

As for furniture Mr. Orford says: "You could make your own furniture if you wanted to but ol' marster would give you a rope bed an' two or three chairs an' dat wus all. De mattress wus made out of a big bag or a tickin' stuffed wid straw—dat wus all de furniture in any of de houses."

"In dem days folks did'nt git sick much like dey do now, but when dey did de fust thing did fer 'em wus to give 'em blue mass. If dey had a cold den dey give 'em blue mass pills. When dey wus very sick de marster sent fer de doctor."

"Our ol' marster wus'nt like some of de other marsters in de community—he never did do much whuppin of his slaves. One time I hit a white man an' ol' marster said he was goin' to cut my arm off an' dat wus de las' I heard of it. Some of de other slaves useter git whuppins fer not workin' an' fer fightin'. My mother got a whuppin once fer not workin'. When dey got so bad ol' marster did'nt bother 'bout whuppin' 'em—he jes' put 'em on de block an' en' sold 'em like he would a chicken or somethin'. Slaves also got whuppins when dey wus caught off the plantation wid out a pass—de Paddie-Rollers whupped you den. I have knowed slaves to run away an' hide in de woods—some of 'em even raised families dere."

"None of us wus allowed to learn to read or to write but we could go to church along wid de white folks. When de preacher talked to de slaves he tol' 'em not to steal fum de marster an' de missus 'cause dey would be stealing fum dere selves—he tol' 'em to ask fer what dey wanted an' it would be givven to 'em."

When Sherman marched through Georgia a number of the slaves on the Orford plantation joined his army. However, a large number remained on the plantation even after freedom was declared. Mr. Orford was one of those who remained. While the Yankee soldiers were in the vicinity of the Orford plantation Mr. Orford, the owner of the plantation, hid in the woods and had some of the slaves bring his food, etc. to him.

Mr. Orford was thirty-five years of age when he left the plantation and at that time he married a twelve year old girl. Since that time he has been the father of twenty-three children, some of whom are dead and some of whom are still alive.

United States. Work Projects Administration

EX-SLAVE INTERVIEW

ANNA PARKES, Age 86
150 Strong Street
Athens, Georgia

Written by:
Sarah H. Hall
Federal Writers' Project
Athens, Georgia

Edited by:
John N. Booth
District Supervisor
Federal Writers' Project
Residencies 6 & 7
Augusta, Georgia

ANNA PARKES

Anna Parkes' bright eyes sparkled as she watched the crowd that thronged the hallway outside the office where she awaited admittance. A trip to the downtown section is a rare event in the life of an 86 year old Negress, and, accompanied by her daughter, she was making the most of this opportunity to see the world that lay so far from the door of the little cottage where she lives on Strong Street. When asked if she liked to talk of her childhood days before the end of the Civil War, she eagerly replied: "'Deed, I does." She was evidently delighted to have found someone who actually wanted to listen to her, and proudly continued:

"Dem days sho' wuz sompin' to talk 'bout. I don't

never git tired of talkin' 'bout 'em. Paw, he wuz Olmstead Lumpkin, and Ma wuz Liza Lumpkin, and us b'longed to Jedge Joe Henry Lumpkin. Us lived at de Lumpkin home place on Prince Avenue. I wuz born de same week as Miss Callie Cobb, and whilst I don't know z'ackly what day I wuz born, I kin be purty sho' 'bout how many years ole I is by axin' how ole Miss Callie is. Fust I 'members much 'bout is totin' de key basket 'round 'hind Ole Miss when she give out de vittals. I never done a Gawd's speck of work but dat. I jes' follered 'long atter Ole Miss wid 'er key basket.

"Did dey pay us any money? Lawsy, Lady! What for? Us didn't need no money. Ole Marster and Ole Miss all time give us plenty good sompin' teat, and clo'es, and dey let us sleep in a good cabin, but us did have money now and den. A heap of times us had nickles and dimes. Dey had lots of comp'ny at Ole Marster's, and us allus act mighty spry waitin' on 'em, so dey would 'member us when dey lef'. Effen it wuz money dey gimme, I jes' couldn't wait to run to de sto' and spend it for candy."

"What else did you buy with the money?", she was asked.

"Nuffin' else," was the quick reply. "All a piece of money meant to me dem days, wuz candy, and den mo' candy. I never did git much candy as I wanted when I wuz chillun."

Here her story took a rambling turn.

"You see I didn't have to save up for nuffin'. Ole Marster and Ole Miss, dey took keer of us. Dey sho' wuz good white folkses, but den dey had to be good white folkses, kaze Ole Marster, he wuz Jedge Lumpkin, and de Jedge wuz bound to make evvybody do right, and he gwine do right his own self 'fore he try to make udder folkses behave deyselvs. Ain't nobody, nowhar, as good to dey Negroes as my white folkses wuz."

"Who taught you to say 'Negroes' so distinctly?" she was asked.

"Ole Marster," she promptly answered, "He 'splained dat us wuz not to be 'shamed of our race. He said us warn't no 'niggers'; he said us wuz 'Negroes', and he 'spected his Negroes to be de best Negroes in de whole land.

"Old Marster had a big fine gyarden. His Negroes wukked it good, and us wuz sho' proud of it. Us lived close in town, and all de Negroes on de place wuz yard and house servants. Us didn't have no gyardens 'round our cabins, kaze all of us et at de big house kitchen. Ole Miss had flowers evvywhar 'round de big house, and she wuz all time givin' us some to plant 'round de cabins.

"All de cookin' wuz done at de big house kitchen, and hit wuz a sho' 'nough big kitchen. Us had two boss cooks, and lots of helpers, and us sho' had plenny of good sompin' teat. Dat's de Gawd's trufe, and I means it. Heap of folkses been tryin' to git me to say us didn't have 'nough teat and dat us never had nuffin' fittin' teat. But ole as I is, I cyan' start tellin' no lies now. I gotter die fo' long, and I sho' wants to be clean in de mouf and no stains or lies on my lips when I dies. Our sompin' teat wuz a heap better'n what us got now. Us had plenny of evvything right dar in de yard. Chickens, ducks, geese, guineas, tukkeys, and de smoke'ouse full of good meat. Den de mens, dey wuz all time goin' huntin', and fetchin' in wild tukkeys, an poddiges, and heaps and lots of 'possums and rabbits. Us had many fishes as us wanted. De big fine shads, and perch, and trouts; dem wuz de fishes de Jedge liked mos'. Catfishes won't counted fittin' to set on de Jedges table, but us Negroes wuz 'lowed to eat all of 'em us wanted. Catfishes mus' be mighty skace now kaze I don't know when ever I is seed a good ole river catfish a-flappin' his tail. Dey flaps dey tails atter you done kilt 'em, and cleaned 'em, and drap 'em in de hot grease to fry. Sometimes dey nigh knock de lid offen de fryin' pan.

"Ole Marster buyed Bill Finch down de country somewhar', and dey called him 'William' at de big house. He wuz de tailor, and he made clo'es for de young marsters. William wuz right smart, and one of his jobs wuz to lock up all de vittals atter us done et much as us wanted. All of us had plenny, but dey won't nuffin' wasted 'round Ole Marster's place.

"Ole Miss wuz young and pretty dem days, and Ole Marster won't no old man den, but us had to call 'em 'Ole Miss,' and 'Ole Marster,' kaze dey chilluns wuz called 'Young Marster' and 'Young Mistess' f'um de very day dey wuz born."

When asked to describe the work assigned to little Negroes, she quickly answered: "Chilluns didn't do nuffin'. Grownup Negroes done all de wuk. All chilluns done wuz to frolic and play. I wuz jes' 'lowed ter tote de key basket kaze I wuz all time hangin' 'round de big house, and wanted so bad to stay close to my ma in de kitchen and to be nigh Ole Miss.

"What sort of clo'es did I wear in dem days? Why Lady, I had good clo'es. Atter my little mistesses wore dey clo'es a little, Ole Miss give 'em to me. Ma allus made me wear clean, fresh clo'es, and go dressed up good all de time so I'd be fittin' to carry de key basket for Ole Miss. Some of de udder slave chilluns had homemade shoes, but I allus had good sto'-bought shoes what my young mistess done outgrowed, or what some of de comp'ny gimme. Comp'ny what had chilluns 'bout my size, gimme heaps of clo'es and shoes, and some times dey didn't look like dey'd been wore none hardly.

"Ole Marster sho' had lots of Negroes 'round his place. Deir wuz Aunt Charlotte, and Aunt Julie, and de two cooks, and Adeline, and Mary, and Edie, and Jimmy. De mens wuz Charlie, and Floyd, and William, and Daniel. I disremembers de res' of 'em.

"Ole Marster never whipped none of his Negroes, not dat I ever heared of. He tole 'em what he wanted done, and give 'em plenny of time to do it. Dey wuz allus skeert effen dey didn't be smart and do right, dey might git sold to some marster dat would beat 'em, and be mean to 'em. Us knowed dey won't many marsters as good to dey slaves as Ole Marster wuz to us. Us would of most kilt ourself wukkin', fo' us would of give him a reason to wanna git rid of us. No Ma'am, Ole Marster ain't never sold no slave, not whilst I kin 'member. Us wuz allus skeert dat effen a Negro git lazy and triflin' he might git sold.

"No Negro never runned away f'um our place. Us didn't have nuffin' to run f'um, and nowhar to run to. Us heared of patterollers but us won't 'fraid none kaze us knowed won't no patteroller gwine tech none of Jedge Lumpkin's Negroes.

"Us had our own Negro church. I b'lieves dey calls it

Foundry Street whar de ole church wuz. Us had meetin' evvy Sunday. Sometimes white preachers, and sometimes Negro preachers done de preachin'. Us didn't have no orgin or pianny in church den. De preacher hysted de hymns. No Ma'am, I cyan' 'member no songs us sung den dat wuz no diffunt f'um de songs now-a-days, 'ceppen' dey got orgin music wid de singin' now. Us had c'lections evvy Sunday in church den, same as now. Ole Marster give us a little change for c'lection on Sunday mawnin' kaze us didn't have no money of our own, and he knowed how big it made us feel ter drap money in de c'lection plate. Us Meferdis had our baptizin's right dar in de church, same as us does now. And 'vival meetin's. Dey jes' broke out any time. Out on de plantations dey jes' had 'vival meetin's in layin'-by times, but here in town us had 'em all durin' de year. Ole Marster used ter say: 'Mo' 'vivals, better Negroes.'

"Evvybody oughter be good and jine de church, but dey sho' oughtn't to jine effen dey still gwine to act like Satan.

"Us chillun would git up long 'fore day Chris'mas mawnin'. Us used ter hang our stockin's over de fire place, but when Chris'mas mawnin' come dey wuz so full, hit would of busted 'em to hang 'em up on a nail, so dey wuz allus layin' on Ma's cheer when us waked up. Us chillun won't 'lowed to go 'round de big house early on Chris'mas mawnin' kaze us mought 'sturb our white folkses' rest, and den dey done already seed dat us got plenny Santa Claus in our own cabins. Us didn't know nuffin' 'bout New Years Day when I wuz chillun.

"When any of his Negroes died Ole Marster wuz mighty extra good. He give plenny of time for a fun'ral sermon in de afternoon. Most of da fun'rals wuz in de yard under de trees by de cabins. Atter de sermon, us would go 'crost de hill to de Negro buyin' ground, not far f'um whar our white folkses wuz buried.

"Us never bothered none 'bout Booker Washin'ton, or Mister Lincum, or none of dem folkses 'way off dar kaze us had our raisin' f'um de Lumpkins and dey's de bes' folkses dey is anywhar'. Won't no Mister Lincum or no Booker Washin'ton gwine to help us like Ole Marster and us knowed dat good and plenny.

"I cyan' 'member much 'bout playin' no special games 'ceppin' 'Ole Hundud.' Us would choose one, and dat one would hide his face agin' a tree whilst he counted to a hundud. Den he would hunt for all de others. Dey done been hidin' whilst he wuz countin'. Us larned to count a-playin' 'Ole Hundud'.

"No Ma'am, us never went to no school 'til atter de War. Den I went some at night. I wukked in de day time atter freedom come. My eyes bothered me so I didn't go to school much.

"Yes Ma'am, dey took mighty good care of us effen us got sick. Ole Marster would call in Doctor Moore or Doctor Carleton and have us looked atter. De 'omans had extra good care when dey chilluns comed. 'Til freedom come, I wuz too little to know much 'bout dat myself, but Ma allus said dat Negro 'omans and babies wuz looked atter better 'fore freedom come dan dey ever wuz anymo'.

"Atter de War wuz over, a big passel of Yankee mens come to our big house and stayed. Dey et and slept dar, and dey b'haved powerful nice and perlite to all our white folkses, and dey ain't bother Jedge Lumpkin's servants none. But den evvybody allus b'haved 'round Jedge Lumpkin's place. Ain't nobody gwine to be brash 'nough to do no devilment 'round a Jedges place.

"Hit was long atter de War 'fo' I married. I cyan' 'member nuffin' 'bout my weddin' dress. 'Pears like to me I been married mos' all of my life. Us jes' went to de preacher man's house and got married. Us had eight chillun, but dey is all dead now 'ceppin' two; one son wukkin' way off f'um here, and my daughter in Athens.

"I knows I wuz fixed a heap better fo' de War, than I is now, but I sho' don't want no slav'ry to come back. It would be fine effen evvy Negro had a marster like Jedge Lumpkin, but dey won't all dat sort."

Anna leaned heavily on her cane as she answered the knock on the front door when we visited her home. "Come in," she invited, and led the way through her scrupulously tidy house to the back porch.

"De sun feels good," she said, "and it sorter helps my rheumatiz. My rheumatiz been awful bad lately. I loves to set here whar I kin see dat my ole hen and little chickens don't git in no mischief." A small bucket containing chicken food was conveniently at hand, so she could scatter it on the ground to call her chickens away from depredations on the flowers. A little mouse made frequent excursions into the bucket and helped himself to the cracked grains in the chicken food. "Don't mind him," she admonished, "he jes' plays 'round my cheer all day, and don't bother nuffin'."

"You didn't tell anything about your brothers and

sisters when you talked to me before," her visitor remarked.

"Well, I jes' couldn't 'member all at onct, but atter I got back home and rested up, I sot here and talked ter myself 'bout old times. My brudder Charles wuz de coachman what drove Ole Marster's carriage, and anudder brudder wuz Willie, and one wuz Floyd. My sisters wuz Jane and Harriet. 'Pears like to me dey wuz more of 'em, but some how I jes' cyan' 'member no more 'bout 'em. My husband wuz Grant Parkes and he tuk care of de gyardens and yards for de Lumpkins.

"I had one chile named Caline, for Ole Miss. She died a baby. My daughter Fannie done died long time ago, and my daughter Liza, she wuks for a granddaughter of Ole Miss. I means, Liza wuks for Mister Eddie Lumpkin's daughter. I done plum clear forgot who Mister Eddie's daughter married.

"I jes' cyan' recollec' whar my boy, Floyd, stays. You oughter know, Lady, hits de town whar de President lives. Yes Ma'am, Washin'ton, dats de place whar my Floyd is. I got one more son, but I done plum forgot his name, and whar he wuz las' time I heared f'um him. I don't know if he's livin' or dead. It sho' is bad to git so old you cyan' tell de names of yo' chilluns straight off widout havin' to stop and study, and den you cyan' allus 'member.

"I done been studyin' 'bout da war times, and I 'members dat Ole Marster wuz mighty troubled 'bout his Negroes when he heared a big crowd of Yankee sojers wuz comin' to Athens. Folkses done been sayin' de Yankees would pick out de bes' Negroes and take 'em 'way wid 'em, and dere wuz a heap of talk 'bout de scandlous way dem Yankee sojers been treatin' Negro 'omans and gals. 'Fore dey got here, Ole Marster sent mos' of his bes' Negroes to Augusta to git 'em out of danger f'um de Fed'rals. Howsome-ever de Negroes dat he kept wid' 'im won't bothered none, kaze dem Fed'rals 'spected de Jedge and didn't do no harm 'round his place.

"In Augusta, I stayed on Greene Street wid a white lady named Mrs. Broome. No Ma'am, I nebber done no wuk. I jes' played and frolicked, and had a good time wid Mrs. Broome's babies. She sho' wuz good to me. Ma, she wukked for a Negro 'oman named Mrs. Kemp, and lived in de house wid her.

"Ole Marster sont for us atter de war wuz over, and us wuz mighty proud to git back home. Times had done changed when us got back. Mos' of Ole Marster's money wuz gone, and he couldn't take keer of so many Negroes, so Ma moved over near de gun fact'ry and started takin' in washin'.

"De wust bother Negroes had dem days wuz findin' a place to live. Houses had to be built for 'em, and dey won't no money to build 'em wid.

"One night, jes' atter I got in bed, some mens come walkin' right in Ma's house widout knockin'. I jerked de kivver up over my head quick, and tried to hide. One of de mens axed Ma who she wuz. Ma knowed his voice, so she said: 'You knows me Mister Blank,' (she called him by his sho' 'nuff name) 'I'm Liza Lumpkin, and you knows I used to b'long to Jedge Lumpkin.' De udders jes' laughed at him and said: 'Boy, she knows you, so you better not say nuffin' else.' Den anudder man axed Ma how she wuz makin' a livin'. Ma knowed his voice too, and she called him by name and tole him us wuz takin' in washin' and livin' all right. Dey laughed at him too, and den anudder one axed her sompin' and she called his name when she answered him too. Den de leader say, 'Boys, us better git out of here. These here hoods and robes ain't doin' a bit of good here. She knows ev'ry one of us and can tell our names.' Den dey went out laughin' fit to kill, and dat wuz de onliest time de Ku Kluxers ever wuz at our house, leastways us s'posed dey wuz Ku Kluxers.

"I don't 'member much 'bout no wuk atter freedom 'ceppin' de wash tub. Maw larned me how to wash and iron. She said: 'Some day I'll be gone f'um dis world, and you won't know nuffin' 'bout takin' keer of yo'self, lessen you larn right now.' I wuz mighty proud when I could do up a weeks washin' and take it back to my white folkses and git sho' 'nuff money for my wuk. I felt like I wuz a grown 'oman den. It wuz in dis same yard dat Ma larned me to wash. At fust Ma rented dis place. There wuz another house here den. Us saved our washin' money and bought de place, and dis is de last of three houses on dis spot. Evvy cent spent on dis place wuz made by takin' in washin' and de most of it wuz made washin' for Mister Eddie Lumpkin's family.

"Heaps of udder Negroes wuz smart like Ma, and dey got along all right. Dese days de young folkses don't try so hard. Things comes lots easier for 'em, and dey got lots better chances dan us had, but dey don't pay no 'tention to nuffin' but spendin' all dey got, evvy day. Boys is wuss'en gals. Long time ago I done give all I got to my daughter. She takes keer of me. Effen de roof leaks, she has it looked atter. She wuks and meks our livin'. I didn't want nobody to show up here atter I die and take nuffin' away f'um her.

"I ain' never had no hard times. I allus been treated good and had a good livin'. Course de rheumatiz done got me right bad, but I is still able to git about and tend to de house while my gal is off at wuk. I wanted to wash today, but I couldn't find no soap. My gal done hid de soap, kaze she say I'se too old to do my own washin' and she wanter wash my clo'es herse'f."

In parting, the old woman said rather apologetically, "I couldn't tell you 'bout no sho' 'nuff hard times. Atter de War I wukked hard, but I ain't never had no hard times".

[HW: Dist. 5
Ex-Slave #83]

"A TALK WITH
G.W. PATTILLO—EX-SLAVE"
[HW: age 78]

Submitted by
Minnie B. Ross

Typed by:
J.C. Russell
1-22-37
[Date Stamp: MAY 8 1937]

[TR: In Informants List, G.W. Pattillio]

G.W. PATTILLO

In the shelter provided by the Department of Public Welfare, lives an old Negro, G.W. Pattillo, who was born in Spaulding County, Griffin, Ga., in the year 1852. His parents, Harriett and Jake Pattillo, had twelve children, of whom he was the second youngest. Their master was Mr. T.J. Ingram. However, they kept the name of their old master, Mr. Pattillo.

Master Ingram, as he was affectionately called by his slaves, was considered a "middle class man," who owned 100 acres of land, with one family of slaves, and was more of a truck farmer than a plantation owner. He raised enough cotton to supply the needs of his family and his slaves and enough cattle to furnish food, but his main crops were corn, wheat, potatoes and truck.

With a few slaves and a small farm, Master Ingram was very lenient and kind to his slaves and usually worked with them in the fields. "We had no special time to begin or end the work for the day. If he got tired he would say, 'Alright, boys, let's stop and rest,' and sometimes we didn't start working until late in the day."

Pattillo's mother was cook and general house servant, so well thought of by the Ingram family that she managed the house as she saw fit and planned the meals likewise. Young Pattillo was considered a pet by everyone and hung around the mistress, since she did not have any children of her own. His job was to hand her the scissors and thread her needles. "I was her special pet," said Pattillo, "and my youngest brother was the master's special pet." Mr. and Mrs. Ingram never punished the children, nor allowed anyone but their parents to do so. If the boy became unruly, Mrs. Ingram would call his mother and say, "Harriett, I think G.W. needs to be taken down a button hole lower."

The master's house, called the "Big House," was a two-story frame structure consisting of 10 rooms. Although not a mansion, it was fairly comfortable. The home provided for Pattillo's family was a three-room frame house furnished comfortably with good home-made furniture.

Pattillo declared that he had never seen anyone on the Ingram Plantation punished by the owner, who never allowed the "paterrollers" to punish them either.

Master Ingram placed signs at different points on his plantation which read thus: "Paterrollers, Fishing and Hunting Prohibited on this Plantation." It soon became known by all that the Ingram slaves were not given passes by their owner to go any place, consequently they were known as "Old Ingram's Free Niggers."

Master Ingram could not write, but would tell his slaves to inform anyone who wished to know, that they belonged to J.D. Ingram. "Once," said Pattillo, "my brother Willis, who was known for his gambling and drinking, left our plantation and no one knew where he had gone. As we sat around a big open fire cracking walnuts, Willis came up, jumped off his horse and fell to the ground. Directly behind him rode a 'paterroller.' The master jumped up and commanded him to turn around and leave his premises. The 'Paterroller' ignored his warning and advanced still further. The master then took his rifle and shot him. He fell to the ground dead and Master Ingram said to his wife, 'Well, Lucy, I guess the next time I speak to that scoundrel he will take heed.' The master then saddled his horse and rode into town. Very soon a wagon came back and moved the body."

The cotton raised was woven into cloth from which their clothing was made. "We had plenty of good clothing and food," Pattillo continued. "The smokehouse was never locked and we had free access to the whole house. We never knew the meaning of a key."

Master Ingram was very strict about religion and attending Church. It was customary for everyone to attend the 9 o'clock prayer services at his home every night. The Bible was read by the mistress, after which the master would conduct prayer. Children as well as grownups were expected to attend. On Sundays, everybody attended church. Separate Churches were provided for the Negroes, with White and Colored preachers conducting the services. White Deacons were also the Deacons of the Colored Churches and a colored man was never appointed deacon of a Church. Only white ministers were priviliged to give the sacrament and do the baptizing. Their sermons were of a strictly religious nature. When a preacher was unable to read, someone was appointed to read the text. The preacher would then build his sermon from it. Of course, during the conference period, colored as well as white ministers were privileged to make the appointments. The Negroes never took up collections but placed their money in an envelope and passed it in. It was their own money, earned with the master's consent, by selling apples, eggs, chickens, etc.

Concerning marriages, Pattillo believes in marriages as they were in the olden days. "Ef two people felt they wuz made for each other, they wuz united within themselves when they done git the master's 'greement, then live together as man and wife, an' that was all. Now, you got to buy a license and pay the preacher."

Loss of life among slaves was a calamity and if a doctor earned a reputation for losing his patients, he might as well seek a new community. Often his downfall would begin by some such comment as, "Dr. Brown lost old man Ingram's nigger John. He's no good and I don't intend to use him." The value of slaves varied, from $500 to $10,000, depending on his or her special qualifications. Tradesmen such as blacksmiths, shoe makers, carpenters, etc., were seldom sold under $10,000. Rather than sell a tradesman slave, owners kept them in order to make money by hiring them out to other owners for a set sum per season. However, before the deal was closed the lessee would have to sign a contract which assured the slave's owner that the slave would receive the best of treatment while in possession.

Pattillo remembers hearing his parents say the North and South had disagreed and Abraham Lincoln was going to free the slaves. Although he never saw a battle fought, there were days when he sat and watched the long line of soldiers passing, miles and miles of them. Master Ingram did not enlist but remained at home to take care of his family and his possessions.

After the war ended, Master Ingram called his slaves together and told them of their freedom, saying, "Mr. Lincoln whipped the South and we are going back to the Union. You are as free as I am and if you wish to remain here you may. If not, you may go any place you wish. I am not rich but we can work together here for both our families, sharing everything we raise equally." Pattillo's family remained there until 1870. Some owners kept their slaves in ignorance of their freedom. Others were kind enough to offer them homes and help them to get a start.

After emancipation, politics began to play a part in the lives of ex-slaves, and many were approached by candidates who wanted to buy their votes. Pattillo tells of an old ex-slave owner named Greeley living in Upson County who bought an ex-slaves vote by giving him as payment a ham, a sack of flour and a place to stay on his plantation. After election, he ordered the ex-slave to get the wagon, load it with his possessions and move away from his plantation. Astonished, the old Negro asked why. "Because," replied old Greeley, "If you allow anyone to buy your vote and rob you of your rights as a free citizen, someone could hire you to set my house on fire."

Pattillo remebers slavery gratefully and says he almost wishes these days were back again.

EX-SLAVE INTERVIEW

ALEC POPE, Age 84
1345 Rockspring Street
Athens, Georgia

Written by:
Sadie B. Hornsby
Federal Writers' Project
Athens, Ga.

Edited by:
Sarah H. Hall
Athens

and
John N. Booth
District Supervisor
Federal Writers' Project
Augusta, Ga.

April 28, 1938
[Date Stamp: MAY 6 1938]

ALEC POPE

Alec lives with his daughter, Ann Whitworth. When asked if he liked to talk about his childhood days, he answered: "Yes Ma'am, but is you one of dem pension ladies?" The negative reply was an evident disappointment to Alec, but it did not hinder his narrative:

"Well, I wuz born on de line of Clarke and Oglethorpe Counties, way down de country. Celia and Willis Pope wuz my ma and pa. Lawdy! Mist'ess, I don't know whar dey come f'um; 'peers lak pa's fust Marster wuz named Pope. Dat's de onlies' last name I ever ricollec' us havin'.

"Dere wuz a passel of us chillun. My sisters wuz Sallie, Phebie Ann, Nelia, and Millie. My brudders wuz Anderson, Osborn, George, Robert, Squire, Jack, and Willis. Willis wuz named for pa and us nicknamed 'im Tuck.

"De slave quarters wuz little log houses scattered here and dar. Some of 'em had two rooms on de fust flo' and a loft up 'bove whar de boys most genially slep' and de gals slep' downstairs. I don't 'member nothin' t'all 'bout what us done 'cept scrap lak chilluns will do.

"Oh! I ain't forgot 'bout dem beds. Dey used cords for springs, and de cords run f'um head to foot; den dey wove 'em 'cross de bed 'til dey looked lak checks. Wheat straw wuz sewed up in ticks for mattresses. When you rolled 'round on one of dem straw mattresses, de straw crackled and sounded lak rain. No Ma'am, I don't know nothin' t'all 'bout my gran'pa and gran'ma.

"I wuz de reg'lar water boy, and I plowed some too. 'Course dere wuz so many on dat plantation it tuk more'n one boy to tote de water. Money? dis Nigger couldn't git no money in dem days.

"Us sho' had plenty somepin' t'eat, sich as meat, and cornbread, and good old wheat bread what wuz made out of seconds. Dere wuz lots of peas, corn, cabbage, Irish 'tatoes, sweet 'tatoes, and chickens, sometimes. Yes Ma'am, sometimes. I laks coffee, but us Niggers didn't have much coffee. Dat wuz for de white folkses at de big house. Cookin' wuz done in de fireplace in great big spiders. Some of de biggest of de spiders wuz called ovens. Dey put coals of fire underneath and more coals on top of de lid. Ma baked bread and 'taters in de ashes. In winter she put de dough in a collard leaf so it wouldn't burn. In summer green corn shucks wuz wrapped 'round de dough 'stid of collard leaves. All de fish and 'possums and rabbits us had wuz cotch right dar on Old Marster's place, 'cause if one of our Niggers got cotch offen our place hit wuz jes' too bad. I sho' does love 'possum, and us had lots of 'em, 'cause my brudder used to ketch 'em by de wholesale wid a dog he had, and dat same dog wuz a powerful good rabbit hound too.

"Us had pretty good clothes most all de year 'round. In summer, shirts, and pants wuz made out of coarse cotton cloth. Sometimes de pants wuz dyed gray. Winter time us had better clothes made out of yarn and us allus had good Sunday clothes. 'Course I wuz jes' a plow boy den and now I done forgot lots 'bout how things looked. Our shoes wuz jes' common brogans, no diff'unt on Sunday, 'ceppin' de Nigger boys what wuz shinin' up to de gals cleaned up deir shoes dat day.

"Our Marster wuz Mr. Mordecai Ed'ards. Well, he wuz pretty good—not too good. He tried to make you do right, but if you didn't he would give you a good brushin'. Miss Martha, Old Marster's old 'oman, warn't good as Old Marster, but she done all right. Dey had a heap of chillun: Miss Susan, Miss Mary, Miss Callie, Miss Alice, and it 'peers to me lak dere wuz two mo' gals, but I can't 'call 'em now. Den dere wuz some boys: Marse Billy, Marse Jim, Marse John, Marse Frank, and Marse Howard. Marse Frank Ed'ards lives on Milledge Avenue now.

"Old Marster and Old Mist'ess lived in a great big fine house what looked to me lak one of dese big hotels does now. Marse Jack Ed'ards wuz de fust overseer I can ricollec'. He wuz kin to Old Marster. Marster had two or three mo' overseers at diff'unt times, but I don't ricollec' dey names. Dere wuz two car'iage drivers. Henry driv de gals 'round and Albert wuz Old Mist'ess' driver. Old Marster had his own hoss and buggy, and most of de time he driv for hisself, but he allus tuk a little Nigger boy namad Jordan 'long to help him drive and to hold de hoss.

"Lawdy! Mist'ess, I couldn't rightly say how many acres wuz in dat plantation. I knowed he had two plantations wid fine houses on 'em. He jes' had droves and droves of Niggers and when dey got scattered out over de fields, dey looked lak blackbirds dere wuz so many. You see I wuz jes' a plow boy and didn't know nothin' 'bout figgers and countin'.

"De overseer got us up 'bout four o'clock in de mornin' to feed de stock. Den us et. Us allus stopped off by dark. Mist'ess dere's a old sayin' dat you had to brush a Nigger in dem days to make 'em do right. Dey brushed us if us lagged in de field or cut up de cotton. Dey could allus find some fault wid us. Marster brushed us some time, but de overseer most gen'ally done it. I 'members dey used to make de 'omans pull up deir skirts and brushed 'em wid a horse whup or a hickory; dey done de mens de same way 'cept dey had to take off deir shirts and pull deir pants down. Niggers sho' would holler when dey got brushed.

"Jails! Yes Ma'am, dey had 'em way down in Lexin'ton. You know some Niggers gwine steal anyhow, and dey put 'em in dere for dat mostly. I didn't never see nobody sold or in chains. De only chains I ever seed wuz on hosses and plows.

"Mist'ess, Niggers didn't have no time to larn to read in no Bible or nothin' lak dat in slav'ry time. Us went to church wid de white folkses if us wanted to, but us warn't 'bleeged to go. De white folkses went to church at Cherokee Corner. Dere warn't no special church for Niggers 'til long atter de War when dey built one out nigh de big road.

"Some of de Niggers run away to de Nawth—some dey got back, some dey didn't. Dem patterollers had lots of fun if dey cotch a Nigger, so dey could brush 'im to hear 'im holler. De onlies' trouble I ever heard 'bout twixt de whites and blacks wuz when a Nigger sassed a white man and de white man shot 'im. H'it served dat Nigger right, 'cause he oughta knowed better dan to sass a white man. De trouble ended wid dat shot.

"De most Niggers ever done for a good time wuz to have little parties wid heaps of fidlin' and dancin'. On Sunday nights dey would have prayer meetin's. Dem patterollers would come and break our prayer meetin's up and brush us if dey cotch us.

"Chris'mas wuz somepin' else. Us had awful good times den, 'cause de white folkses at de big house give us plenty of goodies for Chris'mas week and us had fidlin' and dancin'. Us would ring up de gals and run all 'round 'em playin' dem ring-'round-de-rosie games. Us had more good times at corn shuckin's, and Old Marster allus had a little toddy to give us den to make us wuk faster.

"Oh! No Ma'am, I don't 'member nothin' 'bout what us played when I wuz a little chap, and if I ever knowed anything 'bout Rawhead and Bloody Bones and sich lak I done plumb forgot it now. But I do know Old Marster and

Old Mist'ess sho' wuz powerful good when dey Niggers got sick. Dey put a messenger boy on a mule and sont 'im for Dr. Hudson quick, 'cause to lose a Nigger wuz losin' a good piece of property. Some Niggers wore some sort of beads 'round deir necks to keep sickness away and dat's all I calls to mind 'bout dat charm business.

"I wuz jes' a plow boy so I didn't take in 'bout de surrender. De only thing I ricollects 'bout it wuz when Old Marster told my pa and ma us wuz free and didn't belong to him no more. He said he couldn't brush de grown folks no more, but if dey wanted to stay wid 'im dey could, and dat he would brush dey chilluns if dey didn't do right. Ma told 'im he warn't gwine brush none of her chilluns no more.

"Us lived wid Old Marster 'bout a year, den pa moved up on de big road. Buy land? No Ma'am, Niggers didn't have no money to buy no land wid 'til dey made it. I didn't take in 'bout Mr. Lincoln, only dat thoo' him us wuz sot free. I heard 'em say Mr. Davis wuz de President of de South, and 'bout Booker Washin'ton some of de Niggers tuk him in, but I didn't bodder 'bout him.

"Lawdy! Mist'ess, I didn't marry de fust time 'til long atter de War, and now I done been married three times. I had a awful big weddin' de fust time. De white man what lived on de big road not far f'um us said he never seed sich a weddin' in his life. Us drunk and et, and danced and cut de buck most all night long. Most all my chilluns is dead. I b'lieve my fust wife had 10 or 11 chilluns. I know I had a passel fust and last; and jes' to tell you de trufe, dere jes' ain't no need to stop and try to count de grand chilluns. All three of my wives done daid and I'm lookin' for anudder one to take keer of me now.

"Why did I jine de church? 'Cause I jes' think evvybody oughta jine if dey wanna do right so'se dey can go to Heben. I feels lak a diff'unt man since I done jined and I knows de Lord has done forgive me for all my sins.

"Mist'ess ain't you thoo' axin' me questions yit? Anyhow I wuz thinkin' you wuz one of dem pension ladies." When he was told that the interview was completed, Alec said: "I sho' is glad, 'cause I feels lak takin' a little nap atter I eat dese pecans what I got in my pocket. Goodbye Mist'ess."

United States. Work Projects Administration

[HW: Dist. 5
Ex-Slave #84]

Whitley, Driskell
1-20-37

SLAVERY AS WITNESSED BY ANNIE PRICE
[Date Stamp: MAY 8 1937]

ANNIE PRICE

Mrs. Annie Price was born in Spaulding County, Georgia October 12, 1855. Although only a mere child when freedom was declared she is able to relate quite a few events in her own life as well as some of the experiences of other slaves who lived in the same vicinity as she.

Her mother and father Abe and Caroline were owned by a young married couple named Kennon. (When this couple were married Abe and Caroline had been given as wedding presents by the bride's and the groom's parents). Besides her parents there four brothers and five sisters all of whom were younger than she with one exception. The first thing that she remembers of her mother is that of seeing her working in the "Marster's" kitchen.

Mr. Kennon was described as being a rather young man who was just getting a start in life. His family consisted of his wife and about five children. He was not a mean individual. The plantation on which he lived was a small one, having been given to him by his father (whose plantation adjoined) in order to give him a start. Mr. Kennon owned one other slave besides Mrs. Price and her family while his father owned a large number some of whom he used to lend to the younger Mr. Kennon. Cotton and all kinds of vegetables were raised. There was also some live stock.

As Mr. Kennon owned only a few slaves it was necessary for these few persons to do all of the work. Says Mrs. Price: "My mother had to do everything from cultivating cotton to cooking." The same was true of her father and the other servant. Before the break of day each morning they were all called to prepare for the day's work. Mrs. Price then told how she has seen the men of her plantation and those of the adjoining one going to the fields at this unearthly hour eating their breakfast while sitting astride the back of a mule. After her mother had finished cooking and cleaning the house she was sent to the field to help the men. When it was too dark to see all field hands were permitted to return to their cabins. This same routine was followed each day except Sundays when they were permitted to do much as they pleased. When the weather was too bad for field work they shelled corn and did other types of work not requiring too much exposure. Holidays were unheard of on the Kennon plantation. As a little slave girl the only work that Mrs. Price ever had to do was to pick up chips and bark for her mother to cook with. The rest of the time was spent in playing with the "Marster's" little girls.

"The servants on our plantation always had a plenty of clothes," continued Mrs. Price, "while those on the plantation next to ours (Mrs. Kennon's father) never had enough, especially in the winter." This clothing was given when it was needed and not at any specified time as was the case on some of the other plantations in that community. All of these articles were made on the plantation and the materials that were mostly used were homespun (which was also woven on the premises) woolen goods, cotton goods and calico. It has been mentioned before that the retinue of servants was small in number and so for this reason all of them had a reasonable amount of those clothes that had been discarded by the master and the mistress. After the leather had been cured it was taken to the Tannery where crude shoes called "Twenty Grands" were made. These shoes often caused the wearer no little amount of discomfort until they were thoroughly broken in.

For bedding, homespun sheets were used. The quilts and blankets were made from pieced cotton material along with garments that were unfit for further wear. Whenever it was necessary to dye any of these articles a type of dye made by boiling the bark from trees was used.

In the same manner that clothing was plentiful so was there always enough food. When Mrs. Price was asked if the slaves owned by Mr. Kennon were permitted to cultivate a garden of their own she stated that they did'nt need to do this because of the fact that Mr. Kennon raised everything that was necessary and they often had more than enough. Their week-day diet usually consisted of fried meat, grits, syrup and corn bread for breakfast; vegetables, pot liquor or milk, and corn bread for dinner; and for supper there was milk and bread or fried meat and bread. On Sunday they were given a kind of flour commonly known as the "seconds" from which biscuits were made. "Sometimes", continued Mrs. Price, "my mother brought us the left-overs from the master's table and this was usually a meal by itself". In addition to this Mr. Kennon allowed hunting as well as fishing and so on many days there were fish and roast 'possum. Food on the elder Mr. Kennon plantation was just as scarce as it was plentiful on his son's. When asked how she knew about this Mrs. Price told how she had seen her father take meat from his master's smoke house and hide it so that he could give it to those slaves who invaribly slipped over at night in search of food. The elder Mr. Kennon had enough food but he was too mean to see his slaves enjoy themselves by having full stomachs.

All cooking on Mrs. Price's plantation was done by her mother.

All of the houses on the Kennon plantation were made of logs including that of Mr. Kennon himself. There were only two visible differences in the dwelling places of the slaves and that of Mr. Kennon and there were (1) several rooms instead of the one room allowed the slaves and (2) weatherboard was used on the inside to keep the weather out while the slaves used mud to serve for this purpose. In these crude one-roomed houses (called stalls) there was a bed made of some rough wood. Rope tied from side to side served as the springs for the mattress which was a bag filled with straw and leaves. There were also one or two boxes which were used as chairs. The chimney was made of rocks and mud. All cooking was done here at the fireplace. Mrs. Price says; "Even Old Marster did'nt have a stove to cook on so you know we did'nt." The only available light was that furnished by the fire. Only one family was allowed to a cabin so as to prevent overcrowding. In addition to a good shingle roof each one of these dwellings had a board floor. All floors were of dirt on the plantation belonging to the elder Mr. Kennon.

A doctor was employed to attend to those persons who were sick. However he never got chance to practice on the Kennon premises as there was never any serious illness. Minor cases of sickness were usually treated by giving the patient a dose of castor oil or several doses of some form of home made medicine which the slaves made themselves from roots that they gathered in the woods. In order to help keep his slaves in good health Mr. Kennon required them to keep the cabins they occupied and their surroundings clean at all times.

Mrs. Price said that the slaves had very few amusements and as far as she can remember she never saw her parents indulge in any form of play at all. She remembers, however, that on the adjoining plantation the slaves often had frolics where they sang and danced far into the night. These frolics were not held very often but were usually few and far between.

As there was no church on the plantation Mr. Kennon gave them a pass on Sundays so that they could attend one of the churches that the town afforded. The sermons they heard were preached by a white preacher and on rare occasions by a colored preacher. Whenever the colored pastor preached there were several white persons present to see that [HW: no] doctrine save that laid down by them should be preached. All of the marrying on both plantations [TR: duplicate section removed here] was done by a preacher.

It has been said that a little learning is a dangerous thing and this certainly was true as far as the slaves were concerned, according to Mrs. Price. She says: "If any of us were ever caught with a book we would get a good whipping." Because of their great fear of such a whipping none of them ever attempted to learn to read or to write.

As a general rule Mrs. Price and the other nembers of her family were always treated kindly by the Kennon family. None of them were ever whipped or mistreated in any way. Mrs. Price says that she has seen slaves on the adjoining plantation whipped until the blood ran. She describes the sight in the following manner. "The one to be whipped was tied across a log or to a tree and then his shirt was dropped around his waist and he was lashed with a cow hide whip until his back was raw." Whippings like these were given when a slave was unruly or disobedient or when he ran away. Before a runaway slave could be whipped he had to be caught and the chief way of doing this was to put the blood hounds (known to the slaves as "nigger hounds") on the fugitive's trail. Mrs. Price once saw a man being taken to his master after he had been caught by the dogs. She says that his skin was cut and torn in any number of places and he looked like one big mass of blood. Her father once ran away to escape a whipping.(this was during the Civil War), and he was able to elude the dogs as well as his human pursuers. When asked about the final outcome of this escape Mrs. Price replied that her father remained in hiding until the war was over with and then he was able to show himself without any fear.

She has also seen slaves being whipped by a group of white men when her parents said were the "Paddie-Rollers". It was their duty to whip those slaves who were caught away from their respective plantations without a "pass", she was told.

According to Mrs. Price the jails were built for the "white folks". When a slave did something wrong his master punished him.

She does'nt remember anything about the beginning of the Civil War neither did she understand its significance until Mr. Kennon died as a result of the wounds that he received while in action. This impressed itself on her mind indelibly because Mr. Kennon was the first dead person she had ever seen. The Yankee troops did'nt come near their plantation and so they had a plenty of food to satisfy their needs all during the war. Even after the war was over there was still a plenty of all the necessities of life.

When Mrs. Kennon informed them that they were free to go or to stay as they pleased, her father, who had just come out of hiding, told Mrs. Kennon that he did not want to remain on the plantation any longer than it was necessary to get his family together. He said that he wanted to get out to himself so that he could see how it felt to be free. Mrs. Price says that as young as she was she felt very happy because the yoke of bondage was gone and she knew that she could have a privelege like everybody else. And so she and her family moved away and her father began farming for himself. His was prosperous until his death. After she left the plantation of her birth she lived with her father until she became a grown woman and then she married a Mr. Price who was also a farmer.

Mrs. Price believes that she has lived to reach such

a ripe old age because she has always served God and because she always tried to obey those older than she.

[HW: Dist. 6
Ex-Slave #87]

A FEW FACTS OF SLAVERY BY
CHARLIE PYE—Ex-Slave
[Date Stamp: MAY -- --]

CHARLIE PYE

The writer was much surprised to learn that the person whom she was about to interview was nine years old when the Civil War ended. His youthful appearance at first made her realize that probably he was not an ex-slave after all. Very soon she learned differently. Another surprise followed the first in that his memory of events during that period was very hazy. The few facts learned are related as follows:

Mr. Charlie Pye was born in Columbus, Ga., 1856 and was the ninth child of his parents, Tom Pye and Emmaline Highland. Tom Pye, the father, belonged to Volantine Pye, owner of a plantation in Columbus, Ga. known as the Lynch and Pye Plantation.

Mr. Pye's mistress was Miss Mary Ealey, who later married a Mr. Watts. Miss Ealey owned a large number of slaves, although she did not own a very large plantation. Quite a few of her slaves were hired out to other owners. The workers on the plantation were divided into two or more groups, each group having a different job to do. For instance, there were the plow hands, hoe hands, log cutters, etc. Mr. Pye's mother was a plow hand and besides this, she often had to cut logs. Mr. Pye was too young to work and spent most of his time playing around the yards.

Houses on the Ealey plantation were built of pine poles after which the cracks were filled with red mud. Most of these houses consisted of one room; however, a few were built with two rooms to accommodate the larger families. The beds, called "bunks" by Mr. Pye were nailed to the sides of the room. Roped bottoms covered with a mattress of burlap and hay served to complete this structure called a bed. Benches and a home made table completed the furnishings. There were very few if any real chairs found in the slave homes. The houses and furniture were built by skilled Negro carpenters who were hired by the mistress from other slave owners. A kind slave owner would allow a skilled person to hire his own time and keep most of the pay which he earned.

Plenty of food was raised on the Ealey plantation, but the slave families were restricted to the same diet of corn meal, syrup, and fat bacon. Children were fed "pot likker", milk and bread from poplar troughs, from which they ate with wooden spoons. Grown-ups ate with wooden forks. Slaves were not allowed to raise gardens of their own, although Mr. Pye's uncle was given the privilege of owning a rice patch, which he worked at night.

In every slave home was found a wooden loom which was operated by hands and feet, and from which the cloth for their clothing was made. When the work in the fields was finished women were required to come home and spin one cut (thread) at night. Those who were not successful in completing this work were punished the next morning. Men wore cotton shirts and pants which were dyed different colors with red oak bark, alum and copper. Copper produced an "Indigo blue color." "I have often watched dye in the process of being made," remarked Mr. Pye. Mr. Pye's father was a shoemaker and made all shoes needed on the plantation. The hair was removed from the hides by a process known as tanning. Red oak bark was often used for it produced an acid which proved very effective in tanning hides. Slaves were given shoes every three months.

To see that everyone continued working an overseer rode over the plantation keeping check on the workers. If any person was caught resting he was given a sound whipping. Mr. Pye related the following incident which happened on the Ealey plantation. "A young colored girl stopped to rest for a few minutes and my uncle stopped also and spoke to her. During this conversation the overseer came up and began whipping the girl with a "sapling tree." My uncle became very angry and picked up an axe and hit the overseer in the head, killing him. The mistress was very fond of my uncle and kept him hid until she could "run him." Running a slave was the method they used in sending a slave to another state in order that he could escape punishment and be sold again. You were only given this privilege if it so happened that you were cared for by your mistress and master."

Overseers on the Ealey plantation were very cruel and whipped slaves unmercifully. Another incident related by Mr. Pye was as follows:

"My mother resented being whipped and would run away to the woods and often remained as long as twelve months at a time. When the strain of staying away from her family became too great, she would return home. No sooner would she arrive than the old overseer would tie her to a peach tree and whip her again. The whipping was done by a "Nigger Driver," who followed the overseer around with a bull whip; especially for this purpose. The largest man on the plantation was chosen to be the "Nigger Driver."

"Every slave had to attend church, although there were no separate churches provided for them. However, they were allowed to occupy the benches which were placed in the rear of the church. To attend church on another plantation, slaves had to get a pass or suffer punishment from the "Pader Rollers." (Patrollers)

"We didn't marry on our plantation", remarked Mr. Pye. After getting the consent of both masters the couple jumped the broom, and that ended the so called ceremony. Following the marriage there was no frolic or celebration.

"Sometimes quilting parties were held in the various cabins on the plantation. Everyone would assist in making the winter bed covering for one family one night and the next night for some other family, and so on until everyone had sufficient bed covering.

"A doctor was only called when a person had almost reached the last stages of illness. Illness was often an excuse to remain away from the field. "Blue mass pills", castor oil, etc. were kept for minor aches and pains. When a slave died he was buried as quickly as a box could be nailed together.

"I often heard of people refugeeing during the Civil

War period," remarked Mr. Pye. "In fact, our mistress refugeed to Alabama trying to avoid meeting the Yanks, but they came in another direction. On one occasion the Yanks came to our plantation, took all the best mules and horses, after which they came to my mother's cabin and made her cook eggs for them. They kept so much noise singing, "I wish I was in Dixie" that I could not sleep. After freedom we were kept in ignorance for quite a while but when we learned the truth my mother was glad to move away with us."

"Immediately after the war ex-slave families worked for one-third and one-fourth of the crops raised on different plantations. Years later families were given one-half of the crops raised."

Mr. Pye ended the interview by telling the writer that he married at the age of 35 years and was the father of two children, one of whom is living. He is a Baptist, belonging to Mount Zion Church, and has attended church regularly and believes that by leading a clean, useful life he has lengthened his days on this earth. During his lifetime Mr. Pye followed railroad work. Recently, however, he has had to give this up because of his health.

United States. Work Projects Administration

[HW: Dist. 1
Ex-Slave #91]

SUBJECT: CHARLOTTE RAINES—OGLETHORPE CO.
DISTRICT: W.P.A. NO. 1
RESEARCH WORKER: JOHN N. BOOTH
DATE: JANUARY 18, 1937
[Date Stamp: JAN 26 1937]
[Date Stamp: MAY 8 1937]

CHARLOTTE RAINES

Aunt Charlotte Raines, well up in the seventies at the time of her death some years ago, was an excellent example of the type of negro developed by the economic system of the old South.

When I could first remember, Charlotte was supreme ruler of the kitchen of my home. Thin to emaciation and stooped almost to the point of having a hump on her back she was yet wiry and active. Her gnarled old hands could turn out prodigous amounts of work when she chose to extend herself.

Her voice was low and musical and she seldom raised it above the ordinary tone of conversation; yet when she spoke other colored people hastened to obey her and even the whites took careful note of what she said. Her head was always bound in a snow-white turban. She wore calico or gingham print dresses and white aprons and these garments always appeared to be freshly laundered.

Charlotte seldom spoke unless spoken to and she would never tell very much about her early life. She had been trained as personal maid to one of her ex-master's daughters. This family, (that of Swepson H. Cox) was one of the most cultured and refined that Lexington, in Oglethorpe County, could boast.

Aunt Charlotte never spoke of her life under the old regime but she had supreme contempt for "no count niggers that didn't hav' no white Folks". She was thrifty and frugal. Having a large family, most of her small earnings was spent on them. However, she early taught her children to scratch for themselves. Two of her daughters died after they had each brought several children into the world. Charlotte thought they were being neglected by their fathers and proceeded to take them "to raise myse'f". These grand children were the apple of her eye and she did much more for them than she had done for her own children.

The old woman had many queer ways. Typical of her eccentricities was her iron clad refusal to touch one bite of food in our house. If she wished a dish she was preparing tasted to see that it contained the proper amount of each ingredient she would call some member of the family, usually my grandmother, and ask that he or she sample the food. Paradoxically, she had no compunctions about the amount of food she carried home for herself and her family.

Strange as it may seem, Charlotte was an incorrigible rogue. My mother and my grandmother both say that they have seen her pull up her skirts and drop things into a flour sack which she always wore tied round her waist just for this purpose. I myself have seen this sack so full that it would bump against her knee. She did not confine her thefts to food only. She would also take personal belongings. Another servant in the household once found one of Aunt Charlotte's granddaughters using a compact that she had stolen from her young mistress. The servant took the trinket away from the girl and returned it to the owner but nothing was ever said to Aunt Charlotte although every one knew she had stolen it.

One year when the cherry crop was exceptionally heavy, grandmother had Charlotte make up a huge batch of cherry preserves in an iron pot. While Charlotte was out of the kitchen for a moment she went in to have a look at the preserves and found that about half of them had been taken out. A careful but hurried search located the missing portion hidden in another container behind the stove. Grandmother never said a word but simply put the amount that had been taken out back in the pot.

Charlotte never permitted anyone to take liberties with her except Uncle Daniel, the "man of all work" and another ex-slave. Daniel would josh her about some "beau" or about her over-fondness for her grandchildren. She would take just so much of this and then with a quiet "g'long with you", she would send him on about his business. Once when he pressed her a bit too far she hurled a butcher knife at him.

Charlotte was not a superstitious soul. She did not even believe that the near-by screech of an owl was an omen of death. However, she did have some fearful and wonderful folk remedies.

When you got a bee sting Charlotte made Daniel spit tobacco juice on it. She always gave a piece of fat meat to babies because this would make them healthy all their lives. Her favorite remedy was to put a pan of cold water under the bed to stop "night sweats."

In her last years failing eye-sight and general ill health forced her to give up her active life. Almost a complete shut-in, she had a window cut on the north side of her room so she could "set and see whut went on up at Mis' Molly's" (her name for my grandmother).

She was the perfect hostess and whenever any member of our family went to see how she did during those latter days she always served locust beer and cookies. Once when I took her a bunch of violets she gave me an old coin that she had carried on her person for years. Mother didn't want me to take it because Charlotte's husband had given it to her and she set great store by it. However, the old woman insisted that I be allowed to keep the token arguing it would not be of use to her much longer anyway.

She died about a month later and in accordance with her instructions her funeral was conducted like "white folk's buryin'", that is without the night being filled with wailing and minus the usual harangue at the church. Even in death Charlotte still thought silence golden.

[HW: Dist. 1
Ex-Slave #90]

SUBJECT: FANNY RANDOLPH—EX-SLAVE
Jefferson, Georgia
RESEARCH WORKER: MRS. MATTIE B. ROBERTS
EDITOR: JOHN N. BOOTH
SUPERVISOR: MISS VELMA BELL
DISTRICT: W.P.A. NO. 1
DATE: MARCH 29, 1937
[Date Stamp: MAY 8 1937]

FANNY RANDOLPH

Perhaps the oldest ex-slave living today is found in Jefferson, Georgia. Fanny Randolph is a little old wrinkled-faced woman, but at the time of our visit she was very neat in a calico dress and a white apron with a bandanna handkerchief around her head.

We saw her at the home of a niece with whom she lives, all of her own family being dead. Her room was tidy, and she had a bright log fire burning in the wide old fire place. She readily consented to talk about slavery times.

"Honey, I doan know how ole I is, but I'se been here er long time and I'se been told by folks whut knows, dat I'se, maybe, mo' dan er hunderd years ole. I 'members back er long time befo' de war. My mammy and daddy wuz bofe slaves. My daddy's name wuz Daniel White an' my mammy's name befo' she married wuz Sarah Moon, she b'longed ter Marse Bob Moon who lived in Jackson

County over near whar Winder is now. He wuz er big landowner an' had lots uv slaves."

"When I wuz 'bout nine years ole, Marse Bob tuk me up ter de "big house" ter wait on ole Mistis. I didn't hav' much ter do, jes' had ter he'p 'er dress an' tie 'er shoes an' run eroun' doin' errands fur 'er. Yer know, in dem times, de white ladies had niggers ter wait on 'em an' de big niggers done all de hard wuk 'bout de house an' yard."

"Atter some years my mammy an' daddy bofe died, so I jes' stayed at de "big house" an' wukked on fer Marse Bob an' ole Mistis."

"Atter I growed up, us niggers on Marse Bob's plantation had big times at our corn shuckin's an' dances. Us 'ud all git tergether at one uv de cabins an us 'ud have er big log fire an' er room ter dance in. Den when us had all shucked corn er good while ever nigger would git his gal an' dey would be some niggers over in de corner ter play fer de dance, one wid er fiddle an' one ter beat straws, an' one wid er banjo, an' one ter beat bones, an' when de music 'ud start up (dey gener'ly played 'Billy in de Low Grounds' or 'Turkey in de Straw') us 'ud git on de flo'. Den de nigger whut called de set would say: 'All join hands an' circle to de lef, back to de right, swing corners, swing partners, all run away!' An' de way dem niggers feets would fly!"

"Bye an' bye de war come on, an' all de men folks had ter go an' fight de Yankees, so us wimmen folks an' chillun had er hard time den caze us all had ter look atter de stock an' wuk in de fiel's. Den us 'ud hear all 'bout how de Yankees wuz goin' aroun' an' skeerin' de wimmen folks mos' ter death goin' in dey houses an' making de folks cook 'em stuff ter eat, den tearin' up an' messin' up dey houses an' den marchin' on off."

"Den when ole Mistis 'ud hear de Yankees wuz comin' she'd call us niggers en us 'ud take all de china, silver, and de joolry whut b'longed ter ole Miss an' her family an' dig deep holes out b'hind de smoke-house or under de big house, en bury h'it all 'tell de Yankees 'ud git by."

"Dem wuz dark days, but atter er long time de war wuz over an' dey tole us us wuz free, I didn't want ter leave my white folks so I stayed on fer sometime, but atter while de nigger come erlong whut I married. His name wuz Tom Randolph an' befo' de war he b'longed ter Marse Joshua Randolph, who lived at Jefferson, so den us moved ter Jefferson. Us had thirteen chillun, but dey's all daid now an' my ole man is daid too, so I'se here all by my se'f an' ef h'it warn't fer my two nieces here, who lets me liv' wid 'em I doan know whut I'd do."

"I'se allus tried ter do de right thin' an' de good Lawd is takin' keer uv me fer his prophet say in de Good Book, 'I'se been young and now am ole, yet I'se nebber seed de righteous fersaken ner his seed beggin' bread!' So I ain't worryin' 'bout sumpin' ter eat, but I doan want ter stay here much longer onless h'its de good Lawds will."

Asked if she was superstitious, she said: "Well when I wuz young, I reckin' I wuz, but now my pore ole mine is jes so tired and h'it doan wuk lak h'it uster, so I never does think much 'bout superstition, but I doan lak ter heer er "squinch owl" holler in de night, fer h'it sho is a sign some uv yore folks is goin' ter die, en doan brin' er ax froo de house onless yer take h'it back de same way yer brung h'it in, fer dat 'ill kill de bad luck."

When asked if she believed in ghosts or could "see sights" she said: "Well, Miss, yer know if yer is borned wid er veil over yer face yer can see sights but I has never seed any ghosts er sight's, I warn't born dat way, but my niece, here has seed ghostes, en she can tell yer 'bout dat."

When we were ready to leave we said, "Well, Aunt Fanny, we hope you live for many more years." She replied: "I'se willin' ter go on livin' ez long ez de Marster wants me ter, still I'se ready when de summons comes. De good Lawd has allus giv' me grace ter liv' by, an' I know He'll giv' me dyin' grace when my time comes."

[HW: Dist. 6
Ex-slave #94]

Alberta Minor
Re-search Worker

SHADE RICHARDS, Ex-slave
East Solomon Street
Griffin, Georgia

September 14, 1936
[Date Stamp: MAY 8 1937]

SHADE RICHARDS

Shade Richards was born January 13, 1846 on the Jimpson Neals plantation below Zebulon in Pike County. His father, Alfred Richards had been brought from Africa and was owned by Mr. Williams on an adjoining plantation. His mother, Easter Richards was born in Houston County but sold to Mr. Neal. Shade being born on the plantation was Mr. Neal's property. He was the youngest of 11 children. His real name was "Shadrack" and the brother just older than he was named "Meshack". Sometimes the mothers named the babies but most of the time the masters did. Mr. Neal did Shade's "namin'".

Shade's father came two or three times a month to see his family on Mr. Neal's plantation always getting a "pass" from his master for "niggers" didn't dare go off their own plantation without a "pass". Before the war Shade's grandfather came from Africa to buy his son and take him home, but was taken sick and both father and son died. Shade's earliest recollections of his mother are that she worked in the fields until "she was thru' bornin' chillun" then she was put in charge of the milk and butter. There were 75 or 80 cows to be milked twice a day and she had to have 5 or 6 other women helpers.

Mr. Neal had several plantations in different localities and his family did not live on this one in Pike County but he made regular visits to each one. It had no name, was just called "Neal's Place." It consisted of thirteen hundred acres. There were always two or three hundred slaves on the place, besides the ones he just bought and sold for "tradin'". He didn't like "little nigger men" and when he happened to find one among his slaves he would turn the dogs on him and let them run him down. The boys were not allowed to work in the fields until they were 12 years old, but they had to wait on the hands, such as carrying water, running back to the shop with tools and for tools, driving wagons of corn, wheat etc. to the mill to be ground and any errands they were considered big enough to do. Shade worked in the fields when he became 12 years old.

This plantation was large and raised everything—corn, wheat, cotton, "taters", tobacco, fruit, vegetables, rice, sugar cane, horses, mules, goats, sheep, and hogs. They kept all that was needed to feed the slaves then sent the surplus to Savannah by the "Curz". The stage took passengers, but the "Curz" was 40 or 50 wagons that took the farm surplus to Savannah, and "fetched back things for de house."

Mr. Neal kept 35 or 40 hounds that had to be cooked for. He was "rich with plenty of money" always good to his slaves and didn't whip them much, but his son, "Mr. Jimmy, sure was a bad one". Sometimes he'd use the cow hide until it made blisters, then hit them with the flat of the hand saw until they broke and next dip the victim into a tub of salty water. It often killed the "nigger" but "Mr. Jimmy" didn't care. He whipped Shade's uncle to death.

When the "hog killin' time come" it took 150 nigger men a week to do it. The sides, shoulders, head and jowls were kept to feed the slaves on and the rest was shipped to Savannah. Mr. Neal was good to his slaves and gave them every Saturday to "play" and go to the "wrestling school". At Xmas they had such a good time, would go from house to house, the boys would fiddle and they'd have a drink of liquor at each house. The liquor was plentiful for they bought it in barrels. The plantations took turn about having "Frolics" when they "fiddled and danced" all night.

If it wasn't on your own plantation you sure had to have a "pass". When a slave wanted to "jine the church" the preacher asked his master if he was a "good nigger", if the master "spoke up for you", you were "taken in," but if he didn't you weren't. The churches had a pool for the Baptist Preachers to baptize in and the Methodist Preacher sprinkled.

Mr. Neal "traded" with Dr. by the year and whenever the slaves were hurt or sick he had to come "tend" to them. He gave the families their food by the month, but if it gave out all they had to do was to ask for more and he always gave it to them. They had just as good meals during the week as on Sunday, any kind of meat out of the smoke house, chickens, squabs, fresh beef, shoats, sheep, biscuits or cornbread, rice, potatoes, beans, syrup and any garden vegetables. Sometimes they went fishing to add to their menu.

The single male slaves lived together in the "boy house" and had just as much as others. There were a lot of women who did nothing but sew, making work clothes for the hands. Their Sunday clothes were bought with the money they made off the little "patches" the master let them work for themselves.

Mr. Jimmy took Shade to the war with him. Shade had to wait on him as a body servant then tend to the two horses. Bullets went through Shade's coat and hat many times but "de Lord was takin' care" of him and he didn't get hurt. They were in the battle of Appomatox and "at the surrenderin'," April 8, 1865, but the "evidence warn't sworn out until May 29, so that's when the niggers celebrate emancipation."

Shade's brother helped lay the R.R. from Atlanta to Macon so the Confederate soldiers and ammunition could move faster.

In those days a negro wasn't grown until he was 21 regardless of how large he was. Shade was "near 'bout" grown when the war was over but worked for Mr. Neal four years. His father and mother rented a patch, mule and plow from Mr. Neal and the family was together. At first they gave the niggers only a tenth of what they raised but they couldn't get along on it and after a "lot of mouthin' about it" they gave them a third. That wasn't enough to live on either so more "mouthin" about it until they gave them a half, "and thats what they still gits today."

When the slaves went 'courtin' and the man and woman decided to get married, they went to the man's master for permission then to the woman's master. There was no ceremony if both masters said "alright" they were considered married and it was called "jumpin' the broomstick."

Signs were "more true" in the olden days than now. God lead his people by dreams then. One night Shade dreamed of a certain road he used to walk over often and at the fork he found a lead pencil, then a little farther on he dreamed of a purse with $2.43 in it. Next day he went farther and just like the dream he found the pocketbook with $2.43 in it.

Shade now works at the Kincaid Mill No. 2, he makes sacks and takes up waste. He thinks he's lived so long because he never eats hot food or takes any medicine. "People takes too much medicine now days" he says and when he feels bad he just smokes his corn cob pipe or takes a chew of tobacco.

United States. Work Projects Administration

DORA ROBERTS

Dora Roberts was born in 1849 and was a slave of Joseph Maxwell of Liberty County. The latter owned a large number of slaves and plantations in both Liberty and Early Counties. During the war "Salem" the plantation in Liberty County was sold and the owner moved to Early County where he owned two plantations known as "Nisdell" and "Rosedhu".

Today, at 88 years of age, Aunt Dora is a fine specimen of the fast disappearing type of ante-bellum Negro. Her shrewd dark eyes glowing, a brown paper sack perched saucily on her white cottony hair, and puffing contentedly on an old corn cob pipe, the old woman began her recital what happened during plantation days.

"Dey is powerful much to tell ob de days ob slabry, chile, an' it come to me in pieces. Dis story ain't in no rotation 'cause my mind it don't do dat kinda function, but I tell it as it come ta me. De colored folks had dey fun as well as dey trials and tribulations, 'cause dat Sat'day nigh dance at de plantation wuz jist de finest ting we wanted in dem days. All de slabes fum de udder plantation dey cum ta our barn an' jine in an' if dey had a gal on dis plantation dey lob, den dat wuz da time dey would court. Dey would swing to de band dat made de music. My brother wuz de captain ob de quill band an' dey sure could make you shout an' dance til you quz [TR: wuz?] nigh 'bout exhausted. Atta findin' ya gal ta dat dance den you gits passes to come courtin' on Sundays. Den de most ob dom dey wants git married an' dey must den git de consent fum de massa ceremonies wuz read ober dem and de man git passes fo' de week-end ta syat [TR: stay?] wid his wife. But de slabes dey got togedder an' have dem jump over de broom stick an' have a big celebration an' dance an' make merry 'til morning and it's time fo' work agin.

"We worked de fields an' kep' up de plantation 'til freedom. Ebry Wednesday de massa come visit us an look ober de plantation ta see dat all is well. He talk ta de obersheer an' find out how good de work is. We lub de massa an' work ha'd fo' him.

"Ah kin 'member dat Wednesday night plain as it wuz yesterday. It seems lak de air 'round de quarters an' de big house filled wid excitement; eben de wind seem lak it wuz waitin' fo' som'ting. De dogs an' de pickaninnies dey sleep lazy like 'gainst de big gate waitin' fo' de crack ob dat whip which wuz de signal dat Julius wuz bringin' de master down de long dribe under de oaks. Chile, us all wuz happy knowin' date de fun would start.

"All of a sudden you hear dem chilluns whoop, an' de dogs bark, den de car'age roll up wid a flourish, an' de coachman dressed in de fines' git out an' place de cookie try on de groun'. Den dey all gadder in de circle an' fo' dey git dey supply, dey got ta do de pigeon wing.

"Chile, you ain't neber seen sich flingin' ob de arms an' legs in yo' time. Dem pickaninnies dey had de natural born art ob twistin' dey body any way dey wish. Dat dere ting dey calls truckin' now an' use to be chimmy, ain't had no time wid de dancin' dem chilluns do. Dey claps dey hands and keep de time, while dat old brudder ob mine he blows de quills. Massa he would allus bring de big tray ob 'lasses cookies fo' all de chilluns. Fast as de tray would empty, Massa send ta de barrel fo' more. De niggers do no work dat day, but dey jist celebrate.

"Atta de war broke out we wuz all ca'yhed up to de plantation in Early County to stay 'til atta de war. De day de mancipation wuz read dey wuz sadness an' gladness. De ole Massa he call us all togedder an' wid tears in his eyes he say—'You is all free now an' you can go jist whar you please. I hab no more jurisdiction ober you. All who stay will be well cared for.' But de most ob us wanted to come back to de place whar we libed befo'—Liberty County.

"So he outfitted de wagons wid horses an' mules an' gib us what dey wuz ob privisions on de plantation an' sent us on our way ta de ole plantation in Liberty County. Dare wuz six horses ta de wagons. 'Long de way de wagons broke down 'cause de mules ain't had nothin' ta eat an' most ob dem died. We git in sich a bad fix some ob de people died. When it seem lak we wuz all gwine die, a planter come along de road an' he stopped ta find out what wuz de matter. Wan he heard our story an' who our master wuz he git a message to him 'bout us.

"It seem lak de good Lord musta answered de prayers ob his chillun fo' 'long way down de road we seed our Massa comin' an' he brung men an' horses to git us safely ta de ole home. When he got us dare, I neber see him no more 'cause he went back up in Early County an' atta I work dere at de plantation a long time den I come ta de city whyah my sister be wid one ob my master's oldest daughters—a Mrs. Dunwodies[TR: ?? first letter of name not readable], who she wuz nursin' fo'.

"An' dat's 'bout all dey is ta tell. When I sits an' rocks here on de porch it all comes back ta me. Seems sometimes lak I wuz still dere on de plantation. An' it seem lak it's mos' time fo' de massa ta be comin' ta see how tings are goin'."

Written by Ruth Chitty
Research Worker
District #2
Rewritten by Velma Bell

EX-SLAVE INTERVIEW: AUNT FEREBE ROGERS
Baldwin County
Milledgeville, Ga.

FEREBE ROGERS

More than a century lies in the span of memory of "Aunt Ferebe" Rogers. The interviewers found her huddled by the fireside, all alone while her grandaughter worked on a WPA Project to make the living for them both. In spite of her years and her frail physique, her memory was usually clear, only occasionally becoming too misty for scenes to stand out plainly. Her face lighted with a reminiscent smile when she was asked to "tell us something about old times."

"I 'members a whole heap 'bout slav'ey times. Law, honey, when freedom come I had five chillen. Five chillen and ten cents!" and her crackled laughter was spirited.

"Dey says I'm a hundred and eight or nine years old, but I don't think I'm quite as old as dat. I knows I'se over a hundred, dough.

"I was bred and born on a plantation on Brier Creek in Baldwin County. My ole marster was Mr. Sam Hart.

He owned my mother. She had thirteen chillen. I was de oldest, so I tuck devil's fare.

"My daddy was a ole-time free nigger. He was a good shoe-maker, and could make as fine shoes and boots as ever you see. But he never would work till he was plumb out o' money—den he had to work. But he quit jes' soon as he made a little money. Mr. Chat Morris (he had a regular shoe shop)—he offered him studdy work makin' boots and shoes for him. Was go'n' pay him $300. a year. But he wouldn't take it. Was too lazy. De ole-time free niggers had to tell how dey make dey livin', and if dey couldn't give satisfaction 'bout it, dey was put on de block and sold to de highest bidder. Most of 'em sold for 3 years for $50. My daddy brought $100. when he was sold for three or four years.

"I was on de block twice myself. When de old head died dey was so many slaves for de chillen to draw for, we was put on de block. Mr. John Baggett bought me den; said I was a good breedin' 'oman. Den later, one de young Hart marsters bought me back.

"All de slaves had diff'unt work to do. My auntie was one de weavers. Old Miss had two looms goin' all de time. She had a old loom and a new loom. My husband made de new loom for Old Miss. He was a carpenter and he worked on outside jobs after he'd finished tasks for his marster. He use to make all de boxes dey buried de white folks and de slaves in, on de Hart and Golden Plantations. Dey was pretty as you see, too.

"I was a fiel' han' myself. I come up twix' de plow handles. I warn't de fastes' one wid a hoe, but I didn't turn my back on nobody plowin'. No, _mam_.

"My marster had over a thousand acres o' land. He was good to us. We had plenty to eat, like meat and bread and vegetables. We raised eve'ything on de plantation—wheat, corn, potatoes, peas, hogs, cows, sheep, chickens—jes' eve'ything.

"All de clo'es was made on de plantation, too. Dey spun de thread from cotton and wool, and dyed it and wove it. We had cutters and dem dat done de sewin'. I still got de fus' dress my husband give me. Lemme show it to you."

Gathering her shawl about her shoulders, and reaching for her stick, she hobbled across the room to an old hand-made chest.

"My husband made dis chis' for me." Raising the top, she began to search eagerly through the treasured bits of clothing for the "robe-tail muslin" that had been the gift of a long-dead husband. One by one the garments came out—her daughter's dress, two little bonnets all faded and worn ("my babies' bonnets"), her husband's coat.

"And dat's my husband's mother's bonnet. It use to be as pretty a black as you ever see. It's faded brown now. It was dyed wid walnut."

The chest yielded up old cotton cards, and horns that had been used to call the slaves. Finally the "robe-tail muslin" came to light. The soft material, so fragile with age that a touch sufficed to reduce it still further to rags, was made with a full skirt and plain waist, and still showed traces of a yellow color and a sprigged design.

"My husband was Kinchen Rogers. His marster was

Mr. Bill Golden, and he live 'bout fo' mile from where I stayed on de Hart plantation."

"Aunt Ferebe, how did you meet your husband?"

"Well, you see, us slaves went to de white folks church a-Sunday. Marster, he was a prim'tive Baptis', and he try to keep his slaves from goin' to other churches. We had baptisin's fust Sundays. Back in dem days dey baptised in de creek, but at de windin' up o' freedom, dey dug a pool. I went to church Sundays, and dat's where I met my husband. I been ma'ied jes' one time. He de daddy o' all my chillen'. (I had fifteen in all.)"

"Who married you, Aunt Ferebe. Did you have a license?"

"Who ever heered a nigger havin' a license?" and she rocked with high-pitched laughter.

"Young marster was fixin' to ma'y us, but he got col' feet, and a nigger by name o' Enoch Golden ma'ied us. He was what we called a 'double-headed nigger'—he could read and write, and he knowed so much. On his dyin' bed he said he been de death o' many a nigger 'cause he taught so many to read and write.

"Me and my husband couldn't live together till after freedom 'cause we had diffunt marsters. When freedom come, marster wanted all us niggers to sign up to stay till Chris'man. Bless, yo' soul, I didn't sign up. I went to my husband! But he signed up to stay wid his marster till Chris'man. After dat we worked on shares on de Hart plantation; den we farmed fo'-five years wid Mr. Bill Johnson."

"Aunt Ferebe, are these better times, or do you think slavery times were happier?"

"Well, now, you ax me for de truth, didn't you?—and I'm goin' to tell yo' de truth. I don't tell no lies. Yes, mam, dese has been better times to me. I think hit's better to work for yourself and have what you make dan to work for somebody else and don't git nuttin' out it. Slav'ey days was mighty hard. My marster was good to us (I mean he didn't beat us much, and he give us plenty plain food) but some slaves suffered awful. My aunt was beat cruel once, and lots de other slaves. When dey got ready to beat yo', dey'd strip you' stark mother naked and dey'd say, 'Come here to me, God damn you! Come to me clean! Walk up to dat tree, and damn you, hug dat tree! Den dey tie yo' hands 'round de tree, den tie yo' feets; den dey'd lay de rawhide on you and cut yo' buttocks open. Sometimes dey'd rub turpentine and salt in de raw places, and den beat you some mo'. Oh, hit was awful! And what could you do? Dey had all de 'vantage of you.

"I never did git no beatin' like dat, but I got whuppin's—plenty o' 'em. I had plenty o' devilment in me, but I quit all my devilment when I was ma'ied. I use to fight—fight wid anything I could git my han's on.

"You had to have passes to go from one plantation to 'nother. Some de niggers would slip off sometime and go widout a pass, or maybe marster was busy and dey didn't want to bother him for a pass, so dey go widout one. In eve'y dee-strick dey had 'bout twelve men dey call patterollers. Dey ride up and down and aroun' looking for niggers widout passes. If dey ever caught you off yo' plantation wid no pass, dey beat you all over.

"Yes'm, I 'member a song 'bout—

> 'Run, nigger, run, de patteroller git you,
> Slip over de fence slick as a eel,
> White man ketch you by de heel,
> Run, nigger run!'"

No amount of coaxing availed to make her sing the whole of the song, or to tell any more of the words.

"When slaves run away, dey always put de bloodhounds on de tracks. Marster always kep' one hound name' Rock. I can hear 'im now when dey was on de track, callin', 'Hurrah, Rock, hurrah, Rock! Ketch 'im!'

"Dey always send Rock to fetch 'im down when dey foun' 'im. Dey had de dogs trained to keep dey teef out you till dey tole 'em to bring you down. Den de dogs 'ud go at yo' th'oat, and dey'd tear you to pieces, too. After a slave was caught, he was brung home and put in chains.

"De marsters let de slaves have little patches o' lan' for deyse'ves. De size o' de patch was 'cordin' to de size o' yo' family. We was 'lowed 'bout fo' acres. We made 'bout five hundred pounds o' lint cotton, and sol' it at Warrenton. Den we used de money to buy stuff for Chris'man."

"Did you have big times at Christmas, Aunt Ferebe?"

"Chris'man—huh!—Chris'man warn't no diffunt from other times. We used to have quiltin' parties, candy pullin's, dances, corn shuckin's, games like thimble and sich like."

Aunt Ferebe refused to sing any of the old songs. "No,

mam, I ain't go'n' do dat. I th'oo wid all dat now. Yes, mam, I 'members 'em all right, but I ain't go'n' sing 'em. No'm, nor say de words neither. All dat's pas' now.

"Course dey had doctors in dem days, but we used mostly home-made medicines. I don't believe in doctors much now. We used sage tea, ginger tea, rosemary tea—all good for colds and other ail-ments, too.

"We had men and women midwives. Dr. Cicero Gibson was wid me when my fus' baby come. I was twenty-five years old den. My baby chile seventy-five now."

"Auntie, did you learn to read and write?"

"No, _mam_, I'd had my right arm cut off at de elbow if I'd a-done dat. If dey foun' a nigger what could read and write, dey'd cut yo' arm off at de elbow, or sometimes at de shoulder."

In answer to a query about ghosts, she said—"No, mam, I ain't seed nuttin' like dat. Folks come tellin' me dey see sich and sich a thing. I say hit's de devil dey see. I ain't seed nuttin' yit. No'm, I don't believe in no signs, neither."

"Do you believe a screeeh owl has anything to do with death?"

"Yes, mam, 'fo' one my chillen died, squinch owl come to my house ev'ey night and holler. After de chile die he ain't come no mo'. Cows mooin' or dogs howlin' after dark means death, too.

"No, man, I don't believe in no cunjurs. One cunjur-man come here once. He try his bes' to overcome me, but he couldn't do nuttin' wid me. After dat, he tole my husband he couldn't do nuttin' to me, 'cause I didn't believe in him, and dem cunjur-folks can't hurt you less'n you believes in 'em. He say he could make de sun stan' still, and do wonders, but I knowed dat warn't so, 'cause can't nobody stop de sun 'cep' de man what made hit, and dat's God. I don't believe in no cunjurs.

"I don't pay much 'tention to times o' de moon to do things, neither. I plants my garden when I gits ready. But bunch beans does better if you plants 'em on new moon in Ap'il. Plant butterbeans on full moon in Ap'il—potatoes fus' o' March.

"When de war broke out de damn Yankees come to our place dey done eve'ything dat was bad. Dey burn eve'ything dey couldn't use, and dey tuck a heap o' corn. Marster had a thousand bushels de purtiest shucked corn, all nice good ears, in de pen at de house. Dey tuck all dat. Marster had some corn pens on de river, dough, dey didn't find. I jes' can't tell you all dey done.

"How come I live so long, you say?—I don't know—jes' de goodness o' de Lawd, I reckon. I worked hard all my life, and always tried to do right."

[HW: Dist. 1
Ex-Slave #92]

HENRY ROGERS of WASHINGTON-WILKES
by Minnie Branham Stonestreet
Washington-Wilkes
Georgia
[Date Stamp: MAY 8 1937]

HENRY ROGERS

Henry Rogers of Washington-Wilkes is known by almost every one in the town and county. To the men around town he is "Deacon", to his old friends back in Hancock County (Georgia) where he was born and reared, he is "Brit"; to everybody else he is "Uncle Henry", and he is a friend to all. For forty-one years he has lived in Washington-Wilkes where he has worked as waiter, as lot man, and as driver for a livery stable when he "driv drummers" around the country anywhere they wanted to go and in all kinds of weather. He is proud that he made his trips safely and was always on time. Then when automobiles put the old time livery stables out of business he went to work in a large furniture and undertaking establishment where he had charge of the colored department. Finally he decided to accept a job as janitor and at one time was janitor for three banks in town. He is still working as janitor in two buildings, despite his seventy-three years.

Uncle Henry's "book learning" is very limited, but

he has a store of knowledge gathered here and there that is surprising. He uses very little dialect except when he is excited or worried. He speaks of his heart as "my time keeper". When he promises anything in the future he says, "Please the Lord to spare me", and when anyone gets a bit impatient he bids them, "Be paciable, be paciable". Dismal is one of his favorite words but it is always "dism". When he says "Now, I'm tellin' yer financially" or "dat's financial", he means that he is being very frank and what he is saying is absolutely true.

Regarded highly as the local weather prophet, Uncle Henry gets up every morning before daybreak and scans the heavens to see what kind of weather is on its way. He guards all these "signs" well and under no consideration will he tell them. They were given to him by someone who has passed on and he keeps them as a sacred trust. If asked, upon making a prediction, "How do you know?" Uncle Henry shakes his wise old head and with a wave of the hand says, "Dat's all right, you jess see now, it's goin' ter be dat way". And it usually is!

Seventy-three years ago "last gone June" Uncle Henry was born in the Mt. Zion community in Hancock county (Georgia), seven miles from Sparta. His mother was Molly Navery Hunt, his father, Jim Rogers. They belonged to Mr. Jenkins Hunt and his wife "Miss Rebecca". Henry was the third of eight children. He has to say about his early life:

"Yassum, I wuz born right over there in Hancock county, an' stayed there 'til the year 1895 when Mrs. Riley come fer me to hep' her in the Hotel here in Washington an' I been here ev'ry since. I recollects well living on the Hunt plantation. It wuz a big place an' we had fifteen or twenty slaves"—(The "we" was proudly possessive)—"we wuz all as happy passel o' niggers as could be found anywhere. Aunt Winnie wuz the cook an' the kitchen wuz a big old one out in the yard an' had a fireplace that would 'commodate a whole fence rail, it wuz so big, an' had pot hooks, pots, big old iron ones, an' everything er round to cook on. Aunt Winnie had a great big wooden tray dat she would fix all us little niggers' meals in an' call us up an' han' us a wooden spoon apiece an' make us all set down 'round the tray an' eat all us wanted three times ev'ry day. In one corner of the kitchen set a loom my Mother use to weave on. She would weave way into the night lots of times.

"The fust thing I 'members is follerin' my Mother er 'round. She wuz the housegirl an' seamstress an' everywhere she went I wuz at her heels. My father wuz the overseer on the Hunt place. We never had no hard work to do. My fust work wuz 'tendin' the calves an' shinin' my Master's shoes. How I did love to put a Sunday shine on his boots an' shoes! He called me his nigger an' wuz goin' ter make a barber out o' me if slavery had er helt on. As it wuz, I shaved him long as he lived. We lived in the Quarters over on a high hill 'cross the spring-branch from the white peoples' house. We had comfortable log cabins an' lived over there an' wuz happy. Ole Uncle Alex Hunt wuz the bugler an' ev'ry mornin' at 4:00 o'clock he blowed the bugle fer us ter git up, 'cept Sunday mornin's, us all slept later on Sundays.

"When I wuz a little boy us played marbles, mumble peg, an' all sich games. The little white an' black boys played together, an' ev'ry time 'Ole Miss' whipped her boys she whipped me too, but nobody 'cept my Mistess ever teched me to punish me.

"I recollects one Sadday night ole Uncle Aaron Hunt come in an' he must er been drinkin' or sumpin' fer he got ter singin' down in the Quarters loud as he could 'Go Tell Marse Jesus I Done Done All I Kin Do', an' nobody could make him hush singin'. He got into sich er row 'til they had ter go git some o' the white folks ter come down an' quiet him down. Dat wuz the only 'sturbance 'mongst the niggers I ever 'members.

"I wuz so little when the War come on I don't member but one thing 'bout it an' that wuz when it wuz over with an' our white mens come home all de neighbors, the Simpsons, the Neals, the Allens all living on plantations 'round us had a big dinner over at my white peoples', the Hunts, an' it sho wuz a big affair. Ev'rybody from them families wuz there an' sich rejoicin' I never saw. I won't forgit that time.

"I allus been to Church. As a little boy my folks took me to ole Mt Zion. We went to the white peoples' Church 'til the colored folks had one of they own. The white folks had services in Mt Zion in the mornings an' the niggers in the evenin's."

When a colored person died back in the days when Uncle Henry was coming on, he said they sat up with the dead and had prayers for the living. There was a Mr. Beman in the community who made coffins, and on the Hunt place old Uncle Aaron Hunt helped him. The dead were buried in home-made coffins and the hearse was a one horse wagon.

"When I wuz a growin' up" said Uncle Henry, "I wore a long loose shirt in the summer, an' in the winter plenty of good heavy warm clothes. I had 'nits an' lice' pants an' hickory stripe waists when I wuz a little boy. All these my Mother spun an' wove the cloth fer an' my Mistess made. When I wuz older I had copperas pants an' shirts."

Uncle Henry has many signs but is reluctant to tell them. Finally he was prevailed upon to give several. What he calls his "hant sign" is: "If you runs into hot heat sudden, it is a sho sign hants is somewheres 'round."

When a rooster comes up to the door and crows, if he is standing with his head towards the door, somebody is coming, if he is standing with his tail towards the door, it is a sign of death, according to Uncle Henry. It is good luck for birds to build their nests near a house, and if a male red bird comes around the woodpile chirping, get ready for bad weather for it is on its way.

Uncle Henry is a pretty good doctor too, but he doesn't like to tell his remedies. He did say that life everlasting tea is about as good thing for a cold as can be given and for hurts of any kind there is nothing better than soft rosin, fat meat and a little soot mixed up and bound to the wound. He is excellent with animals and when a mule, dog, pig or anything gets sick his neighbors call him in and he doctors them and usually makes them well.

As for conjuring, Uncle Henry has never known much about it, but he said when he was a little fellow he heard the old folks talk about a mixture of devil's snuff and cotton stalk roots chipped up together and put into a little bag and that hidden under the front steps. This was to make all who came up the steps friendly and peacable even if they should happen to be coming on some other mission.

After the War the Rogers family moved from the Hunts' to the Alfriend plantation adjoining. As the Alfriends were a branch of the Hunt family they considered they were still owned as in slavery by the same "white peoples". They lived there until Uncle Henry moved to Washington-Wilkes in 1895.

Christmas was a great holiday on the plantation. There was no work done and everybody had a good time with plenty of everything good to eat. Easter was another time when work was laid aside. A big Church service took place Sunday and on Monday a picnic was attended by all the negroes in the community.

There were Fourth of July celebrations, log rollings, corn shuckings, house coverings and quilting parties. In all of these except the Fourth of July celebration it was a share-the-work idea. Uncle Henry grew a bit sad when he recalled how "peoples use ter be so good 'bout hep'in' one 'nother, an' now dey don't do nothin' fer nobody lessen' dey pays 'em." He told how, when a neighbor cleared a new ground and needed help, he invited all the men for some distance around and had a big supper prepared. They rolled logs into huge piles and set them afire. When all were piled high and burning brightly, supper was served by the fire light. Sometimes the younger ones danced around the burning logs. When there was a big barn full of corn to be shucked the neighbors gladly gathered in, shucked the corn for the owner, who had a fiddler and maybe some one to play the banjo. The corn was shucked to gay old tunes and piled high in another barn. Then after a "good hot supper" there was perhaps a dance in the cleared barn. When a neighbor's house needed covering, he got the shingles and called in his neighbors and friends, who came along with their wives. While the men worked atop the house the women were cooking a delicious dinner down in the kitchen. At noon it was served amid much merry making. By sundown the house was finished and the friends went home happy in the memory of a day spent in toil freely given to one who needed it.

All those affairs were working ones, but Uncle Henry told of one that marked the end of toil for a season and that was the Fourth of July as celebrated on the Hunt and Alfriend plantations. He said: "On the evenin' of the third of July all plows, gear, hoes an' all sich farm tools wuz bro't in frum the fields an' put in the big grove in front o' the house where a long table had been built. On the Fo'th a barbecue wuz cooked, when dinner wuz ready all the han's got they plows an' tools, the mules wuz bro't up an' gear put on them, an' den ole Uncle Aaron started up a song 'bout the crops wuz laid by an' res' time had come, an' everybody grabbed a hoe er sumpin', put it on they shoulder an' jined the march 'round an' round the table behind Uncle Aaron singin' an' marchin', Uncle Aaron linin' off the song an' ev'ry body follerin' him. It wuz a sight to see all the han's an' mules er goin' 'round the table like that. Den when ev'ry body wuz might nigh 'zausted, they stopped an' et a big barbecue dinner. Us use ter work hard to git laid by by de Fo'th so's we could celebrate. It sho' wuz a happy time on our plantations an' the white peoples enjoyed it as much as us niggers did.

"Us use ter have good times over there in Hancock County", continued Uncle Henry. Ev'rybody wuz so good an' kind ter one 'nother; 't'ain't like that now—no mam, not lak it use ter be. Why I 'members onst, when I fust growed up an' wuz farmin' fer myself, I got sick way long up in the Spring, an' my crop wuz et up in grass when one evenin' Mr. Harris—(he wuz overseein' fer Mr. Treadwell over on the next plantation to the Alfriends)—come by. I wuz out in the field tryin' ter scratch 'round as best I could, Mr. Harris say: 'Brit, you in de grass mighty bad.' I say: 'Yassir, I is, but I been sick an' couldn't hep' myself, that's how come I so behind.' He say: 'Look lak you needs hep'.' 'Yassir,' I says, 'but I ain't got nobody to work but me.' Dat's all he said. Well sir, the nex' mornin' by times over comes Mr. Harris wid six plows an' eight hoe han's an' they give me a whole day's work an' when they finished that evenin' they want a sprig of grass in my crop; it wuz clean as this floor, an' I'se tellin' yer the truth. Dat's the way peoples use ter do, but not no mo'—everybody too selfish now, an' they think ain't nobody got responsibilits (responsibilities) but them."

Speaking of his early life Uncle Henry continued: "When I growed up I broke race horses fer white mens an' raced horses too, had rooster fights an' done all them kind o' things, but I 'sought 'ligion an' found it an' frum that day to this I ain't never done them things no mo'. When I jined the Church I had a Game rooster named 'Ranger' that I had won ev'ry fight that I had matched him in. Peoples come miles ter see Ranger fight; he wuz a Warhorse Game. After I come to be a member of the Church I quit fightin' Ranger so Mr. Sykes come over an' axed me what I would take fer him, I told him he could have him—I warn't goin' to fight wid him any mo'. He took him an' went over three states, winnin' ev'ry fight he entered him in an' come home wid fifteen hundred dollars he made on Ranger. He give me fifty dollars, but I never wanted him back. Ranger wuz a pet an' I could do anything wid 'im. I'd hold out my arm an' tell him to come up an' he'd fly up on my arm an' crow. He'd get on up on my haid an' crow too. One rainy day 'fore I give him away he got in the lot an' kilt three turkeys an' a gobbler fer my Mistess. She got mighty mad an' I sho wuz skeered 'til Marse took mine an' Ranger's part an' wouldn't let her do nothin' wid us."

Forty-seven years ago Uncle Henry married Annie Tiller of Hancock County. They had four children, three of whom are living. About his courtship and marriage he has to say: "I wuz at Sunday School one Sunday an' saw Annie fer the fust time. I went 'round where she wuz an' wuz made 'quainted with her an' right then an' there I said to myself, 'She's my gal'. I started goin' over to see her an' met her folks. I liked her Pa an Ma an' I would set an' talk with them an' 'pear not to be payin' much 'tention to Annie. I took candy an' nice things an' give to the family, not jest to her. I stood in with the ole folks an' 't'warn't long 'fore me an' Annie wuz married." Uncle Henry said he took Annie to Sparta to his Pastor's home for the marriage and the preacher told him he charged three dollars for the ceremony. "But I tole him I warnt goin' to give him but er dollar an' a half 'cause I wuz one of his best payin' members an' he ought not to charge me no more than dat. An' I never paid him no mo' neither, an' dat wuz er plenty."

Though he is crippled in his "feets" he is hale and hearty and manages to work without missing a day. He is senior Steward in his church and things there go about like he says even though he isn't a preacher. All the members seem to look to him for "consulation an' 'couragement". In all his long life he has "never spoke a oath if I knows it, an' I hates cussin'." He speaks of his morning devotions as "havin' prayers wid myself". His blessing at mealtime is the same one he learned in his "white peoples'" home when he was a little boy:

> "We humbly thank Thee, our Heavenly Father,
> for what we have before us."

Uncle Henry says: "I loves white peoples an' I'm a-livin' long 'cause in my early days dey cared fer me an' started me off right—they's my bes' frien's."

[HW: Dist. 5
E.F. Driskell
12/30/36

JULIA RUSH, Ex-Slave
109 years old]

[TR: The beginning of each line on the original typewritten pages for this interview is very faint, and some words have been reconstructed from context. Questionable entries are followed by [??]; words that could not be deciphered are indicated by [--].]

JULIA RUSH

Mrs. Julia Rush was born in 1826 on Saint Simons Island, Georgia. Mrs. Rush, her mother, and three sisters were the property of a Frenchman named Colonel De Binien, a very wealthy land owner. Mrs. Rush does not remember her father as he was sold away from his family when she was a baby.

As a child Mrs. Rush served as playmate to one of the Colonel's daughters and so all that she had to do was to play from morning till night. When she grew older she started working in the kitchen in the master's house. Later she was sent to the fields where she worked side by side with her mother and three sisters from sunup until sundown. Mrs. Rush says that she has plowed so much that she believes she can "outplow" any man.

Instead of the white overseer usually found on plantations the Colonel used one of the slaves to act as foreman of the field hands. He was known to the other slaves as the "Nigger Driver" and it was he who awakened all every morning. It was so dark until torch lights had to be used to see by. Those women who had babies took them along to the field in a basket which they placed on their heads. All of the hands were given a certain amount of work to perform each day and if the work was not completed a whipping might be forthcoming. Breakfast was sent to the field to the hands and if at dinner time they were not too far away from their cabins they were permitted to go home[??]. At night they prepared their own meals in their individual cabins.

All food on the colonel's plantation was issued daily from the corn house. Each person was given enough corn to make a sufficient amount of bread for the day when ground. Then they went out and dug their potatoes from the colonel's garden. No meat whatsoever was issued. It was up to the slaves to catch fish, oysters, and other sea food for their meat supply. All those who desired to were permitted to raise chickens, watermelons and vegetables. There was no restriction on any as to what must be done with the produce so raised. It could be sold or kept for personal consumption.

Colonel De Binien always saw that his slaves had sufficient clothing. In the summer months the men were given two shirts, two pairs of pants, and two pairs of underwear. All of these clothes were made of cotton and all were sewed on the plantation. No shoes were worn in the summer. The women were given two dresses, two underskirts, and two pairs of underwear. When the winter season approached another issue of clothes was given. At this time shoes were given. They were made of heavy red leather and were known as "brogans".

The slave quarters on the plantation were located behind the colonel's cabin[??]. All were made of logs. The chinks in the walls were filled with mud to keep the weather out. The floors were of wood in order to protect the occupants from the dampness. The only furnishings were a crude bed and several benches. All cooking was done at the large fireplace in the rear of the one room.

When Colonel De Binion's [TR: earlier, De Binien] wife died he divided his slaves among the children. Mrs. Rush was given to her former playmate who was at the time married and living in Carrollton, Georgia. She was very mean and often punished her by beating her on her forearm for the slightest offence. At other times she made her husband whip her (Mrs. Rush) on her bare back with a cowhide whip. Mrs. Rush says that her young Mistress thought that her husband was being intimate with her and so she constantly beat and mistreated her. On one occasion all of the hair on her head (which was long and straight) was cut from her head by the young mistress.

For a while Mrs. Rush worked in the fields where she plowed and hoed the crops along with the other slaves. Later she worked in the master's house where she served as maid and where she helped with the cooking. She was often hired out to the other planters in the vicinity. She says that she liked this because she always received better treatment than she did at her own home. These persons who hired her often gave her clothes as she never received a sufficient amount from her own master.

The food was almost the same here as it had been at

the other plantation. At the end of each week she and her fellow slaves were given a "little bacon, vegetables, and some corn meal."[HW: ?] This had to last for a certain length of time. If it was all eaten before the time for the next issue that particular slave had to live as best he or she could. In such an emergency the other slaves usually shared with the unfortunate one.

There was very little illness on the plantation where Mrs. Rush lived. Practically the only medicine ever used was castor oil and turpentine. Some of the slaves went to the woods and gathered roots and herbs from which they made their own tonics and medicines.

According to Mrs. Rush the first of the month was always sale day for slaves and horses. She was sold on one of those days from her master in Carrollton to one Mr. Morris, who lived in Newman, Ga. Mr. Morris paid $1100.00 for her. She remained with him for a short while and was later sold to one Mr. Ray who paid the price of $1200.00. Both of these masters were very kind to her, but she was finally sold back to her former master, Mr. Archibald Burke of Carrollton, Ga.

Mrs. Rush remembers that none of the slaves were allowed away from their plantation unless they held a pass from their master. Once when she was going to town to visit some friends she was accosted by a group of "Paddle-Rollers" who gave her a sound whipping when she was unable to show a pass from her master.

Mrs. Rush always slept in her masters' houses after leaving Colonel De Binien. When she was in Carrollton her young mistress often made her sleep under the house when she was angry with her.

After the war was over with and freedom was declared Mr. Burke continued to hold Mrs. Rush. After several unsuccessful attempts she was finally able to escape. She went to another part of the state where she married and started a family of her own.

Because of the cruel treatment that she received at the hands of some of her owners[??] Mrs. Rush says that the mere thought of slavery makes her blood boil. Then there are those, under whom she served, who treated her with kindness, whom she holds no malice against.

As far as Mrs. Rush knows the war did very little damage to Mr. Burke. He did not enlist as a soldier.

United States. Work Projects Administration

[HW: Dist. 1
Ex-Slave #96]

[HW: Good ghost story on page 4.]
[HW: "revolution drummer" parts very good.]

EX-SLAVE INTERVIEW
NANCY SETTLES, Ex-slave, Age 92
2511 Wheeler Road
(Richmond County)
Augusta, Georgia

By: (Mrs.) MARGARET JOHNSON
Augusta, Georgia
[Date Stamp: MAY 8 1937]

NANCY SETTLES

Nancy Settles was born 15 miles from Edgefield in South Carolina on the plantation of Mr. Berry Cochran.

Until about five months ago, Nancy had been bed-ridden for three years. Her speech is slow, and at times it is difficult to understand her, but her mind is fairly clear. Her eyes frequently filled with tears, her voice becoming so choked she could not talk. "My Marster and Missis, my husban' and eight of my chaps done lef me. De Lawd mus be keepin' me here fur some reason. Dis here chile is all I got lef'." The "Chile" referred to was a woman about 69. "My fust chap was born in slavery. Me and my husband lived on diffunt plantashuns till after Freedom come. My Ma and my Pa lived on diffunt places too. My Pa uster come evy Sadday evenin' to chop wood out uv de wood lot and pile up plenty fur Ma till he come agin. On Wensday evenin', Pa uster come after he been huntin' and bring in possum and coon. He sho could get 'em a plenty.

"Ma, she chop cotton and plow, and I started choppin' cotton when I wuz twelve years old. When I was a gal I sure wuz into plenty devilment."

"What kind of devilment?"

"Lawdy Miss, evy time I heayd a fiddle, my feets jes' got to dance and dancin' is devilment. But I ain't 'lowed to dance nothin' but de six-handed reel.

"I uster take my young Misses to school ev'y day, but de older Misses went to boadin' school and come home ev'y Friday an' went back on Monday. No ma'am, I never learn to read and write but I kin spell some."

"Nancy, did you go out at night and were you ever caught by the patrol?"

"No, ma'am, I never wuz caught by de patterol; my Pa wuz the one I was scart uv."

"Did you always have enough to eat, and clothes to wear?"

"Yes ma'am, Marster put out a side uv meat and a barrul o' meal and all uv us would go and git our rations fur de week."

"Suppose some one took more than his share, and the supply ran short."

"Lawd Ma'am, we knowed better'n to do dat kinder thing. Eve'ybody, had er garden patch an' had plenty greens and taters and all dat kinder thing. De cloth fur de slave close wuz all made on the place and Missis see to mekkin' all de close we wear."

"My Missis died endurin' of de war, but Marster he live a long time. Yes, Ma'am, we went to Church an to camp meetin' too. We set up in de galley, and ef dey too many uv us, we set in de back uv de church. Camp meetin' wuz de bes'. Before Missis died I wuz nussin' my young miss baby, and I ride in de white foke's kerrage to camp meetin' groun' and carry de baby. Lawdy, I seen de white folks and de slaves too shoutin' an gittin' 'ligion plenty times."

"Nancy, were the slaves on your place ever whipped?"

"Yes'm sometimes when de wouldn' mine, but Marster allus whip 'em hissef, he ain't let nobody else lay er finger on his slaves but him. I heayd 'bout slaves been whipped but I tink de wuz whipped mostly cause de Marsters _could_ whip 'em."

"Nancy do you know any ghost stories, or did you ever see a ghost?"

"No, Ma'am, I ain't never see a ghos' but I heayd de drum!"

"What drum did you hear—war drums?"

"No, ma'am de drum de little man beats down by Rock Crick. Some say he is a little man whut wears a cap and goes down the crick beating a drum befo' a war. He wuz a Revolushun drummer, and cum back to beat the drum befo' de war. But some say you can hear de drum 'most any spring now. Go down to the Crick and keep quiet and you hear Brrr, Brrr, Bum hum, louder and louder and den it goes away. Some say dey hav' seen de little man, but I never seen him, but I heayd de drum, 'fo de war, and ater dat too. There was a white man kilt hisself near our place. He uster play a fiddle, and some time he come back an play. I has heayd him play his fiddle, but I ain't seen him. Some fokes say dey is seen him in the wood playin' and walkin' 'bout."

"Nancy I am glad you are better than you were the last time I came to see you."

"Yes, Ma'am, I is up now. I prayed to God and tell Him my trouble and he helped me get about again. This po chile uv mine does what she kin to pay de rent and de Welfare gives us a bit to eat but I sho do need er little wood, cause we is back on de rent and my chile jes scrap 'bout to pick up trash wood and things to burn."

Slave Narratives

PLANTATION LIFE as viewed by ex-slave

WILL SHEETS, Age 76
1290 W. Broad Street
Athens, Georgia

Written by:
Sadie B. Hornsby
Athens

Edited by:
Sarah H. Hall
Athens

Leila Harris
and
John N. Booth
District Supervisor
Federal Writers' Project
Augusta, Georgia
[Date Stamp: MAY 13 1938]

WILL SHEETS

Old Will Sheets readily complied with the request that he tell of his experiences during slavery days. "No'm I don't mind, its been many a long day since anybody axed me to talk 'bout things dat far back, but I laks to have somebody to talk to 'cause I can't git 'bout no more since I los' both of my footses, and I gits powerful lonesome sometimes.

"I was borned in Oconee County, not far f'um whar Bishop is now. It warn't nothin' but a cornfield, way back in dem times. Ma was Jane Southerland 'fore she married my pa. He was Tom Sheets. Lawsy Miss! I don't know whar dey cone f'um. As far as I knows, dey was borned and raised on deir Marsters' plantations. Dar was seven of us chilluns. I was de oldes'; James, Joe, Speer, Charlie, and Ham was my brudders, and my onlies' sister was Frances.

"You ax me 'bout my gram'ma and gram'pa? I can't tell you nothin' t'all 'bout 'em. I jus' knows I had 'em and dat's all. You see Ma was a house gal and de mos' I seed of her was when she come to de cabin at night; den us chilluns was too sleepy to talk. Soon as us et, us drapped down on a pallet and went fast asleep. Niggers is a sleepy-headed set.

"I was a water boy, and was 'spected to tote water f'um de spring to de house, and to de hands in de fiel'. I helped Mandy, one of de colored gals, to drive de calves to de pasture and I toted in a little wood and done little easy jobs lak dat. Lawsy Miss! I never seed no money 'til atter de War. If I had a had any money what could I have done wid it, when I couldn't leave dat place to spend it?

"Dare ain't much to tell 'bout what little Nigger chillun done in slavery days. Dem what was big enough had to wuk, and dem what warn't, played, slep' and scrapped. Little Niggers is bad as game chickens 'bout fightin'. De quarters whar us lived was log cabins chinked wid mud to keep out de rain and wind. Chimblies was made out of fiel' rock and red clay. I never seed a cabin wid more dan two rooms in it.

"Beds warn't fancy dem days lak dey is now; leastwise I didn't see no fancy ones. All de beds was corded; dey had a headboard, but de pieces at de foot and sides was jus' wide enough for holes to run de cords thoo', and den de cords was pegged to hold 'em tight. Nigger chillun slep' on pallets on de flo'.

"Marse Jeff Southerland was a pore man, but he fed us all us could eat sich as turnips, cabbages, collards, green corn, fat meat, cornbread, 'taters and sometimes chicken. Yes Ma'am, chicken dinners was sorter special. Us didn't have 'em too often. De cookin' was all done at de big house in a open fireplace what had a rack crost it dat could be pulled out to take de pots off de fire. 'Fore dey started cookin', a fire was made up ready and waitin'; den de pots of victuals was hung on de rack and swung in de fireplace to bile. Baking was done in skillets. Us cotched rabbits three and four at a time in box traps sot out in de plum orchard. Sometimes us et 'em stewed wid dumplin's and some times dey was jus' plain biled, but us laked 'em bes' of all when dey was fried lak chickens.

"Oh! dem 'possums! How I wisht I had one right now. My pa used to ketch 40 or 50 of 'em a winter. Atter dey married, Ma had to stay on wid Marse Jeff and Pa was 'bliged to keep on livin' wid Marster Marsh Sheets. His marster give him a pass so dat he could come and stay wid Ma at night atter his wuk was done, and he fetched in de 'possums. Dey was baked in de white folkses kitchen wid sweet 'tatoes 'roun' 'em and was barbecued sometimes. Us had fishes too what was mighty good eatin'. Dere warn't but one gyarden on de plantation.

"Slave chillun didn't wear nothin' in summer but shirts what looked lak gowns wid long sleeves. Gals and boys was dressed in de same way whe dey was little chaps. In winter us wore shirts made out of coarse cloth and de pants and little coats was made out of wool. De gals wore wool dresses." He laughed and said: "On Sunday us jus' wore de same things. Did you say shoes? Lawsy Miss! I was eight or nine 'fore I had on a pair of shoes. On frosty mornin's when I went to de spring to fetch a bucket of water, you could see my feet tracks in de frost all de way dar and back.

"Miss Carrie, my Mist'ess, was good as she knowed how to be. Marse and Mist'ess had two gals and one boy, Miss Anna, Miss Callie, and Marster Johnny.

"Marse Jeff was a good man; he never whupped and slashed his Niggers. No Ma'am, dere warn't nobody whupped on Marse Jeff's place dat I knows 'bout. He didn't have no overseer. Dere warn't no need for one 'cause he didn't have so many slaves but what he could do de overseein' his own self. Marse Jeff jus' had 'bout four mens and four 'oman slaves and him and young Marse Johnny wukked in de fiel' 'long side of de Niggers. Dey went to de fiel' by daybreak and come in late at night.

"When Marse Jeff got behind wid his crop, he would hire slaves f'um other white folkses, mostly f'um Pa's marster, dat's how Pa come to know my Ma.

"Dere was 'bout a hunderd acres in our plantation countin' de woods and pastures. Dey had 'bout three or four acres fenced in wid pine poles in a plum orchard. Dat's whar dey kep' de calves.

"Dere was a jail at Watkinsville, but Marse Jeff never had none of his slaves put in no jail. He didn't have so many but what he could make 'em behave. I never seed no slaves sold, but I seed 'em in a wagon passin' by on deir way to de block. Marse Jeff said dey was takin' 'em a long ways off to sell 'em. Dat's why dey was a-ridin'.

"Miss Anna larned Ma her A.B.C's. She could read a little, but she never larned to write.

"Slaves went to de white folkses church if dey went a t'all. I never could sing no tune. I'se lak my Ma; she warn't no singer. Dat's how come I can't tell you 'bout de songs what dey sung den. I 'members de fus' time I seed anybody die; I was 'bout eight years old, and I was twelve 'fore I ever seed a funeral. No Ma'am, us chilluns didn't go to no baptizin's—Ma went, but us didn't.

"Didn't none of Marse Jeff's Niggers run off to no North, but I heared of a Nigger what did on de place whar my Pa was at. De only thing I knowed what might a made him run to de North was dat Niggers thought if dey got dar dey would be in Heb'en. Dem patterollers was somepin' else. I heared folkses say dey would beat de daylights mos' out of you if dey cotched you widout no pass. Us lived on de big road, and I seed 'em passin' mos' anytime. I mos' know dere was plenty trouble twixt de Niggers and de white folkses. Course I never heared tell of none, but I'm sho' dere was trouble jus' de same," he slyly remarked.

"Marse Jeff wukked dem few Niggers so hard dat when dey got to deir cabins at night dey was glad to jus' rest. Dey all knocked off f'um wuk Sadday at 12 o'clock. De 'omans washed, patched, and cleaned up de cabins, and de mens wukked in dey own cotton patches what Marse Jeff give 'em. Some Niggers wouldn't have no cotton patch 'cause dey was too lazy to wuk. But dey was all of 'em right dar Sadday nights when de frolickin' and dancin' was gwine on. On Sundays dey laid 'round and slep'. Some went to church if dey wanted to. Marster give 'em a pass to keep patterollers f'um beatin' 'em when dey went to church.

"Us chilluns was glad to see Chris'mas time come 'cause us had plenty to eat den; sich as hogshead, backbones, a heap of cake, and a little candy. Us had apples what had been growed on de place and stored away special for Chris'mas. Marse Jeff bought some lallahoe, dat was syrup, and had big old pones of lightbread baked for us to sop it up wid. What us laked best 'bout Chris'mas was de good old hunk of cheese dey give us den and de groundpeas. Don't you know what groundpeas is? Dem's goobers (peanuts). Such a good time us did have, a-parchin' and a-eatin' dem groundpeas! If dere was oranges us didn't git none. Marse Jeff give de grown folkses plenty of liquor and dey got drunk and cut de buck whilst it lasted. New Year's Day was de time to git back to wuk.

"Marse Jeff was sich a pore man he didn't have no corn shuckin's on his place, but he let his Niggers go off to 'em and he went along hisself. Dey had a big time a-hollerin' and singin' and shuckin' corn. Atter de shuckin' was all done dere was plenty to eat and drink—nothin' short 'bout dem corn shuckin's.

"When slaves got sick, dey didn't have no doctor dat I knowed 'bout. Miss Carrie done de doctorin' herself. Snake root tea was good for colds and stomach mis'ries. Dey biled rabbit tobacco, pine tops, and mullein together; tuk de tea and mixed it wid 'lasses; and give it to us for diffunt ailments. If dey done dat now, folkses would live longer. Ma put asafiddy (asafetida) sacks 'round our necks to keep off sickness.

"Ma said us was gwine to be free. Marse Jeff said us warn't, and he didn't tell us no diffunt 'til 'bout Chris'mas atter de War was done over wid in April. He told us dat us was free, but he wanted us to stay on wid him, and didn't none of his Niggers leave him. Dey all wukked de same as dey had before dey was sot free only he paid 'em wages atter de War.

"I 'members dem Yankees comin' down de big road a-stealin' as dey went 'long. Dey swapped deir bags of bones for de white folkses good fat hosses. I never seed so many pore hosses at one time in my life as dey had. Dem Yankees stole all da meat, chickens, and good bedclothes and burnt down de houses. Dey done devilment aplenty as dey went 'long. I 'members Marse Jeff put one of his colored mens on his hoss wid a coffeepot full of gold and sont him to de woods. Atter dem Yankees went on he sont for him to fetch back de gold and de fine hoss what he done saved f'um de sojer mens.

"I heared tell of dem Ku Kluxers, but I never seed 'em. Lawsy Miss! What did Niggers have to buy land wid 'til atter dey wukked long enough for to make some money? Warn't no schoolin' done 'round whar us lived. I was 10 years old 'fore I ever sot foots in a schoolhouse. De nearest school was at Shady Grove.

"It was a long time atter de War 'fore I married. Us didn't have no weddin'; jus' got married. My old 'oman had on a calico dress—I disremembers what color. She looked good to me though. Us had 16 chilluns in all; four died. I got 22 grandchillun and one great grandchild. None of 'em has jobs to brag 'bout; one of 'em larned to run a store.

"I think Mr. Lincoln was a great man, 'cause he sot us free. When I thinks back, it warn't no good feelin' to be bound down lak dat. Mr. President Davis wanted us to stay bound down. No Ma'am, I didn't lak dat Mr. Davis atter I knowed what he stood for. 'Course dere is plenty what needs to be bound down hard and fast so dey won't git in no trouble. But for me I trys to behave myself, and I sho' had ruther be free. I guess atter all it's best dat slavery days is over. 'Bout dat Booker Washin'ton man, de Niggers what tuk him in said he done lots of good for his race, and I reckon he did.

"Somepin' 'nother jus' made me jine de church. I wanted to do better'n what I was doin'. De Lord says it's best for folkses to be 'ligious.

"No Ma'am, I don't 'spect to live as long as my Ma lived, 'cause dese legs of mine since I done los' both of my footses wid blood pizen atter gangreen sot in, sho' gives me a passel of trouble. But de Lord is good to me and no tellin' how long I'se gwine to stay here. Miss, you sho' tuk me way back yonder, and I laks to talk 'bout it. Yes, Ma'am, dat's been a long time back."

Slave Narratives

ROBERT SHEPHERD, Age 91
386 Arch Street
Athens, Georgia

Written by:
Grace McCune [HW: (White)]
Athens

Edited by:
Sarah H. Hall
Athens

Leila Harris
Augusta

and
John N. Booth
District Supervisor
Federal Writers' Project
Residencies 6 & 7

ROBERT SHEPHERD

R obert lives in a small house so old and in such bad repair that a strong wind would no doubt tumble it down. Large holes in the roof can be plainly seen from the gateway. The neat yard, filled with old-fashioned flowers, is enclosed by a makeshift fence of rusty wire sagging to the ground in places, and the gate rocks on one hinge. There was some evidence that a porch had extended across the front of the cottage, but it is entirely gone now and large rocks serve as steps at the doorway.

Knocks and calls at the front of the house were unanswered and finally Robert was found working in his garden behind the house. He is a tiny old man, and his large sun hat made him seem smaller than he actually was. He wore a clean but faded blue shirt and shabby gray pants much too large for him. His shoes, bound to his feet with strips of cloth, were so much too large that it was all he could do to shuffle along. He removed his hat and revealed white hair that contrasted with his black face, as he smiled in a friendly way. "Good morning, Missy! How is you?" was his greeting. Despite his advanced age, he keeps his garden in excellent condition. Not a blade of grass was to be seen. Asked how he managed to keep it worked so efficiently he proudly answered: "Well Miss, I jus' wuks in it some evvy day dat comes 'cept Sundays and, when you keeps right up wid it dat way, it ain't so hard. Jus' look 'round you! Don't you see I got de bestest beans and squashes, 'round here, and down under dem 'tater vines, I kin tell you, dem roots is jus' full of 'taters. My Old Marster done larnt me how to gyarden. He allus made us raise lots of gyarden sass such as: beans, peas, roas'in' ears, collards, turnip greens, and ingons (onions). For a fact, dere was jus' 'bout all de kinds of veg'tables us knowed anything 'bout dem days right dar in our Marster's big old gyarden. Dere was big patches of 'taters, and in dem wheatfields us growed enough to make bread for all de folks on dat dere plantation. Us sho' did have plenty of mighty good somepin t'eat.

"I would ax you to come in and set down in my house to talk," he said, "but I don't 'spect you could climb up dem dere rocks to my door, and dem's all de steps I got." When Robert called to his daughter, who lived next door, and told her to bring out some chairs, she suggested that the interview take place on her porch. "It's shady and cool on my porch," she said, "and Pa's done been a-diggin' in his garden so long he's plum tuckered out; he needs to set down and rest." After making her father comfortable, she drew up a bucket of water from the well at the edge of the porch and, after he had indulged in a long drink of the fresh water, he began his story.

"I was borned on Marster Joe Echols' plantation in Oglethorpe County, 'bout 10 miles from Lexin'ton, Georgy. Mammy was Cynthia Echols 'fore she married up wid my daddy. He was Peyton Shepherd. Atter Pappy and Mammy got married, Old Marse Shepherd sold Pappy to Marse Joe Echols so as dey could stay together.

"Marse Joe, he had three plantations, but he didn't live on none of 'em. He lived in Lexin'ton. He kept a overseer on each one of his plantations and dey had better be good to his Niggers, or else Marse Joe would sho' git 'em 'way from dar. He never 'lowed 'em to wuk us too hard, and in bad or real cold weather us didn't have to do no outside wuk 'cept evvyday chores what had to be done, come rain or shine, lak milkin', tendin' de stock, fetchin' in wood, and things lak dat. He seed dat us had plenty of good somepin t'eat and all de clothes us needed. Us was lots better off in dem days dan us is now.

"Old Marster, he had so many Niggers dat he never knowed 'em all. One day he was a-ridin' 'long towards one of his plantations and he met one of his slaves, named William. Marse Joe stopped him and axed him who he was. William said: 'Why Marster, I'se your Nigger. Don't you know me?' Den Marster, he jus' laughed and said: 'Well, hurry on home when you gits what you is gwine atter.' He was in a good humor dat way most all de time. I kin see him now a-ridin' dat little hoss of his'n what he called Button, and his little fice dog hoppin' 'long on three legs right side of de hoss. No Ma'am, dere warn't nothin' de matter wid' dat little dog; walkin' on three legs was jus' his way of gittin' 'round.

"Marster never let none of de slave chillun on his plantation do no wuk 'til dey got fifteen—dat was soon 'nough, he said. On all of his plantations dere was one old 'oman dat didn't have nothin' else to do but look atter and cook for de nigger chillun whilst dey mammies was at wuk in de fields. Aunt Viney tuk keer of us. She had a big old horn what she blowed when it was time for us to eat, and us knowed better dan to git so fur off us couldn't hear dat horn, for Aunt Viney would sho' tear us up. Marster had done told her she better fix us plenty t'eat and give it to us on time. Dere was a great long trough what went plum 'cross de yard, and dat was whar us et. For dinner us had peas or some other sort of veg'tables, and cornbread. Aunt Viney crumbled up dat bread in de trough and poured de veg'tables and pot-likker over it. Den she blowed de horn and chillun come a-runnin' from evvy which away. If us et it all up, she had to put more victuals in de trough. At nights, she crumbled de cornbread in de trough and poured buttermilk over it. Us never had nothin' but cornbread and buttermilk at night. Sometimes dat trough would be a sight, 'cause us never stopped to wash our hands, and 'fore us had been eatin' more dan a minute or two what was in de trough would look lak de red mud what had come off of our hands. Sometimes Aunt Viney would fuss at us and make us clean it out.

"Dere was a big sand bar down on de crick what made

a fine place to play, and wadin' in de branches was lots of fun. Us frolicked up and down dem woods and had all sorts of good times—anything to keep away from Aunt Viney 'cause she was sho' to have us fetchin' in wood or sweepin' de yards if us was handy whar she could find us. If us was out of her sight she never bothered 'bout dem yards and things. Us was skeered to answer dat horn when us got in Marster's 'bacco. He raised lots of 'bacco and rationed it out to mens, but he never 'lowed chillun to have none 'til dey was big enough to wuk in de fields. Us found out how to git in his 'bacco house and us kept on gittin' his 'bacco 'fore it was dried out 'til he missed it. Den he told Aunt Viney to blow dat horn and call up all de chillun. I'se gwine to whup evvy one of 'em, he would 'clare. Atter us got dere and he seed dat green 'bacco had done made us so sick us couldn't eat, he jus' couldn't beat us. He jus' laughed and said: 'It's good enough for you.'

"Aunt Martha, she done de milkin' and helped Aunt Nancy cook for de slaves. Dey had a big long kitchen up at de big house whar de overseer lived. De slaves what wuked in de field never had to do deir own cookin'. It was all done for 'em in dat big old kitchen. Dey cooked some of de victuals in big old washpots and dere was sho' a plenty for all. All de cookin' was done in big fireplaces what had racks made inside to hang pots on and dey had big old ovens for bakin', and thick iron skillets, and long-handled fryin' pans. You jus' can't 'magine how good things was cooked dat way on de open fire. Nobody never had no better hams and other meat dan our Marster kept in dem big old smokehouses, and his slaves had meat jus' lak white folks did. Dem cooks knowed dey had to cook a plenty and have it ready when it was time for de slaves to come in from de fields. Miss Ellen, she was the overseer's wife, went out in de kitchen and looked over evvything to see that it was all right and den she blowed de bugle. When de slaves heared dat bugle, dey come in a-singin' from de fields. Dey was happy 'cause dey knowed Miss Ellen had a good dinner ready for 'em.

"De slave quarters was long rows of log cabins wid chimblies made out of sticks and red mud. Dem chimblies was all de time ketchin' fire. Dey didn't have no glass windows. For a window, dey jus' cut a openin' in a log and fixed a piece of plank 'cross it so it would slide when dey wanted to open or close it. Doors was made out of rough planks, beds was rough home-made frames nailed to de side of de cabins, and mattresses was coarse, home-wove ticks filled wid wheat straw. Dey had good home-made kivver. Dem beds slept mighty good.

"Dere warn't many folks sick dem days, 'specially 'mongst de slaves. When one did die, folks would go 12 or 15 miles to de buryin'. Marster would say: 'Take de mules and wagons and go but, mind you, take good keer of dem mules.' He never seemed to keer if us went—fact was, he said us ought to go. If a slave died on our place, nobody went to de fields 'til atter de buryin'. Marster never let nobody be buried 'til dey had been dead 24 hours, and if dey had people from some other place, he waited 'til dey could git dar. He said it warn't right to hurry 'em off into de ground too quick atter dey died. Dere warn't no undertakers dem days. De homefolks jus' laid de corpse out on de coolin' board 'til de coffin was made. Lordy Miss! Ain't you never seed one of dem coolin' boards? A coolin' board was made out of a long straight plank raised a little at de head, and had legs fixed to make it set straight. Dey wropt 'oman corpses in windin' sheets.

Uncle Squire, de man what done all de wagon wuk and buildin' on our place, made coffins. Dey was jus' plain wood boxes what dey painted to make 'em look nice. White preachers conducted de funerals, and most of de time our own Marster done it, 'cause he was a preacher hisself. When de funeral was done preached, dey sung _Harps From De Tomb_, den dey put de coffin in a wagon and driv slow and keerful to de graveyard. De preacher prayed at de grave and de mourners sung, _I'se Born To Die and Lay Dis Body Down_. Dey never had no outside box for de coffin to be sot in, but dey put planks on top of de coffin 'fore dey started shovellin' in de dirt.

"Fourth Sundays was our meetin' days, and evvybody went to church. Us went to our white folks' church and rid in a wagon 'hind deir car'iage. Dere was two Baptist preachers—one of 'em was Mr. John Gibson and de other was Mr. Patrick Butler. Marse Joe was a Methodist preacher hisself, but dey all went to de same church together. De Niggers sot in de gallery. When dey had done give de white folks de sacrament, dey called de Niggers down from de gallery and give dem sacrament too. Church days was sho' 'nough big meetin' days 'cause evvybody went. Dey preached three times a day; at eleven in de mornin', at three in de evenin', and den again at night. De biggest meetin' house crowds was when dey had baptizin', and dat was right often. Dey dammed up de crick on Sadday so as it would be deep enough on Sunday, and dey done de baptizin' 'fore dey preached de three o'clock sermon. At dem baptizin's dere was all sorts of shoutin', and dey would sing _Roll Jordan, Roll_, _De Livin' Waters_, and _Lord I'se Comin' Home_.

"When de craps was laid by and most of de hardest wuk

of de year done up, den was camp-meetin' time, 'long in de last of July and sometimes in August. Dat was when us had de biggest times of all. Dey had great big long tables and jus' evvything good t'eat. Marster would kill five or six hogs and have 'em carried dar to be barbecued, and he carried his own cooks along. Atter de white folks et dey fed de Niggers, and dere was allus a plenty for all. Marster sho' looked atter all his Niggers good at dem times. When de camp-meetin' was over, den come de big baptizin': white folks fust, den Niggers. One time dere was a old slave 'oman what got so skeered when dey got her out in de crick dat somebody had to pull her foots out from under her to git her under de water. She got out from dar and testified dat it was de devil a-holdin' her back.

"De white ladies had nice silk dresses to wear to church. Slave 'omans had new calico dresses what dey wore wid hoopskirts dey made out of grapevines. Dey wore poke bonnets wid ruffles on 'em and, if de weather was sort of cool, dey wore shawls. Marster allus wore his linen duster. Dat was his white coat, made cutaway style wid long tails. De cloth for most all of de clothes was made at home. Marse Joe raised lots of sheep and de wool was used to make cloth for de winter clothes. Us had a great long loom house whar some of de slaves didn't do nothin' but weave cloth. Some cyarded bats, some done de spinnin', and dere was more of 'em to do de sewin'. Miss Ellen, she looked atter all dat, and she cut out most of de clothes. She seed dat us had plenty to wear. Sometimes Marster would go to de sewin' house, and Mist'ess would tell him to git on 'way from dar and look atter his own wuk, dat her and Aunt Julia could run dat loom house. Marster, he jus' laughed den and told us chillun what was hangin' round de door to jus' listen to dem 'omans cackle. Oh, but he was a good old boss man.

"Us had water buckets, called piggens, what was made out of cedar and had handles on de sides. Sometimes us sawed off little vinegar kegs and put handles on 'em. Us loved to drink out of gourds. Dere was lots of gourds raised evvy year. Some of 'em was so big dey was used to keep eggs in and for lots of things us uses baskets for now. Dem little gourds made fine dippers.

"Dem cornshuckin's was sho' 'nough big times. When us got all de corn gathered up and put in great long piles, den de gittin' ready started. Why dem 'omans cooked for days, and de mens would git de shoats ready to barbecue. Marster would send us out to git de slaves from de farms 'round about dar.

"De place was all lit up wid light'ood-knot torches and bonfires, and dere was 'citement a-plenty when all de Niggers got to singin' and shoutin' as dey made de shucks fly. One of dem songs went somepin lak dis: 'Oh! my haid, my pore haid, Oh! my pore haid is 'fected.' Dere warn't nothin' wrong wid our haids—dat was jus' our way of lettin' our overseer know us wanted some likker. Purty soon he would come 'round wid a big horn of whiskey, and dat made de 'pore haid' well, but it warn't long 'fore it got wuss again, and den us got another horn of whiskey. When de corn was all shucked den us et all us could and, let me tell you, dat was some good eatin's. Den us danced de rest of de night.

"Next day when us all felt so tired and bad, Marster he would tell us 'bout stayin' up all night, but Mist'ess tuk up for us, and dat tickled Old Marster. He jus' laughed and said: 'Will you listen to dat 'oman?' Den he would make some of us sing one of dem songs us had done been singin' to dance by. It goes sort of lak dis: 'Turn your pardner 'round! Steal 'round de corner, 'cause dem Johnson gals is hard to beat! Jus' glance 'round and have a good time! Dem gals is hard to find!' Dat's jus' 'bout all I can ricollect of it now.

"Us had big 'possum hunts, and us sho' cotched a heap of 'em. De gals cooked 'em wid 'taters and dey jus' made your mouth water. I sho' wish I had one now. Rabbits was good too. Marster didn't 'low no huntin' wid guns, so us jus' took dogs when us went huntin'. Rabbits was kilt wid sticks and rocks 'cept when a big snow come. Dey was easy to track to dey beds den, and us could jus' reach in and pull 'em out. When us cotch 'nough of 'em, us had big rabbit suppers.

"De big war was 'bout over when dem yankees come by our place and jus' went through evvything. Dey called all de slaves together and told 'em dey was free and didn't b'long to nobody no more, and said de slaves could take all dey wanted from de smokehouses and barns and de big house, and could go when and whar dey wanted to go. Dey tried to hand us out all de meat and hams, but us told 'em us warn't hongry, 'cause Marster had allus done give us all us wanted. When dey couldn't make none of us take nothin', dey said it was de strangest thing dey had done ever seed, and dat dat man Echols must have sho' been good to his Niggers.

"When dem yankees had done gone off Marster come out to our place. He blowed de bugle to call us all up to de house. He couldn't hardly talk, 'cause somebody had done told him dat dem yankees couldn't talk his Niggers into stealin' nothin'. Marster said he never knowed 'fore how good us loved him. He told us he had done tried to be good to us and had done de best he could for us and dat he was mighty proud of de way evvy one of us had done 'haved ourselfs. He said dat de war was over now, and us was free and could go anywhar us wanted to, but dat us didn't have to go if us wanted to stay dar. He said he would pay us for our wuk and take keer of us if us stayed or, if us wanted to wuk on shares, he would 'low us to wuk some land dat way. A few of dem Niggers drifted off, but most of 'em stayed right dar 'til dey died."

A sad note had come into Robert's voice and he seemed to be almost overcome by the sorrow aroused by his reminiscences. His daughter was quick to perceive this and interrupted the conversation: "Please Lady," she said. "Pa's too feeble to talk any more today. Can't you let him rest now and come back again in a day or two? Maybe he will be done 'membered things he couldn't call back today."

The front door was open when Robert's house was next visited, and a young girl answered the knock. "Come in," she said. The little house was as dilapidated in the interior as it was on the outside. Bright June sunshine filtered through the many gaps in the roof arousing wonder as to how the old man managed to remain inside this house during heavy rains. The room was scrupulously clean and neat. In it was a very old iron bed, a dresser that was minus its mirror, two chairs, and a table, all very old and dilapidated. The girl laughed when she called attention to a closet that was padlocked. "Dat's whar Grandpa keeps his rations," she said, and then volunteered the information: "He's gone next door to stay wid Ma, whilst

I clean up his house. He can't stand no dust, and when I sweeps, I raises a dust." The girl explained a 12 inch square aperture in the door, with a sliding board fastened on the inside by saying: "Dat's Grandpa's peep-hole. He allus has to see who's dar 'fore he unfastens his door."

Robert was sitting on the back porch and his daughter was ironing just inside the door. Both seemed surprised and happy to see the interviewer and the daughter placed a comfortable chair for her as far as the dimensions of the small porch would permit from the heat of the charcoal bucket and irons. Remembering that his earlier recollections had ended with the close of the Civil War, Robert started telling about the days "atter freedom had done come."

"Me, I stayed right on dar 'til atter Marster died. He was sick a long, long time, and one morning Old Mist'ess, she called to me. 'Robert,' she said, 'you ain't gwine to have no Marster long, 'cause he's 'bout gone.' I called all de Niggers up to de big house and when dey was all in de yard, Mist'ess, she said: 'Robert, you been wid us so long, you kin come in and see him 'fore he's gone for good.' When I got in dat room I knowed de Lord had done laid His hand on my good Old Marster, and he was a-goin' to dat Home he used to preach to us Niggers 'bout, and it 'peared to me lak my heart would jus' bust. When de last breath was done gone, I went back out in de yard and told de other Niggers, and dere was sho' cryin' and prayin' 'mongst 'em, 'cause all of 'em loved Marster. Dat was sho' one big funeral. Mist'ess said she wanted all of Marster's old slaves to go, 'cause he loved 'em so, and all of us went. Some what had done been gone for years come back for Marster's funeral.

"Next day, atter de funeral was over, Mist'ess, she said: 'Robert, I want you to stay on wid me 'cause you know how he wanted his wuk done.' Den Mist'ess' daughter and her husband, Mr. Dickenson, come dar to stay. None of de Niggers laked dat Mr. Dickenson and so most of 'em left and den, 'bout 2 years atter Marster died, Mist'ess went to 'Lanta (Atlanta) to stay wid another of her daughters, and she died dar. When Mist'ess left, I left too and come on here to Athens, and I been here ever since.

"Dere warn't much town here den, and 'most all 'round dis here place was woods. I wuked 'bout a year for Mr. John McCune's fambly on de old Pitner place, den I went to wuk for Mr. Manassas B. McGinty. He was a cyarpenter and built most of de fine houses what was put up here dem days. I got de lumber from him to build my house. Dere warn't but two other houses 'round here den. My wife, Julie, washed for de white folks and helped 'em do deir housewuk. Our chillun used to come bring my dinner. Us had dem good old red peas cooked wid side meat in a pot in de fireplace, and ashcake to go wid 'em. Dat was eatin's. Julie would rake out dem coals and kivver 'em wid ashes, and den she would wrop a pone of cornbread dough in collard or cabbage leaves and put it on dem ashes and rake more ashes over it. You had to dust off de bread 'fore you et it, but ashcake was mighty good, folks what lived off of it didn't git sick lak dey does now a-eatin' dis white flour bread all de time. If us had any peas left from dinner and supper, Julie would mash 'em up right soft, make little cakes what she rolled in corn meal, and fry 'em for breakfast. Dem sausage cakes made out of left-over peas was mighty fine for breakfast.

"When de chillun started out wid my dinner, Julie allus made two of 'em go together and hold hands all de way so dey wouldn't git lost. Now, little chillun jus' a few years old goes anywhar dey wants to. Folks don't look atter dey chillun lak dey ought to, and t'ain't right. Den, when night come, chillun went right off to bed. Now, dey jus' runs 'round 'most all night, and it sho' is a-ruinin' dis young genrayshun (generation). Dey don't take no keer of deirselfs. My own grandchillun is de same way.

"I left Mr. McGinty and went to wuk for Mr. Bloomfield in de mill. Mr. Bill Dootson was our boss, and he was sho' a good man. Dem was good times. I wuked inside de mill and 'round de yard too, and sometimes dey sont me to ride de boat wid de cotton or sometimes wid cloth, whatever dey was sendin'. Dere was two mills den. One was down below de bridge on Oconee Street, and de old check factory was t'other side of de bridge on Broad Street. Dey used boats to carry de cotton and de cloth from one mill to de other.

"Missy, can you b'lieve it? I wuked for 68¢ a day and us paid for our home here. Dey paid us off wid tickets what us tuk to de commissary to git what us needed. Dey kept jus' evvything dat anybody could want down dar at de comp'ny store. So us raised our nine chillun, give 'em plenty to eat and wear too and a good roof over deir haids, all on 68¢ a day and what Julie could make wukin' for de white folks. 'Course things warn't high-priced lak dey is now, but de main diff'unce is dat folks didn't have to have so many kinds of things to eat and wear den lak dey does now. Dere warn't nigh so many ways to throw money 'way den.

"Dere warn't so many places to go; jus' church and

church spreads, and Sundays, folks went buggy ridin'. De young Niggers, 'specially dem what was a-sparkin', used to rent buggies and hosses from Mr. Selig Bernstein. He kept a big livery stable den and he had a hoss named Buckskin. Dat was de hoss what evvybody wanted 'cause he was so gentle and didn't skeer de 'omans and chilluns. Mr. Bernstein is a-livin' yit, and he is sho' a good man to do business wid. Missy, dere was lots of good white folks den. Most of dem old ones is done passed on. One of de best of 'em was Mr. Robert Chappell. He done passed on, but whilst he lived he was mighty good to evvybody and de colored folks sho' does miss him. He b'lieved in helpin' 'em and he give 'em several churches and tried his best to git 'em to live right. If Mr. Robert Chappell ain't in Heb'en, dere ain't no use for nobody else to try to git dar. His granddaughter married Jedge Matthews, and folks says she is most as good as her granddaddy was."

Robert chuckled when he was asked to tell about his wedding. "Miss," he said, "I didn't have no sho' 'nough weddin'. Me and Julie jus' jumped over de broom in front of Marster and us was married. Dat was all dere was to it. Dat was de way most of de slave folks got married dem days. Us knowed better dan to ax de gal when us wanted to git married. Us jus' told our Marster and he done de axin'. Den, if it was all right wid de gal, Marster called all de other Niggers up to de big house to see us jump over de broom. If a slave wanted to git married to somebody on another place, den he told Marster and his Marster would talk to de gal's Marster. Whatever dey 'greed on was all right. If neither one of 'em would sell one of de slaves what wanted to git married, den dey let 'em go ahead and jump over de broom, and de man jus' visited his wife on her Marster's place, mostly on Wednesday and Sadday nights. If it was a long piece off, he didn't git dar so often. Dey had to have passes den, 'cause de patterollers would git 'em sho' if dey didn't. Dat meant a thrashin', and dey didn't miss layin' on de stick, when dey cotch a Nigger.

"Dese days, de boys and gals jus' walks off and don't say nothin' to nobody, not even to dey mammies and daddies. [TR: written in margin: "Elopement"] Now take dis daughter of mine—Callie is her name—she runned away when she was 'bout seventeen. Dat day her mammy had done sont her wid de white folks' clothes. She had on brass-toed brogan shoes, a old faded cotton dress dat was plum up to her knees,—dem days, long dresses was stylish—and she wore a old bonnet. She was totin' de clothes to Mrs. Reese and met up wid dat Davenport boy. Dey traips'd up to de courthouse, got a license, and was married 'fore me and Julie knowed nothin' 'bout it. Julie sho' did light out from hyar to go git Callie. She brung her back and kept her locked up in de house a long time 'fore she would let her live wid dat Nigger.

"Us had our troubles den, but dey warn't lak de troubles us has now. Now, it seems lak dem was mighty good days back when Arch Street was jus' a path through de woods. Julie, she's done been gone a long time, and all of our chillun's daid 'cept three, and two of 'em is done gone up north. Jus' me and my Callie and de grandchillun is all dat's left here. Soon I'se gwine to be 'lowed to go whar Julie is and I'se ready any time, 'cause I done been here long 'nough."

When the visitor arose to take her departure Robert said: "Good-bye Missy, come back to see me and Callie again 'cause us laked your 'pearments (appearance) de fust time you was here. Jus' trust in de Lord, Miss, and He will take keer of you wharever you is."

United States. Work Projects Administration

PLANTATION LIFE, AS VIEWED BY AN EX-SLAVE

TOM SINGLETON, Ex-Slave, Age 94
Athens, Georgia

Written by:
Sadie B. Hornsby
Research Worker
Federal Writers' Project
Athens, Georgia

Edited by:
Leila Harris
Editor
Federal Writers' Project
Augusta, Georgia
[Date Stamp: APR 27 1938]

TOM SINGLETON

Uncle Tom lives alone in a one room cabin, about two and one half miles from town, on Loop-de-Loop road, not far from the Brooklyn section of Athens. He states that he lives alone because: "I wuz raised right and de Niggers dis day and time ain't had no raisin'. I just can't be bothered wid havin' 'em 'round me all de time. Dey ain't my sort of folkses." Uncle Tom says he will be 94 years old on May 15th of this year, but many believe that he is much older.

When asked if he felt like talking about his experiences and observances while he was a slave, he said: "I don't know, Missie; I got a pow'ful hurtin' in my chest, and I'm too old to 'member much, but you ax me what you want to know and I'll try to tell you. I wuz born in Lumpkin County on Marster Joe Singleton's place. My ma wuz named Nancy Early, and she belonged to Marster Joe Early what lived in Jackson County. My pa's name wuz Joe Singleton. I don't 'member much 'bout my brothers and sisters. Ma and Pa had 14 chillun. Some of deir boys wuz me and Isaac, Jeff, Moses, and Jack; and deir gals wuz: Celia, Laura, Dilsey, Patsey, Frankie, and Elinor. Dese wuz de youngest chillun. I don't 'member de fust ones. I don't ricollect nothin' t'all 'bout my grandma and grandpa, cause us wuz too busy to talk in de daytime, and at night us wuz so whupped out from hard wuk us just went off to sleep early and never talked much at no time. All I knows 'bout 'em is dat I heared folkses say my gran'pa wuz 107 years old when he died. Folkses don't live dat long now-a-days.

"De slave quarters wuz in rows and had two rooms and a shed. Dey had beds made out of poles fastened together wid pegs and 'cross 'em wuz laid de slats what dey spread de wheat straw on. Us had good kivver 'cause our Marster wuz a rich man and he believed in takin' keer of his Niggers. Some put sheets dat wuz white as snow over de straw. Dem sheets wuz biled wid home-made soap what kept 'em white lak dat. Udder folkses put quilts over de straw. At de end of de slave quarters wuz de barns and cow sheds, and a little beyond dem wuz de finest pasture you ever seed wid clear water a-bubblin' out of a pretty spring, and runnin' thoo' it. Dar's whar dey turned de stock to graze when dey warn't wukkin' 'em."

When Tom was asked if he ever made any money, a mischievous smile illumined his face. "Yes ma'am, you see I plowed durin' de day on old Marster's farm. Some of de white folks what didn't have many Niggers would ax old Marster to let us help on dey places. Us had to do dat wuk at night. On bright moonshiny nights, I would cut wood, fix fences, and sich lak for 'em. Wid de money dey paid me I bought Sunday shoes and a Sunday coat and sich lak, cause I wuz a Nigger what always did lak to look good on Sunday.

"Yes ma'am, us had good clo'es de year 'round. Our summer clothes wuz white, white as snow. Old Marster said dey looked lak linen. In winter us wore heavy yarn what de women made on de looms. One strand wuz wool and one wuz cotton. Us wore our brogan shoes evvy day and Sunday too. Marster wuz a merchant and bought shoes from de tanyard. Howsomever, he had a colored man on his place what could make any kind of shoes.

"Lawdy! Missie, us had evvythin' to eat; all kinds of greens, turnips, peas, 'tatoes, meat and chickens. Us wuz plumb fools 'bout fried chicken and chicken stew, so Marster 'lowed us to raise plenty of chickens, and sometimes at night us Niggers would git together and have a hee old time. No Ma'am, us didn't have no gyardens. Us didn't need none. Old Marster give us all de vittuls us wanted. Missie, you oughta seed dem big old iron spiders what dey cooked in. 'Course de white folkses called 'em ovens. De biscuits and blackberry pies dey cooked in spiders, dey wuz somethin' else. Oh! don't talk 'bout dem 'possums! Makes me hungry just to think 'bout 'em. One night when pa and me went 'possum huntin', I put a 'possum what us cotched in a sack and flung it 'cross my back. Atter us started home dat 'possum chewed a hole in de sack and bit me square in de back. I 'member my pa had a little dog." Here he stopped talking and called a little black and white dog to him, and said: "He wuz 'bout de size of dis here dog, and pa said he could natchelly jus' make a 'possum de way he always found one so quick when us went huntin'." The old man sighed, and looking out across the field, continued: "Atter slav'ry days, Niggers turned dey chilluns loose, an' den de 'possums an' rabbits most all left, and dere ain't so many fishes left in de rivers neither."

Tom could not recall much about his first master: "I wuz four year old when Marster Dr. Joe Singleton died. All I 'members 'bout him; he wuz a big man, and I sho' wuz skeered of him. When he cotch us in de branch, he would holler at us and say: 'Come out of dar 'fore you git sick.' He didn't 'low us to play in no water, and when, he hollered, us lit a rag. Dere wuz 'bout a thousand acres in Marse Joe's plantation, he owned a gold mine and a copper mine too. Old Marster owned 'bout 65 Niggers in all. He bought an' sold Niggers too. When Old Marster wanted to send news, he put a Nigger on a mule an' sont de message.

"Atter Marse Joe died, old Mist'ess run de farm 'bout six years. Mist'ess' daughter, Miss Mattie, married Marster Fred Lucas, an' old Mist'ess sold her share in de plantation den. My pa, my sister, an' me wuz sold on de block at de sheriff's sale. Durin' de sale my sister cried all de time, an' Pa rubbed his han' over her head an' face, an' he said: 'Don't cry, you is gwine live wid young Miss Mattie.' I didn't cry none, 'cause I didn't care. Marse Fred bought us, an' tuk us to Athens to live, an' old Mist'ess went to live wid her chilluns.

"Marse Fred didn't have a very big plantation; jus' 'bout 70 or 80 acres I guess, an' he had 'bout 25 Niggers.

He didn't have no overseer. My pa wuz de one in charge, an' he tuk his orders from Marse Fred, den he went out to de farm, whar he seed dat de Niggers carried 'em out. Pa wuz de carriage driver too. It wuz his delight to drive for Marster and Mist'ess.

"Marster and Mist'ess had eight chillun: Miss Mattie, Miss Mary, Miss Fannie, Miss Senie, Mr. Dave, Mr. Joe, Mr. Frank and Mr. Freddy. Dey lived in a big house, weather-boarded over logs, an' de inside wuz ceiled.

"Marster an' Mist'ess sho' wuz good to us Niggers. Us warn't beat much. De onliest Nigger I 'member dey whupped wuz Cicero. He wuz a bad boy. My Marster never did whup me but onct. Mist'ess sont me up town to fetch her a spool of thread. I got to playin' marbles an' 'fore I knowed it, it wuz dinner time. When I got home, Mist'ess wuz mad sno' 'nough. Marster cotch me an' wore me out, but Mist'ess never touched me. I seed Niggers in de big jail at Watkinsville an' in de calaboose in Athens. Yes Ma'am! I seed plenty of Niggers sold on de block in Watkinsville. I ricollects de price of one Nigger run up to $15,000. All de sellin' wuz done by de sheriffs an' de slave Marsters.

"Marster Fred Lucas sold his place whar he wuz livin' in town to Major Cook, an' moved to his farm near Princeton Factory. Atter Major Cook got kilt in de War, Marse Fred come back to town an' lived in his house again.

"No Ma'am, dey warn't no schools for Niggers in slav'ry time. Mist'ess' daughters went to Lucy Cobb. Celia, my sister, wuz deir nurse, an' when all our little missies got grown, Celia wuz de house gal. So when our little missies went to school dey come home an' larnt Celia how to read an' write. 'Bout two years atter freedom, she begun to teach school herself.

"Us had our own churches in town, an' de white folkses furnished our preachers. Once dey baptised 75 in de river below de Check Factory; white folkses fust, and Niggers last.

"Oh! dem patterrollers! Dey wuz rough mens. I heared 'em say dey would beat de stuffin' out of you, if dey cotch you widout no pass.

"Yes Ma'am! dar always wuz a little trouble twixt de white folkses an' Niggers; always a little. Heaps of de Niggers went Nawth. I wuz told some white men's livin' in town hyar helped 'em git away. My wife had six of 'er kinfolkses what got clean back to Africa, an' dey wrote back here from dar.

"Us had parties an' dances at night. Sometimes Mist'ess let Celia wear some of de little missies' clo'es, 'cause she wanted her to outshine de other Nigger gals. Dey give us a week at Christmas time, an' Christmas day wuz a big day. Dey give us most evvythin': a knot of candy as big as my fist, an' heaps of other good things. At corn shuckin's Old Marster fotched a gallon keg of whiskey to de quarters an' passed it 'round. Some just got tipsy an' some got low down drunk. De onliest cotton pickin' us knowed 'bout wuz when us picked in de daytime, an' dey warn't no good time to dat. A Nigger can't even sing much wid his head all bent down pickin' cotton.

"Folkses had fine times at weddin's dem days. Dar wuz more vittuls dan us could eat. Now dey just han' out a little somethin'. De white folkses had a fine time too.

Dey let de Niggers git married in deir houses. If it wuz bad weather, den de weddin' wuz most genully in de hall, but if it wuz a pretty day, dey married in de yard.

"I can't 'member much 'bout de games us played or de songs us sung. A few of de games wuz marbles, football, an' town ball. 'Bout dem witches, I don't know nothin'. Some of de folkses wore a mole foot 'roun' dey neck to keep bad luck away: some wore a rabbit's foot fer sharpness, an' it sholy did fetch sharpness. I don't know nothin' 'tall 'bout Rawhead and Bloody Bones, but I heared tell he got atter Mist'ess' chillun an' made 'em be good. Dey wuz pow'ful skeert of 'im.

"Old Marster an' Mist'ess looked atter deir Niggers mighty well. When dey got sick, de doctor wuz sont for straight away. Yes Ma'am, dey looked atter 'em mighty well. Holly leaves an' holly root biled together wuz good for indigestion, an' blackgum an' blackhaw roots biled together an' strained out an' mixed wid whiskey wuz good for diffunt mis'ries. Some of de Niggers wore little tar sacks 'roun' dey necks to keep de fever 'way.

"Yes Ma'am.' I wuz in de War 'bout two years, wid young Marster Joe Lucas. I waited on him, cooked for him, an' went on de scout march wid him, for to tote his gun, an' see atter his needs. I wuz a bugger in dem days!

"I 'members I wuz standin' on de corner of Jackson Street when dey said freedom had come. Dat sho' wuz a rally day for de Niggers. 'Bout a thousand in all wuz standin' 'roun' here in Athens dat day. Yes Ma'am, de fust time de yankees come thoo' dey robbed an' stole all dey could find an' went on to Monroe. Next to come wuz de gyards to take charge of de town, an' dey wuz s'posed to set things to goin' right.

"Atter de War I stayed on wid Marse Fred, an' wukked for wages for six years, an' den farmed on halves wid him. Some of de Niggers went on a buyin' spree, an' dey bought land, hand over fist. Some bought eight an' nine hundred acres at a time."

When asked to tell about his wedding, a merry twinkle shone in his eyes: "Lawdy, Missie, dis ole Nigger nebber married 'til long atter de War. Us sho' did cut up jack. Us wuz too old to have any chillun, but us wuz so gay, us went to evvy dance 'til 'bout six years ago. She died den, an' lef' me all by myse'f.

"Dat Mr. Abyham Lincoln wuz a reg'lar Nigger god. Us b'lieved dat Mr. Jeff. Davis wuz all right too. Booker Washin'ton give a speech here onct, an' I wuz dar, but de Niggers made sich a fuss over him I couldn't take in what he said."

Asked what he thinks about slavery, now that it is over, he replied: "I think it is all right. God intended it. De white folks run de Injuns out, but dey is comin' back for sho'. God said every nation shall go to deir own land 'fore de end.

"I just jined de church right lately. I had cut de buck when I wuz a young chap, and God has promised us two places, heb'en an' hell. I thinks it would be scand'lous for anybody to go to hell, so I 'cided to jine up wid de crowd goin' to heb'en."

After the interview, he called to a little Negro boy that had wandered into the house: "Moses! gimme a drink of water! Fotch me a chaw of 'bacco, Missie done tuck me up de crick, down de branch, now she's a gwine 'roun'. Hurry! boy, do as I say, gimme dat water. Nigger chillun, dis day an' time, is too lazy to earn deir bread. I wuz sorry to see you come, Missie 'cause my chest wuz a hurtin' so bad, but now I'se sorry to see you go." Out of breath, he was silent for a moment, then grinned and said: "I wuz just lookin' at de Injun on dis here nickle, you done gimme. He looks so happy! Good-bye, Missie, hurry an' come back! You helped dis old Nigger lots, but my chest sho' do hurt."

United States. Work Projects Administration

Slave Narratives

[HW: Dist. 6
Ex slave 100]

Mary A. Crawford
Re-search Worker

CHARLIE TYE SMITH, Ex-slave
East Solomon Avenue,
Griffin, Georgia

September 16, 1936
[Date Stamp: MAY 8 1937]

CHARLIE TYE SMITH

Charlie Tye Smith was born in Henry County, near Locust Grove, Georgia, on June 10, 1850 (as nearly as he can tell). His mother kept his age for him and had him tell it to her over and over when he was a little boy. The old fellow is well and rather alert, despite his eighty-six years.

Mr. Jim Smith, of Henry County, was Charlie's owner and according to Charlie's version, "sho wuz a mighty good Marster". Mr. Smith owned a large plantation, and also "around one hundred and fifty, to two hundred Darkies". Charlie recalls that the slaves were well treated, seldom "whupped", and never "onmercifully". "Ole Miss", too, [HW: was] "powerful good" to the darkies, most especially to the "Chillun."

The old man related the following incident in proof of Miss Nancy's goodness. About every two weeks "ole

Miss" would have "ole Uncle Jim" bake "a whole passel of ginger cakes and tote 'em down to the cabins and jest pitch 'em out by de handfuls to de chillun!" The old man smiled broadly as he concluded the ginger cake story and said, "Charlie allus got his share. Miss Nancy seed to that, kase I wuz one of ole Miss's best little darkies". The interviewer inquired as to how so many ginger cakes could have been baked so easily, and he replied that "ole Marse" had a big rock-oven down at the spring about like what they boil syrup cane juice in today.

The slaves on "Marse Jim's" place were allowed about four holidays a year, and a week at Christmas, to frolic. The amusements were dancing ("the break-down"), banjo playing, and quill blowing. Sometimes when the "patarol" was in a good humor, he would take about twenty-five or thirty "Niggers" and go fishing at night. This kind of fishing was mostly seining, and usually "they got plenty o' fish".

Charlie, true to his race, is quite superstitious and on many occasions "went into the cow lot on Christmas night and found the cows down on their knees 'a-lowin". He also witnessed the "sun shoutin" on Christmas morning and "made sho" to get up jest in time to see the sun as it first "showed itself." Here Charlie did some very special gesticulating to illustrate.

The Negroes were required to go to Church on Sunday. They called it "gwine to meetin'", often leaving at sun up and walking ten or twelve miles to the meeting house, staying all day and late into the night.

If "ole Marse" happened to be in a good humor on Sunday, he would let the Darkies use the "waggins" and mules. The little "Niggers" never went to meetin' as they were left at home to take care of the house and "nuss" the babies. There were no Sunday Schools in those days. When the grown folks got back late in the night, they often "had to do some tall knocking and banging to get in the house—'cause the chillun were so dead asleep, and layin' all over the floor".

When asked if the slaves wouldn't be awfully tired and sleepy the next morning after they stayed up so late, he replied that they were "sho tired" but they had better turn out at four o'clock when ole Marse "blowed the horn!" They [TR: then?] he added with a chuckle, "the field was usually strowed with Niggers asleep in the cotton rows when they knocked off for dinner".

"No, Miss, the Marster never give us no money (here he laughed), for we didn't need none. There wasn't nothing to buy, and we had plenty to eat and wear".

"Yes, Mr. Jim and Miss Nancy believed in whuppin' and kep the raw hide hanging by the back door, but none o' Mr. Jim's Niggers evah got beat till dey bled".

Charlie Tye recalls vividly when the Yankees passed through and graphically related the following incident. "The Yankees passed through and caught "ole Marse" Jim and made him pull off his boots and run bare-footed through a cane brake with half a bushel of potatoes tied around his neck; then they made him put his boots back on and carried him down to the mill and tied him to the water post. They were getting ready to break his neck when one of Master's slaves, "ole Peter Smith", asked them if they intended to kill "Marse Jim", and when they said "Yes", Peter choked up and said, "Well, please, suh, let me die wid ole Marse! Well, dem Yankees let ole Marse loose and left! Yes, Missy, dat's de truf 'case I've heered my daddy tell it many's the time!"

Charlie is not working at all now as he is too old and is supported by the Griffin Relief Association. For forty-five years he served as janitor in the various public schools of Griffin.

PLANTATION LIFE, AS VIEWED BY AN EX-SLAVE

GEORGIA SMITH, Age 87
286 Augusta Ave.
Athens, Georgia

Written by:
Miss Grace McCune
Research Worker
Federal Writers' Project
Athens, Georgia

Edited by:
Mrs. Sarah H. Hall
Editor
Federal Writers' Project
Athens, Georgia

WPA Residency No. 6
April 6, 1938

GEORGIA SMITH

The cold, rainy, and altogether disagreeable weather on the outside was soon forgotten when the interviewer was admitted to the neat little home of Aunt Georgia Smith and found the old woman enjoying the cheerful warmth of her blazing fire.

Aunt Georgia appeared to be quite feeble. She was not only willing, but eager to talk of her experiences, and explained that her slow and rather indistinct articulation is one of the several bad after effects of her recent stroke of paralysis.

"My pappy was Blackstone Smith, and he b'longed to Marse Jeb Smith. My mammy was Nancy Chappell, owned by Mistus Peggie Chappell.

"I stayed wid my mammy on Mistus Chappell's plantation in Oglethorpe County, near old Antioch Church. W'en I was 'bout five or six years ole my mammy died. Den my pappy done come an' got me, an' I was to stay wid 'im on Marster Smith's place. Dey was good to me dar, but I warn't satisfied, an' I cried for Old Mistus.

"I'd jes' go 'roun' snifflin', an' not eatin' nuffin', an' one day w'en us was pickin' peaches, Marster Smith tole my pappy he better take dat chile back to her old mistus, 'fo' she done git sick fer sho'.

"Hit was de next day w'en dey ax me did I want to see Old Mistus an' I jes' cry an' say, 'yassum.' Den Marster say: 'Blackstone, hitch a mule to dat wagon, an' take dat chile right back to her Old Mistus.' I tell 'em I can walk, but dey made me ride in de wagon, an' I sho' was glad I was goin' back home.

"I seed Old Mistus 'fo' I got dar, an' jumped out of de wagon an' run to 'er. W'en she seed me, she jes' grabbed me, an' I thought she was a laughin', but when I seed dat she was cryin', I tole 'er not to cry, dat I warn't goin' to leave 'er no mo'.

"Mistus sho' was good to me, but she was good to all 'er niggers, an' dey all loved 'er. Us allus had plenny of evvything, she made us wear plenny of good warm clo'es, an' us wo'e flannel petticoats when hit was cole weather. Chillun don't wear 'nuff clo'es dese days to keep 'em warm, an nuffin' on deir legs. Hits a wonder dey doan' freeze.

"I diden' stay at de quarters with de udder niggers. Mistus kep' me in de big 'ouse wid 'er, an' I slep' on a cotton mattress on de floor by de side of 'er bed. She had a stick dat she used to punch me wid w'en she wannid somepin' in de night, an' effen I was hard to wake, she sho' could punch wid dat stick.

"Mistus diden' ever have us niggers whipped 'lessen it jes' had to be done. An' if us chilluns was bad, fussin' an' fightin', Mistus would git 'er a stick, but us would jes' run an' hide, an' Mistus would forgit all 'bout it in jes' a little w'ile.

"Marster was dead, an' us had a overseer, but he was good to us jes' lak' Mistus was. Hit was a big old plantation, wid lots of niggers. W'en de overseer would try to larn de chilluns to plow an' dey diden' want to larn, dey would jes' play 'roun'. Sometimes dey snuck off to de udder side of de fiel' an' hunnid for lizards. Dey would hold a lizard's head wid a stick, an' spit 'bacco juice in 'is mouf an' turn 'im loose. De 'bacco juice would make de lizard drunk, and he would run 'roun' an' 'roun'. Dey would cotch snakes, kill dem an' hang de skins on trees so hit would rain an' dey wouldn't have to wuk in de fiel'.

"De quarters was built away f'um de big 'ouse. Dey was cabins made of logs an' dey all had dey own gardens whar dey raised all kinds of vegetables an' allus had plenny of hog meat. De cookin' was done on a big fireplace an' in brick ovens. 'Taters was baked in de ashes, an' dey sho' was good.

"Dey had big times huntin' an' fishin' w'en de wuk was over. Dey cotch lots of 'possums, an' had big 'possum suppers. De 'possums was roasted with plenny of 'taters, butter an' red pepper. Us would eat an' dance most of de night w'en us had a 'possum supper.

"De rabbits was so bad in de gardens dat dey tuk white rags an' tied 'em on sticks stuck up in de ground. Rabbits woulden' come 'roun' den, cyaze dey was 'fraid of dem white rags flyin' on de sticks.

"Mistus b'lieved in lookin' atter her niggers w'en dey was sick. She would give 'em medicine at home. Candy an' tea, made wid ho'e houn' an' butterfly root tea was good for worms; dewberry wine, lak'wise dewberry root tea was good for de stomach ache; samson snake root an' poplar bark tea was good medicine for coles an' so'e th'oats, an' w'en you was in pain, de red pepper bag would sho' help lots sometimes. If de homemade medicine diden' cyore 'em, den Mistus sont for de doctor.

"Slaves went to de white folkses chu'ch an' sot up in de gallery. Dey stayed all day at chu'ch, an' had big dinners on de groun'. Dem was sho' 'nough good dinners. Us had big times on meetin' days.

"Our slaves had prayer meetin' twict a week in deir quarters, 'til dey got 'roun' to all de cabins den dey would start over again. Dey prayed an' sung all de old songs, and some of 'em as I 'member are: 'Roll Jordan Roll,'—'Better Mind How you Step on de Cross,'—'Cause You Ain' Gon 'er be Here Long,'—'Tell de Story Bye an' Bye,'—'All God's Chilluns are a Gatherin' Home,' an' 'We'll Understand Better Bye an' Bye.' Dey really could sing dem old songs. Mistus would let me go to dem cabin prayer meetin's an' I sho' did enjoy 'em.

"W'en slaves died dey jes' tuk 'em off an buried 'em. I doan' 'member 'em ever havin' a funeral, 'til way atter freedom done come an' niggers got dey own chu'ches.

"I 'member one night dey had a quiltin' in de quarters. De quilt was up in de frame, an' dey was all jes' quiltin' an' singin', 'All God's Chilluns are a Gatherin' Home,' w'en a drunk man wannid to preach, an' he jumped up on de quilt. Hit all fell down on de flo', an' dey all got fightin' mad at 'im. Dey locked 'im in de smokehouse 'til mornin', but dey diden' nobody tell Mistus nuffin' 'bout it.

"Us chilluns had to pick peas; two baskets full 'fo' dinner an' two 'fo' night, an' dey was big baskets too. I 'member dere was a white widow 'oman what lived near our place, an' she had two boys. Mistus let dem boys pick 'em some peas w'en us would be pickin', an' us would run 'em off, cause us diden' lak' po' white trash. But Mistus made us let 'em pick all dey wannid.

"I was 'bout twelve years old w'en freedom come, an' was big 'nough to wait on Mistus good den. I 'member how I used to run to de spring wid a little tin bucket w'en she wannid a fresh drink of water.

"Mos' of de slaves stayed with Mistus atter freedom come, 'cause dey all loved her, an' dey diden' have no place to go. Mistus fed 'em jes' lak' she had allus done and paid 'em a little money too. Us diden' never have no fussin' an' fightin' on our place, an' de Ku Klux Klan never come 'roun' dar, but de niggers had to have a ticket if dey lef' de place on Sunday. Dat was so de paddyrollers woulden' whip 'em if dey cotch 'em.

"All de niggers on de udder places, called us free niggers long 'fo' freedom come, 'cause we diden' have no whippin' post, an' if any of us jes' had to be whipped, Mistus would see dat dey warn't beat bad 'nough to leave no stripes.

"My pappy left de old Smith plantation, soon atter he got 'is freedom, an' went to Augusta, Georgia whar he died in jes' 'bout two years.

"I waked up one mornin' an' heered Mistus makin' a funny fuss. She was tryin' to git up an' pullin' at her gown. I was plum skeert an' I runned atter some of de udder folkses. Dey come a runnin' but she never did speak no mo', an' diden' live but jes' a few hours longer. De white folkses made me go to 'er funeral. Dere sho' was a big crowd of folkses dar, 'cause evvybody loved Mistus; she was so good to evvybody. Dey diden' preach long, mos'ly jes' prayed an' sung Mistus' favorite songs: 'All God's Chillun are a Gatherin' Home,' and', 'We'll Understand Bye an' Bye.'

"I lef' de old place not long atter Mistus died, 'cause hit was too lonesome dar an' I missed her so much, I come to town an' jes' wukked for white folkses. I doan' 'member all of 'em. But I cain' wuk no mo' now, an' hit woan' be so long 'til I see my old Mistus again, an' den I can still wait on her, an' we woan' have to part no mo'."

[HW: Dist. 2
Ex Slave 101]

EX-SLAVE INTERVIEW:
MARY SMITH
910 Spruce Street
Augusta, Georgia
(Richmond County)

BY: (Mrs.) Margaret Johnson
Editor
Fed. Writer's Proj.
Augusta, Georgia
[Date Stamp: MAY 8 1937]

MARY SMITH

Such a hovel, such squalor it would be hard to imagine. Only first hand observation could be a reliable witness to such conditions.

Into a tiny room was squeezed a double and a single bed with a passage-way barely wide enough to walk between the two beds. The door from the small porch could be opened only enough to allow one to enter, as the head on the single bed was against it. A small fire burned in the open fire place. An old man, ragged but respectful, and two old women were sitting in the room, one on a broken chair, the other on an empty nail keg. As we entered the room one of the old women got up, took a badly clipped and handleless teacup from the hearth and offered it to a girl lying in the single bed, in a smother of dirty quilts.

Mary was a squat figure, her head tied up in a dirty towel, her dress ragged and dirty, and much too small for her abundant figure. She welcomed us telling us the "po chile was bad sick" but she would talk to us. As the door of the lean-to kitchen was open, it offered a breath of outside air, even though polluted with the garbage scattered on the ground, and the odors from chickens, cats and dogs meandering about.

Mary's round face was unwrinkled, but the wisps of wool showing beneath her "head rag" were grey, and her eyes were rheumy with age. She was entirely toothless and her large tongue rolled ceaselessly in her mouth, chewing nothing.

Her articulation necessarily was very poor. "I wus seven yeres old when Freedum cum. My ma and pa belonged to Mr. McNorrell of Burke County. Miss Sally was a good lady and kind to evebody. My marster was a good man cuz he was a preacher, I never member him whuppin' anybody. I 'members slavry, yes mam, I 'members all the slaves' meals wus cooked in de yard, in big pots hung up on hooks on a iron bar. The fust wurk I ever done wus to push fire wood under dem pots. Mostly I stayed home and minded de baby. My ma uster pin a piece of fat back on my dres' before she went to de fiel' and when de baby cry I tek him up and let 'em suck 'em. My brudder you see sittin' in dere, he de baby I uster mine. My pa wuz the blacksmith on the plantashun, and he mek all de plows and tings like dat. My ma tek me to de fiel when I wuz 'bout sever yeres ole and teach me to chop cotton, I don't member what happen when freedom come, tings wuz 'bout de same, fur as we chillun knowed."

Elizabeth Watson
M.G. 7/15/37

MELVIN SMITH, Ex-Slave, 96 Years
[Date Stamp: JUL 28 1937]

MELVIN SMITH

"Yes'm, I show does 'member all 'about my white folks an' th' war 'cause I was twenty-four year ole when th' war was over. I was born in 1841 an' that makes me 'bout eighty-seven now, don't it?"

Old Melvin Smith sat back in his chair with a smile of satisfaction on his face. He was seated on the narrow porch of his little cabin with the bright sunshine beaming down upon him. But his blind eyes could not notice the glare from the sun. His wife and daughter appeared from around the corner of the house and took their places near him to hear again the story that they had heard many times before.

"My white folks lived in Beaufort, South Ca'lina, an' that's whar I was born," Melvin continued. "My old Miss, I called her Miss Mary, took care of me 'till I was eight year old. Then she give me back to my ma. You see, it was this a-way. My ma an' pa was sold in Beaufort; I don't know whar they come from before that. When I was born Miss Mary took me in th' big house with her an' thar I stayed, jest like I told you, 'till I was eight. Old Miss jest wanted me to be in th' room with her an' I slep' on a pallet right near her bed. In the daytime I played in th' yard an' I pick up chips for old Miss. Then when I got most big enuff to work she give me back to my ma.

"Then I live in a cabin like the rest of th' niggers. Th' quarters was stretched out in a line behind Marse Jim's house. Ever' nigger fam'ly had a house to theyselves. Me an' my pa an' ma, they names was Nancy an' Henry Smith, live in a cabin with my sisters. They names was Saphronia an' Annie. We had beds in them cabins made out of cypress. They looked jest like they do now. Ever'body cooked on th' fire place. They had pots an' boilers that hung over th' fire an' we put th' vittles in thar an' they cooked an' we et 'em. 'Course we never et so much in th' cabin 'cause ever mornin' th' folks all went to th' field. Ma an' Pa was field hands an' I worked thar too when I got big enuff. Saphronia an' Annie, they worked to th' big house. All th' nigger chillun stayed all day with a woman that was hired to take care of them."

When asked about the kind of food they ate, Melvin replied:

"We had enuff for anybody. Th' vittles was cooked in great big pots over th' fire jest like they was cookin' for stock. Peas in this pot, greens in that one. Corn-bread was made up an' put back in th' husks an' cooked in th' ashes. They called that a ash cake. Well, when ever'thing was done th' vittles was poured in a trough an' we all et. We had spoons cut out of wood that we et with. Thar was a big lake on th' plantation whar we could fish an' they show was good when we had 'em for supper. Sometimes we go huntin' an' then we had possum an' squirrel to eat. Th' possums was best of all."

Melvin was asked to tell something about his master's family.

"Old Marster was name Jim Farrell an' his wife was Miss Mary. They had three chillun name Mary, Jim an' Martha. They live in a big white house sot off from th' road 'bout two an' a half mile from Beaufort. Marster was rich I reckon 'cause he had 'bout a sixteen horse farm an' a whole hoodle of niggers. If you measured 'em it would a-been several cowpens full. Heap of them niggers worked in Marster's house to wait on th' white folks. They had a heap of comp'ny so they had to have a heap of niggers. Marster was good to his niggers but he had a overseer that was a mean man. He beat th' niggers so bad that Marster showed him th' road an' told him to git. Then th' Boss an' his son looked after th' hands theyselves 'till they could git another one. That overseer's name was Jimmy.

"Ever' mornin' at four clock th' overseer blowed a conchshell an' all us niggers knowed it was time to git up an' go to work. Sometimes he blowed a bugle that'd wake up the nation. Ever'body worked from sunup 'till sundown. If we didn't git up when we was s'posed to we got a beatin'. Marster'd make 'em beat the part that couldn't be bought." Melvin chuckled at his own sly way of saying that the slaves were whipped through their clothes.

"In the summertime," he continued, "We wore shirts that come down to here." Melvin measured to his ankle. "In the wintertime we wore heavy jeans over them shirts an' brogan shoes. They made shoes on the plantation but mine was store-bought. Marster give us all the vittles an' clothes we needed. He was good to ever'body. I 'member all the po' white trash that lived near us. Marster all time send 'em meat an' bread an' help 'em with they crop. Some of 'em come from Goldsboro, North Ca'lina to git a crop whar we lived. They was so sorry they couldn't git no crop whar they come frum, so they moved near us. Sometimes they even come to see the niggers an' et with us. We went to see them, too, but we had more to eat than them. They was sorry folks."

After a pause, Melvin asked:

"Did you ever hear how the niggers was sold? They was put on a stage on the courthouse square an' sold kinder like they was stock. The prettiest one got the biggest bid. They said that they was a market in North Ca'lina but I never see'd it. The ones I saw was jest sold like I told you. Then they went home with they marsters. If they tried to run away they sont the hounds after them. Them dogs would sniff around an' first news you knowed they caught them niggers. Marster's niggers run away some but they always come back. They'd hear that they could have a better time up north so they think they try it. But they found out that they wasn't no easy way to live away from Marster. He always took 'em back, didn't beat 'em nor nothin'. I run away once myself but I never went nowhere." Melvin's long body shook with laughter as he thought of his prank. He shifted in his chair and then began:

"I was 'bout sixteen an' I took a notion I was grown. So I got under the house right under Marster's dinin' room an' thar I stayed for three months. Nobody but the cook knowed whar I was. They was a hole cut in the floor so ever' day she lifted the lid an' give me something to eat. Ever' day I sneaked out an' got some water an' walked about a bit but I never let nobody see me. I jest got biggety like chillun does now. When I got ready to come out for good I went 'way round by the barn an' come up so nobody know whar I been. Ol' Miss was standin' in the yard an' she spy me an' say, 'Jim," she always call all us niggers Jim 'cause that was Marster's name. She say, "Jim, whar you been so long?' I say, 'I been to Mr. Jones's workin' but I don't like the way they treat me. You all treats me better over here so I come back home.' I say, 'You ain't gonna whip me is you, Miss?' Ol' Miss say, 'No, I ain't gonna whip you this time but if you do such a thing again I'm gonna use all the leather on this place on you." So I went on 'bout my business an' they never bothered me."

Melvin was asked about the church he attended. To this he replied:

"The niggers had a church in the bush arbor right thar on the place. Preacher Sam Bell come ever' Sunday mornin' at ten clock an' we sot thar an' listened to him 'till 'leven thirty. Then we tear home an' eat our dinner an' lie round till four-thirty. We'd go back to church an' stay 'bout hour an' come home for supper. The preacher was the onliest one that could read the Bible. When a nigger joined the church he was baptized in the creek near the bush arbor." And in a low tone he began to speak the words of the old song though he became somewhat confused.

> "Lord, remember all Thy dying groans,
> And then remember me.
> While others fought to win the prize
> And sailed through bloody sea.

"Through many dangers, toils an' snares,

I have already come.

I once was lost but now am found,

Was blind but now I see."

"I've knowed that song for a long time. I been a member of the church for sixty year."

When asked about the war, Melvin became somewhat excited. He rose feebly to his feet and clasped his walking stick as if it were a gun.

"I see'd the Yankee soldiers drill right thar in front of our house," he said. "They'd be marchin' 'long this way (Melvin stumblingly took a few steps across the porch) an' the cap'n say, 'Right' an' they turn back this here way." Melvin retraced his steps to illustrate his words. "Cap'n say, 'Aim' an' they aim." He lifted his stick and aimed. "Cap'n say, 'Fire' an' they fire. I see'd 'em most ever' day. Ol' Marster was a cap'n in our army. I hear big guns a-boomin' all a-time an' the sights I did see! Streets jest runnin' with blood jest like it was water. Here lay a man on this side with his legs shot off; on that thar side they was a man with his arms shot off. Some of them never had no head. It was a terrible sight. I wasn't scared 'cause I knowed they wouldn't hurt me. Them Yankees never bothered nothin' we had. I hear some folks say that they stole they vittles but they never bothered ours 'cause they had plenty of they own. After the war Marster called us together an' say, 'You is free an' can go if you want to' an' I left, so that's all I know."

A few days later a second visit was made to Melvin. This time he was on the inside of his little cabin and was all alone. He came forward, a broad smile on his face, when he heard familiar voices.

"I been thinkin' 'bout what I told you an' I b'lieve that's 'bout all I 'member," he said.

Then he was asked if he remembered any days when the slaves did not have to work.

"Yes'm," was the reply. "We never worked on Christmas or the Fourth of July. Marster always give us big sacks of fruit an' candy on Christmas an' a barbecue the Fourth of July. We never worked none New Year's Day, neither. We jest sot around an' et chicken, fish an' biscuit. Durin' the week on Wednesday an' Thursday night we had dances an' then they was a lot of fiddlin' an' banjo playin'. We was glad to see days when we never had to work 'cause then we could sleep. It seem like the niggers had to git up soon's they lay down. Marster was good to us but the overseer was mean. He wan't no po' white trash; he was up-to-date but he like to beat on niggers."

When asked if he has been happier since he was freed, he replied:

"In a sense the niggers is better off since freedom come. Ol' Marster was good an' kind but I like to be free to go whar I please. Back then we couldn't go nowhar 'less we had a pass. We don't have no overseer to bother us now. It ain't that I didn't love my Marster but I jest likes to be free. Jest as soon as Marster said I didn't b'long to nobody no more I left an' went to Tallahassee. Mr. Charlie Pearce come an' wanted some hands to work in orange groves an' fish for him so that's what I done. He took a whole crew. While we was down thar Miss Carrie Standard, a white lady, had a school for the colored folks. 'Course, my ol' Miss had done taught me to read an' write out of the old blue back Webster but I had done forgot how. Miss Carrie had 'bout fifteen in her class.

"I stayed in Tallahassee three years an' that's whar I married the first time. I was jest romancin' about an' happened to see Ca'line Harris so I married her. That was a year after the war. We never had no preacher but after we been goin' together for such a long time folks say we married. We married jest like the colored folks does now. When I left Tallahassee I moved to another place in Florida, thirteen mile from Thomasville, Ga. I stay thar 'bout thirty-seven year. My first wife died an' I married another. The second one lived twenty-one year an' I married again. The one what's livin' now is my third one. In 1905 she had a baby that was born with two lower teeth. It never lived but a year. In all, I've had twenty-three chillun. They most all lives in Florida an' I don't know what they doin' or how many chillun they got. I got four gran'-chillun livin' here."

Melvin was asked to tell what he knew of the Ku Klux Klan. He answered:

"I don't know nothin' 'bout that, I hear somethin' 'bout it but I never b'lieved in it. I b'lieve in h'ants, though. I ain't never see'd one but I'se heard 'em. When you walkin' 'long an' a twig snaps an' you feel like you want to run an' your legs won't move an' your hair feels like it's goin' to rise off your head, that's a ha'nt after you. That sho is the evil sperrit. An' if you ain't good somethin' bad'll happen to you."

When asked why he joined the church, he replied:

"So many people is tryin' to live on flowery beds of ease that the world is in a gamblin' position an' if it wasn't for the Christian part, the world would be destroyed. They ask God for mercy an' He grants it. When they git in trouble they can send a telegram wire an' git relief from on high."

United States. Work Projects Administration

PLANTATION LIFE as viewed by Ex-Slave

NANCY SMITH, Age about 80
129 Plum Street
Athens, Georgia

Written by:
Grace McCune
Athens

Edited by:
Sarah H. Hall
Athens

and
John N. Booth
District Supervisor
Federal Writers' Project
Residencies 6 & 7

NANCY SMITH

Nancy Smith was in bed when the interviewer called. The aged Negress appeared to be quite feeble but, even though she was alone in the house, her head was tied up in a snowy white cloth and the sickroom was neat and clean. The bowl of fresh flowers on her bedside table was no gayer than Nancy's cheerful chuckle as she repeated the doctor's instructions that she must stay in bed because of a weak heart. "Lawsy Chile," she said, "I ain't dead yit." Nancy stated that the grandson who lives with her has been preparing breakfast and cleaning the room since she has been bedridden, and that a niece who lives nearby comes in occasionally during the day to look after her.

Asked if she felt strong enough to talk about the old plantation days, she answered: "I jus' loves to talk 'bout old times, and I spends a lot of dis lonesome time here by myself jus' a-studyin' 'bout dem days. But now listen, Chile, and understand dis. I warn't no plantation Negro. Our white folks was town folks, dey was. My Mammy and Daddy was Julia and Jack Carlton. Dey belonged to old Marster, Dr. Joe Carlton, and us lived right here in town in a big white house dat had a upstairs and a downstairs in it. Our house stood right whar de courthouse is now. Marster had all dat square and his mother, Mist'ess Bessie Carlton, lived on de square de other side of Marse Joe's. His office was on de corner whar de Georgia (Georgian) Hotel is now, and his hoss stable was right whar da Cain's boardin' house is. Honey, you jus' ought to have seed Marse Joe's hoss stable for it sho' was a big one.

"No Mam, I don't know 'zactly how old I is. I was born 'fore de war, and Marse Joe kept de records of all of us and evvything, but somehow dem books got lost. Folks said I was 'bout de age of Marse Joe's son, Dr. Willie. Marster had three boys: Dr. Joe, Jr., Dr. Willie, and Dr. Jimmie, and dere was one little Mist'ess. She was Miss Julia. Us all played 'round in de yard together.

"Daddy, he was de car'iage driver. He driv Marse Joe 'round, 'cept when Mist'ess wanted to go somewhar. Den Daddy driv de coach for her, and Marse Joe let another boy go wid him.

"De biggest, bestest fireplace up at de big house was in de kitchen whar Mammy done de cookin'. It had a great wide hearth wid four big swingin' racks and four big old pots. Two of de ovens was big and two was little. Dat was better cookin' 'rangements and fixin's dan most of de other white folks in dis town had den. When dat fire got good and hot and dere was plenty of ashes, den Mammy started cookin' ash cakes and 'taters. One of Mammy's good ash-roasted 'taters would be awful good right now wid some of dat good old home-made butter to go wid it. Marster allus kept jus' barrels and barrels of good old home-made 'lasses sirup, 'cause he said dat was what made slave chilluns grow fast and be strong. Folks don't know how to have plenty of good things to eat lak us had den. Jus' think of Marse Joe's big old plantation down nigh de Georgia Railroad whar he raised our somepin' t'eat: vegetables sich as green corn, 'taters, cabbages, onions, collards, turnip greens, beans, peas—more than I could think up all day—and dere was plenty of wheat, rye, and corn for our bread.

"Out dar de pastur's was full of cows, hogs and sheep, and dey raised lots of chickens and turkeys on dat farm. Dey clipped wool from dem sheep to weave wid de cotton when dey made cloth for our winter clothes.

"Marster had a overseer to look atter his plantation, but us chillun in town sho'ly did love to be 'lowed to go wid him or whoever went out dar when dey needed somepin' at de big house from de farm. Dey needed us to open and shut gates and run errands, and whilest dey was gittin' up what was to be took back to town, us would run 'round seein' evvything us could.

"Honey, de clothes us wore den warn' t lak what folks has now. Little gals jus' wore slips cut all in one piece, and boys didn't wear nothin' but long shirts 'til dey was big enough to wuk in de fields. Dat was summertime clothes. In winter, dey give us plenty of warm clothes wid flannel petticoats and brass-toed shoes. Grown-up Negroes had dresses what was made wid waisties and skirts sewed together. Dey had a few gathers in de skirts, but not many. De men wore homespun britches wid galluses to hold 'em up. White folks had lots better clothes. Mist'ess' dresses had full, ruffled skirts and, no foolin', her clothes was sho'ly pretty. De white menfolks wore plain britches, but dey had bright colored coats and silk vests dat warn't lak de vests de men wears now. Dem vests was more lak fancy coats dat didn't have no sleeves. Some folks called 'em 'wescoats.' White chillun never had no special clothes for Sunday.

"Miss Julia used to make me sweep de yard wid a little brushbroom and I had to wear a bonnet den to keep dust out of my hair. Dat bonnet was ruffled 'round de front and had staves to hold de brim stiff, but in de back it didn't have no ruffle; jus' de bottom of de crown what us called de bonnet tail. Dem bonnets looked good enough in front but mighty bob-tailed in de back.

"Dey used to have big 'tracted meetin's in Pierce's Chapel nigh Foundry Street and Hancock Avenue, and us was allus glad for dem meetin' times to come. Through de week dey preached at night, but when Sunday come it was all day long and dinner on de ground. Pierce's Chapel was a old fashioned place, but you forgot all 'bout dat when Brother Thomas got in de pulpit and preached dem old time sermons 'bout how de devil gwine to git you if you don't repent and be washed in de blood of de Lamb. De call to come up to de mourner's bench brought dem Negroes jus' rollin' over one another in de 'citement. Soon dey got happy and dere was shoutin' all over de place. Some of 'em jus' fell out. When de 'tracted meetin' closed and de baptizin' dey come, dat was de happiest time of all. Most of de time dere was a big crowd for Brother Thomas to lead down into de river, and dem Negroes riz up out of de water a-singin': _Lord, I'm comin' Home_, _Whar de Healin' Waters Flow_, _Roll, Jordan Roll_, _All God's Chillun Got Wings_, and sich lak. You jus' knowed dey was happy.

"No Mam, I don't 'member much 'bout folks dyin' in dem days 'cause I never did love to go 'round dead folks. De first corpse I ever seed was Marse Joe's boy, young Marse Jimmy. I was skeered to go in dat room 'til I had done seed him so peaceful lak and still in dat pretty white casket. It was a sho' 'nough casket, a mighty nice one; not lak dem old home-made coffins most folks was buried in. Hamp Thomas, a colored man dat lived right below us, made coffins for white folks and slaves too. Some of dem coffins was right nice. Dey was made out of pine mostly, and sometimes he painted 'em and put a nice linin' over cotton paddin'. Dat made 'em look better dan de rough boxes de porest folks was buried in. Mammy said dat when slaves died out on de plantation day wropped de 'omans in windin' sheets and laid 'em on coolin' boards 'til de coffins was made, Dey put a suit of homespun clothes on de mens when dey laid 'em out. Dey jus' had a prayer when dey buried plantation slaves, but when de crops was laid by, maybe a long time atter de burial, dey would have a white man come preach a fun'ral sermon and de folks would all sing: _Harps (Hark) From De Tomb_ and _Callin' God's Chillun Home_.

"Dere warn't no patterollers in town, but slaves had

to have passes if dey was out atter 9:00 o'clock at night or de town marshal would put a fine on 'em if dey couldn't show no pass.

"De fust I knowed 'bout de war was when Marse Joe's brother, Marse Bennie Carlton, left wid de other sojers and pretty soon he got kilt. I was little den, and it was de fust time I had ever seed our Mist'ess cry. She jus' walked up and down in de yard a-wringin' her hands and cryin'. 'Poor Benny's been killed,' she would say over and over.

"When dem yankee sojers come, us warn't much skeered 'cause Marse Joe had done told us all 'bout 'em and said to spect 'em 'fore long. Sho' 'nough, one day dey come a-lopin' up in Marse Joe's yard. Dey had dem old blue uniforms on and evvy one of 'em had a tin can and a sack tied to his saddle. Marster told us dey kept drinkin' water in dem cans and dey called 'em canteens. De sacks was to carry deir victuals in. Dem fellows went all through out big house and stole whatever dey wanted. Dey got all of Mist'ess' best silver 'cause us didn't have no time to hide it atter us knowed dey was nigh 'round de place. Dey tuk all de somepin' t'eat dere was in de big house. When dey had done et all dey wanted and tuk evvything else dey could carry off, dey called us Negroes up 'fore deir captain, and he said all of us was free and could go any time and anywhar us wanted to go. Dey left, and us never seed 'em in dat yard no more. Marse Joe said all of us dat wanted to could stay on wid him. None of us had nowhar else to go and 'sides nobody wanted to go nowhar else, so evvy one of Marse Joe's Negroes stayed right on wid him dat next year. Us warn't skeered of dem Kluxers (Ku Klux Klan) here in town, but dey was right bad out on de plantations.

"'Bout de time I was old enough to go to school, Daddy moved away from Marse Joe's. Us went over to de other side of de river nigh whar de old check mill is. Dey had made guns dar durin' de war, and us chillun used to go and look all through dat old mill house. Us played 'long de river banks and went swimmin' in de river. Dem was de good old days, but us never realized it den.

"I never went to school much, 'cause I jus' couldn't seem to larn nothin'. Our teachers said I didn't have no talent for book larnin'. School was taught in Pierce's Chapel by a Negro man named Randolph, and he sho'ly did make kids toe da mark. You had better know dem lessons or you was gwine to git fanned out and have to stay in atter school. Us got out of school evvy day at 2:00 o'clock. Dat was 'cause us was town chillun. I was glad I didn't live in de country 'cause country schools kept de chillun all day long.

"It was sort of funny to be able to walk out and go in town whenever us wanted to widout gittin' Marster's consent, but dere warn't nothin' much to go to town for 'less you wanted to buy somepin. A few stores, mostly on Broad Street, de Town Hall, and de Fire Hall was de places us headed for. Us did love to hang 'round whar dat fire engine was, 'cause when a fire broke out evvybody went, jus' evvybody. Folks would form lines from de nearest cisterns and wells and pass dem buckets of water on from one to another 'til dey got to de man nighest de fire.

"Soon as I was big enough, I went to wuk for white folks. Dey never paid me much in cash money, but things was so much cheaper dan now dat you could take a little cash and buy lots of things. I wukked a long time for a yankee fambly named Palmer dat lived on Oconee Street right below de old Michael house, jus' 'fore you go down de hill. Dey had two or three chillun and I ain't never gwine to forgit de day dat little Miss Eunice was runnin' and playin' in de kitchen and fell 'gainst de hot stove. All of us was skeered most to death 'cause it did seem den lak her face was plumb ruint, and for days folks was 'most sho' she was gwine to die. Atter a long, long time Miss Eunice got well and growed up to be a fine school teacher. Some of dem scars still shows on her face.

"Me and Sam Smith got married when I was 17. No Chile, us didn't waste no money on a big weddin' but I did have a right pretty weddin' dress. It was nice and new and was made out of white silk. My sister was a-cookin' for Mrs. White at dat time, and dey had a fine two-room kitchen in de back yard set off from de big house. My sister lived in one of dem rooms and cooked for de Whites in de other one. Mrs. White let us git married in her nice big kitchen and all de white folks come out from de big house to see Brother Thomas tie de knot for us. Den me and Sam built dis very same house whar you is a-settin', and I done been livin' here ever since.

"Us was livin' right here when dey put on dem fust new streetcars. Little bitty mules pulled 'em 'long and sometimes dey had a right hard time draggin' dem big old cars through mud and bad weather. Now and den day got too frisky and run away; dat was when dem cars would rock and roll and you wished you could git off and walk. Most of de time dem little mules done good and us was jus' crazy 'bout ridin' on de streetcars."

When Nancy tired of talking she tactfully remarked: "I spects I better git quiet and rest now lak de doctor ordered, but I'm mighty glad you come, and I hopes you'll be back again 'fore long. Most folks don't take up no time wid old wore-out Negroes. Good-bye, Missy."

United States. Work Projects Administration

Slave Narratives

PLANTATION LIFE AS VIEWED BY EX-SLAVE

NELLIE SMITH, Age 78
660 W. Hancock Avenue
Athens, Georgia

Written by:
Miss Grace McCune
Athens

Edited by:
Mrs. Sarah H. Hall
Athens

and
John N. Booth
District Supervisor
Federal Writers' Project
Residencies 6 & 7
Augusta Georgia

September 2, 1938

NELLIE SMITH

Large pecan trees shaded the small, well-kept yard that led to Nellie Smith's five-room frame house. The front porch of her white cottage was almost obscured by a white cloud of fragrant clematis in full blossom, and the yard was filled with roses and other flowers.

A small mulatto woman sat in the porch swing, a walking stick across her lap. Her straight, white hair was done in a prim coil low on the neck, and her print dress and white apron were clean and neat. In answer to the visitor's inquiry, she smiled and said: "This is Nellie Smith. Won't you come in out of the hot sun? I just knows you is plumb tuckered out. Walkin' around in this hot weather is goin' to make you sick if you don't be mighty careful.

"'Scuse me for not gittin' up. I can't hardly make it by myself since I fell and got hurt so bad. My arm was broke and it looks lak my old back never will stop hurtin' no more. Our doctor says I'll have to stay bandaged up this way two or three weeks longer, but I 'spects that's on account of my age. You know old folks' bones don't knit and heal quick lak young folks' and, jus' let me tell you, I've done been around here a mighty long time. Are you comfortable, Child? Wouldn't you lak to have a glass of water? I'll call my daughter; she's back in the kitchen."

Nellie rapped heavily on the floor with her walking stick, and a tall, stout, mulatto in a freshly laundered house frock made her appearance. "This is my daughter, Amanda," said Nellie, and, addressing her off-spring, she continued: "Bring this lady a drink of water. She needs it after walkin' 'way out here in this hot sun." Ice tinkled in the glass that the smiling Amanda offered as she inquired solicitously if there was anything else she could do. Amanda soon went back to her work and Nellie began her narrative.

"Lordy, Honey, them days when I was a child, is so far back that I don't s'pect I can 'member much 'bout 'em. I does love to talk about them times, but there ain't many folks what keers anything 'bout listening to us old folks these days. If you don't mind we'll go to my room where it'll be more comfortable." Amanda appeared again, helped Nellie to her room, and placed her in a large chair with pillows to support the broken arm. Amanda laughed happily when she noticed her mother's enthusiasm for the opportunity to relate her life story. "Mother likes that," she said, "and I'm so glad you asked her to talk about those old times she thinks so much about. I'll be right back in the kitchen ironing; if you want anything, just call me."

Nellie now began again: "I was born right near where the Coordinate College is now; it was the old Weir place then. I don't know nothin' 'bout my Daddy, but my Mother's name was Harriet Weir, and she was owned by Marster Jack Weir. He had a great big old plantation then and the homeplace is still standin', but it has been improved and changed so much that it don't look lak the same house. As Marse Jack's sons married off he give each one of 'em a home and two slaves, but he never did sell none of his slaves, and he told them boys they better not never sell none neither.

"Slaves slept in log cabins what had rock chimblies at the end. The rocks was put together with red clay. All the slaves was fed at the big house kitchen. The fireplace, where they done the cookin', was so big it went 'most across one end of that big old kitchen. It had long swingin' cranes to hang the pots on, and there was so many folks to cook for at one time that often there was five or six pots over the fire at the same time. Them pots was large too—not lak the little cookin' vessels we use these days. For the bakin', they had all sizes of ovens. Now Child, let me tell you, that was good eatin'. Folks don't take time enough to cook right now; They are always in too big a hurry to be doin' something else and don't cook things long enough. Back in dem days they put the vegetables on to cook early in the mornin' and biled 'em 'til they was good and done. The biggest diffunce I see is that folks didn't git sick and stay sick with stomach troubles then half as much as they does now. When my grandma took a roast out of one of them old ovens it would be brown and juicy, with lots of rich, brown gravy. Sweet potatoes baked and browned in the pan with it would taste mighty fine too. With some of her good biscuits, that roast meat, brown gravy, and potatoes, you had food good enough for anybody. I just wish I could taste some more of it one more time before I die.

"Why, Child, two of the best cake-makers I ever knew used them old ovens for bakin' the finest kinds of pound cakes and fruit cakes, and evvybody knows them cakes was the hardest kinds to bake we had in them days. Aunt Betsey Cole was a great cake-baker then. She belonged to the Hulls, what lived off down below here somewhere but, when there was to be a big weddin' or some 'specially important dinner in Athens, folks 'most always sent for Aunt Betsey to bake the cakes. Aunt Laura McCrary was a great cake-maker too; she baked the cake for President Taft when he was entertained at Mrs. Maggie Welch's home here.

"In them days you didn't have to be runnin' to the store evvy time you wanted to cook a extra good meal; folks raised evvything they needed right there at home. They had all the kinds of vegetables they knowed about then in their own gardens, and there was big fields of corn, rye, and wheat. Evvy big plantation raised its own cows for plenty of milk and butter, as well as lots of beef cattle, hogs, goats, and sheep. 'Most all of 'em had droves of chickens, geese, and turkeys, and on our place there were lots of peafowls. When it was goin' to rain them old peafowls set up a big holler. I never knew rain to fail after them peafowls started their racket.

"All our clothes and shoes was home-made, and I mean by that they growed the cotton, wool, and cattle and made the cloth and leather on the plantation. Summer clothes was made of cotton homespun, and cotton and wool was wove together for winter clothin'. Marse Jack owned a man what he kept there to do nothin' but make shoes. He had another slave to do all the carpenterin' and to make all the coffins for the folks that died on the plantation. That same carpenter made 'most all the beds the white folks and us slaves slept on. Them old beds— they called 'em teesters—had cords for springs; nobody never heard of no metal springs them days. They jus' wove them cords criss-cross, from one side to the other and from head to foot. When they stretched and sagged they was tightened up with keys what was made for that purpose.

"Jus' look at my room," Nellie laughed. "I saw you lookin' at my bed. It was made at Wood's Furniture Shop, right here in Athens, and I've had it ever since I got married the first time. Take a good look at it, for there ain't many lak it left." Nellie's pride in her attractively furnished room was evident as she told of many offers she has had for this furniture, but she added: "I want to keep it all here to use myself jus' as long as I live. Shucks, I done got plumb off from what I was tellin' you jus' ravin' 'bout my old furniture and things.

"My Mother died when I was jus' a little girl and she's buried in the old family graveyard on the Weir place, but there are several other slaves buried there and I don't know which grave is hers. Grandma raised me, and I was jus' gittin' big enough to handle that old peafowl-tail fly brush they used to keep the flies off the table when we were set free.

"It wasn't long after the War when the Yankees come to Athens. Folks had to bury or hide evvything they could, for them Yankees jus' took anything they could git their hands on, 'specially good food. They would catch up other folks' chickens and take hams from the smokehouses, and they jus' laughed in folks' faces if they said anything 'bout it. They camped in the woods here on Hancock Avenue, but of course it wasn't settled then lak it is now. I was mighty scared of them Yankees and they didn't lak me neither. One of 'em called me a little white-headed devil.

"One of my aunts worked for a northern lady that they called Mrs. Meeker, who lived where the old Barrow home is now. Evvy summer when she went back up North she would leave my aunt and uncle to take care of her place. It was right close to the Yankees' camp, and the soldiers made my aunt cook for them sometimes. I was livin' with her then, and I was so scared of 'em that I stayed right by her. She never had to worry 'bout where I was them days, for I was right by her side as long as the Yankees was hangin' 'round Athens. My uncle used to say that he had seen them Yankees ride to places and shoot down turkeys, then make the folks that owned them turkeys cook and serve 'em. Folks used to talk lots 'bout the Yankees stoppin' a white 'oman on the street and takin' her earrings right out of her ears to put 'em on a Negro 'oman; I never saw that, I jus' heard it.

"After the war was over Grandpa bought one of the old slave cabins from Marse Jack and we lived there for a long time; then we moved out to Rock Spring. I was about eight or nine years old then, and they found out I was a regular tomboy. The woods was all 'round Rock Spring then, and I did have a big time climbin' them trees. I jus' fairly lived in 'em durin' the daytime, but when dark come I wanted to be as close to Grandpa as I could git.

"One time, durin' those days at Rock Spring, I wanted to go to a Fourth of July celebration. Those celebrations was mighty rough them days and Grandpa didn't think that would be a good place for a decent little girl, so he didn't want me to go. I cried and hollered and cut up something awful. Grandma told him to give me a good thrashin' but Grandpa didn't lak to do that, so he promised me I could go to ride if I wouldn't go to that celebration. That jus' tickled me to death, for I did lak to ride. Grandpa had two young mules what was still wild, and when he said I could ride one of 'em Grandma tried hard to keep me off of it, for she said that critter would be sure to kill me, but I was so crazy to go that nobody couldn't tell me nothin'. Auntie lent me her domino coat to wear for a ridin' habit and I sneaked and slipped a pair of spurs, then Grandpa put a saddle on the critter and helped me to git up on him. I used them spurs, and then I really went to ride. That mule showed his heels straight through them woods and way on out in the country. I couldn't stop him, so I jus' kept on kickin' him with them spurs and didn't have sense to know that was what was makin' him run. I thought them spurs was to make him mind me, and all the time I was I lammin' him with the spurs I was hollerin': 'Stop! Oh, Stop!' When I got to where I was too scared to kick him with the spurs or do nothin' 'cept hang on to that saddle, that young mule quit his runnin' and trotted home as nice and peaceable as you please. I never did have no more use for spurs.

"Grandpa used to send me to Phinizy's mill to have corn and wheat ground. It would take all day long, so they let me take a lunch with me, and I always had the best sort of time when I went to mill. Uncle Isham run the mill then and he would let me think I was helpin' him. Then, while he helped me eat my lunch, he would call me his little 'tomboy gal' and would tell me about the things he used to do when he was 'bout my age.

"My first schoolin' was in old Pierce's Chapel that set right spang in the middle of Hancock Avenue at Foundry Street. Our teacher was a Yankee man, and we were mighty surprised to find out that he wasn't very hard on us. We had to do something real bad to git a whippin', but when we talked or was late gittin' to school we had to stand up in the back of the schoolroom and hold up one hand. Pierce's chapel was where the colored folks had preachin' then—preachin' on Sunday and teachin' on week days, all in the same buildin'. A long time before then it had been the white folks' church, and Preacher Pierce was the first one to preach there after it was built, so they named it for him. When the white folks built them a new church they gave the old chapel to the colored folks, and, Honey, there was some real preachin' done in that old place. Me, I was a Methodist, but I was baptized just lak the Baptists was down there in the Oconee River.

"Me and my first husband was too young to know what we was doin' when we got married, but our folks give us a grand big weddin'. I think my weddin' cake was 'bout the biggest one I ever saw baked in one of them old ovens in the open fireplace. They iced it in white and decorated it with grapes. A shoat was cooked whole and brought to the table with a big red apple in his mouth. You know a shoat ain't nothin' but a young hog that's done got bigger than a little pig. We had chicken and pies and just evvything good that went to make up a fine weddin' supper.

"Our weddin' took place at night, and I wore a white dress made with a tight-fittin' waist and a long, full skirt that was jus' covered with ruffles. My sleeves was tight at the wrists but puffed at the shoulders, and my long veil of white net was fastened to my head with pretty flowers. I was a mighty dressed up bride. The bridegroom wore a real dark-colored cutaway coat with a white vest. We did have a swell weddin' and supper, but there wasn't no dancin' 'cause we was all good church folks.

"We was so young we jus' started out havin' a good time and didn't miss nothin' that meant fun and frolic. We was mighty much in love with each other too. It didn't seem long before we had three children, and then one night he was taken sick all of a sudden and didn't live but a little while. Soon as he was taken sick I sent for the doctor, but my husband told me then he was dyin' fast and that he wasn't ready to die. He said: 'Nellie, here we is with these three little children and neither one of us had been fit to raise 'em. Now I've got to leave you and you will have to raise one of 'em, but the other two will come right on after me.'"

For several moments Nellie was still and quiet; then she raised her head and said: "Honey, it was jus' lak he said it would be. He was gone in jus' a little while and it wasn't two weeks 'fore the two youngest children was gone lak their daddy. I worried lots after my husband and babies was taken. I wanted to be saved to raise my little girl right, and I was too proud to let anybody know how troubled I was or what it was all about, so I kept it to myself. I lost weight, I couldn't sleep, and was jus' dyin' away with sin. I would go to church but that didn't git me no relief.

"One day a dear, good white lady sent for me to come to the hotel where she was stayin'. She had been a mighty good friend to me for a long, long time, and I had all the faith in the world in her. She told me that she had a good job for me and wanted me to take it because it would let me keep my little girl with me. She said her best friend's maid had died and this friend of hers needed someone to work for her. 'I want you to go there and work for her,' said the white lady, 'for she will be good to you and your child. I've already talked with her about it.'

"I took her advice and went to work for Mrs. R.L. Bloomfield whose husband operated the old check mill. Honey, Mrs. Bloomfield was one of God's children and one of the best folks I have ever known. Right away she told her cook: 'Amanda, look after Nellie good 'cause she's too thin.' It wasn't long before Mrs. Bloomfield handed me a note and told me to take it to Dr. Carlton. When he read it he laughed and said; 'Come on Nellie, I've got to see what's wrong with you.' I tried to tell him I wasn't sick, but he examined me all over, then called to see Mrs. Bloomfield and told her that I didn't need nothin' but plenty of rest and to eat enough good food. Bless her dear old heart, she done evvything she could for me, but there wasn't no medicine, rest, or food that could help the trouble that was wearin' me down then.

"Soon they started a revival at our church. One night I wanted to go, but Aunt Amanda begged me not to, for she said I needed to go to bed and rest; later she said she would go along with me to hear that preachin'. Honey, I never will forgit that night. The text of the sermon was: 'Come unto me all you weary and heavy laden, and I will give you rest.' When they began callin' the mourners to come up to the mourners' bench something seemed to be jus' a-pullin' me in that direction, but I was too proud to go. I didn't think then I ever could go to no mourners' bench or shout. After a while they started singin' _Almost Persuaded_, and I couldn't wait; I jus' got up and run to that blessed mourners' bench and I prayed there. Honey, I shouted too, for I found the Blessed Lord that very night and I've kept Him right with me ever since. I don't aim to lose Him no more. Aunt Amanda was most nigh happy as I was and, from that night when the burden was lifted from my heart, I begun gittin' better.

"I worked on for Mrs. Bloomfield 'til I got married again, and then I quit work 'cept for nursin' sick folks now and then. I made good money nursin' and kept that up 'til I got too old to work outside my own family.

"My second husband was Scott Smith. We didn't have no big, fancy weddin' for I had done been married and had all the trimmin's one time. We jus' had a nice quiet weddin' with a few close friends and kinfolks invited. I had on a very pretty, plain, white dress. Again I was blessed with a good husband. Scott fixed up that nice mantelpiece you see in this room for me, and he was mighty handy about the house; he loved to keep things repaired and in order. Best of all, he was jus' as good to my little girl as he was to the girl and boy that were born to us later. All three of my children are grown and married now, and they are mighty good to their old mother. One of my daughters lives in New York.

"Soon after we married, we moved in a big old house called the old White place that was jus' around the corner from here on Pope Street. People said it was haunted, and we could hear something walkin' up and down the stairs that sounded lak folks. To keep 'em from bein' so scared, I used to try to make the others believe it was jus' our big Newfoundland dog, but one night my sister heard it. She got up and found the dog lyin' sound asleep on the front porch, so it was up to me to find out what it was. I walked up the stairs without seein' a thing, but, Honey, when I put my foot on that top step such a feelin' come over me as I had never had before in all my life. My body trembled 'til I had to hold tight to the stair-rail to keep from fallin', and I felt the hair risin' up all over my head. While it seemed like hours before I was able to move, it was really only a very few seconds. I went down those stairs in a hurry and, from that night to this day, I have never hunted ghosts no more and I don't aim to do it again, never.

"I've been here a long time, Honey. When them first street lights was put up and lit, Athens was still mostly woods. Them old street lights would be funny to you now, but they was great things to us then, even if they wasn't nothin' but little lanterns what burned plain old lamp-oil hung out on posts. The Old Town Hall was standin' then right in the middle of Market (Washington) Street, between Lumpkin and Pulaski Streets. The lowest floor was the jail, and part of the ground floor was the old market place. Upstairs was the big hall where they held court, and that was where they had so many fine shows. Whenever any white folks had a big speech to make they went to that big old room upstairs in Town Hall and spoke it to the crowd.

"You is too young to remember them first streetcars what was pulled by little bitsy Texas mules with bells around their necks. Hearing them bells was sweet music to us when they meant we was goin' to git a ride on them streetcars. Some folks was too precise to say 'streetcars'; they said 'horsecars', but them horsecars was pulled through the streets by mules, so what's the diffunce? Sometimes them little mules would mire up so deep in the mud they would have to be pulled out, and sometimes, when they was feelin' sassy and good, they would jus' up and run away with them streetcars. Them little critters could git the worst tangled up in them lines." Here Nellie laughed heartily. "Sometimes they would even try to climb inside the cars. It was lots of fun ridin' them cars, for you never did know what was goin' to happen before you got back home, but I never heard of no real bad streetcar accidents here."

Nellie now began jumping erratically from one subject to another. "Did you notice my pretty flowers and ferns on the front porch?" she asked. "I jus' know you didn't guess what I made them two hangin' baskets out of. Them's the helmets that my son and my son-in-law wore when they was fightin' in the World War. I puts my nicest flowers in 'em evvy year as a sort of memorial to the ones that didn't git to fetch their helmets back home. Yes Mam, I had two stars on my service flag and, while I hated mighty bad that there had to be war, I wanted my family to do their part.

"Honey, old Nellie is gittin' a little tired, but jus' you listen to this: I went to meetin' one night to hear the first 'oman preacher that ever had held a meetin' in this town. She was meanin' to preach at a place out on Rock Spring Street, and there was more folks there than could git inside that little old weather-boarded house. The place was packed and jammed, but me and Scott managed to git in. When I saw an old Hardshell Baptist friend of mine in there, I asked her how come she was at this kind of meetin'. 'Curiosity, my child,' she said, 'jus' plain old curiosity.' The 'oman got up to preach and, out of pure devilment, somebody on the outside hollered; 'The house is fallin' down.' Now Child, I know it ain't right to laugh at preachin's of any sort, but that was one funny scene. Evvybody was tryin' to git out at one time; such cryin', prayin', and testifyin' to the Lord I ain't never heard before. The crowd jus' went plumb crazy with fright. I was pushed down and trampled over in the rush before Scott could git me out; they mighty near killed me." The old woman stopped and laughed until the tears streamed down her face. "You know, Honey," she said, when she could control her voice sufficiently to resume her story, "Niggers ain't got no sense at all when they gits scared. When they throwed one gal out of a window, she called out: 'Thank you, Lord,' for the poor thing thought the Lord was savin' her from a fallin' buildin'. Poor old Martha Holbrook,"—The sentence was not finished until Nellie's almost hysterical giggles had attracted her daughter who came to see if something was wrong—"Martha Holbrook," Nellie repeated, "was climbin' backwards out of a window and her clothes got fastened on a nail. She slipped on down and there she was with her legs kickin' around on the outside and the rest of her muffled up in her clothes. It looked lak her clothes was jus' goin' to peel off over her head. It took the menfolks a long time to git her uncaught and out of that predicament in the window. Pretty soon the folks began to come to their senses and they found there wasn't nothin' wrong with the house 'cept that some doors and windows had been torn out by the crowd. They sho did git mad, but nobody seemed to know who started that ruction. My old Hardshell Baptist friend came up then and said: 'Curiosity brought us here, and curiosity like to have killed the cat.'"

Seeing that Nellie was tired, the visitor prepared to leave. "Goodbye and God bless you," were the old woman's farewell words. At the front door Amanda said: "I haven't heard my Mother laugh that way in a long, long time, and I jus' know she is goin' to feel more cheerful after this. Thank you for givin' her this pleasure, and I hope you can come back again."

Slave Narratives

EX-SLAVE INTERVIEW
with
PAUL SMITH, Age 74
429 China Street
Athens, Georgia

Written by:
Miss Grace McCune
Athens

Edited by:
Mrs. Sarah H. Hall
Athens

Mrs. Leila Harris
Augusta

and
John N. Booth
District Supervisor
Federal Writers' Project
Residencies 6 & 7
Augusta, Georgia

PAUL SMITH

Paul Smith's house stands on China Street, a narrow rutted alley deriving its name from the large chinaberry tree that stands at one end of the alley.

Large water oaks furnish ample shade for the tidy yard where an old well, whose bucket hanging from a rickety windlass frame, was supplying water for two Negro women, who were leaning over washtubs. As they rubbed the clothes against the washboards, their arms kept time to the chant of _Lord I'se Comin' Home_. Paul and two

Negro men, barefooted and dressed in overalls rolled to their knees, were taking their ease under the largest tree, and two small mulatto children were frolicking about with a kitten.

As the visitor approached, the young men leaped to their feet and hastened to offer a chair and Paul said: "Howdy-do, Missy, how is you? Won't you have a cheer and rest? I knows you is tired plumb out. Dis old sun is too hot for folkses to be walkin' 'round out doors," Turning to one of the boys he continued: "Son, run and fetch Missy some fresh water; dat'll make her feel better. Jus' how far is you done walked?" asked Paul. Then he stopped one of the women from the washing and bade her "run into the house and fetch a fan for Missy."

Paul is a large man, and a fringe of kinky white hair frames his face. His manner is very friendly for, noticing that the visitor was looking with some curiosity at the leather bands that encircled his wrists, the old man grinned. "Dem's jus' to make sho' dat I won't have no rheumatiz," he declared. "Mind if I cuts me a chaw of 'baccy? I'se jus' plumb lost widout no 'baccy."

Paul readily agreed to give the story of his life. "I can't git over it, dat you done walked way out here from de courthouse jus' to listen to dis old Nigger talk 'bout dem good old days.

"Mammy belonged to Marse Jack Ellis, and he owned de big old Ellis Plantation in Oglethorpe County whar I was borned. Marse Jack give mammy to his daughter, young Miss Matt, and when her and Marse Nunnally got married up, she tuk my mammy 'long wid her. Mistess Hah'iet (Harriet) Smith owned my daddy. Him and mammy never did git married. My granddaddy and grandmammy was owned by Marse Jim Stroud of Oconee County, and I dug de graves whar bofe of 'em's buried in Mars Hill graveyard.

"All I knows 'bout slavery time is what I heared folkses say, for de war was most over when I was borned, but things hadn't changed much, as I was raised up.

"I warn't but 'bout 2 years old when young Miss Matt tuk my mammy off, and she put me out 'cause she didn't want me. Missy, dey was sho good to me. Marse Jack's wife was Mistess Lizzie. She done her best to raise me right, and de ways she larnt me is done stayed wid me all dese years; many's de time dey's kept old Paul out of trouble. No Mam, I ain't never been in no jailhouse in all my days, and I sho ain't aimin' to de nothin' to make 'em put me dar now.

"In dem days, when chillun got big enough to eat, dey was kept at de big house, 'cause deir mammies had to wuk off in de fields and Old Miss wanted all de chillun whar she could see atter 'em. Most times dere was a old slave 'oman what didn't have nothin' else to do 'cept take keer of slave chillun and feed 'em. Pickaninnies sho had to mind too, 'cause dem old 'omans would evermore lay on de switch. Us et out of wooden trays, and for supper us warn't 'lowed nothin' but bread and milk.

"Long as us was little, us didn't have to wuk at nothin' 'cept little jobs lak pickin' up chips, bringin' in a little wood, and sometimes de biggest boys had to slop de hogs. Long 'bout de fust of March, dey tuk de pants 'way from all de boys and give 'em little shirts to wear from den 'til frost. Yes Mam, dem shirts was all us boys had to wear in summer 'til us was big enough to wuk in de fields. Gals jus' wore one piece of clothes in summertime too; dey wore a plain cotton dress. All our clothes, for summer and winter too, was made right dere on dat plantation. Dey wove de cloth on de looms; plain cotton for summer, and cotton mixed wid a little wool for winter. Dere was a man on de plantation what made all our brogans for winter. Marster made sho us had plenty of good warm clothes and shoes to keep us warm when winter come.

"Folkses raised deir livin', all of it, at home den. Dey growed all sorts of gyarden truck sech as corn, peas, beans, sallet, 'taters, collards, ingons, and squashes. Dey had big fields of grain. Don't forgit dem good old watermillions; Niggers couldn't do widout 'em. Marster's old smokehouse was plumb full of meat all de time, and he had more cows, hogs, sheep, goats, chickens, turkeys, geese, and de lak, dan I ever larnt how to count. Dere warn't no runnin' off to de sto' evvy time dey started cookin' a company meal.

"Dem home-made cotton gins was mighty slow. Us never seed no fast sto'-bought gins dem days. Our old gins was turned by a long pole what was pulled around by mules and oxen, and it tuk a long time to git de seeds out of de cotton dat way. I'se seed 'em tie bundles of fodder in front of de critters so dey would go faster tryin' to git to de fodder. Dey grez dem gins wid homemade tar. De big sight was dem old home-made cotton presses. When dem old mules went round a time or two pullin' dat heavy weight down, dat cotton was sho pressed.

"Us chillun sho did lak to see 'em run dat old gin, 'cause 'fore dey ever had a gin Marster used to make us pick a shoe-full of cotton seeds out evvy night 'fore us went to bed. Now dat don't sound so bad, Missy, but did you ever try to pick any seeds out of cotton?

"Course evvybody cooked on open fireplaces dem days, and dat was whar us picked out dem cotton seeds, 'round dat big old fireplace in de kitchen. All de slaves et together up dar at de big house, and us had some mighty good times in dat old kitchen. Slave quarters was jus' little one room log cabins what had chimblies made of sticks and red mud. Dem old chimblies was all de time a-ketchin' on fire. De mud was daubed 'twixt de logs to chink up de cracks, and sometimes dey chinked up cracks in de roof wid red mud. Dere warn't no glass windows in dem cabins, and dey didn't have but one window of no sort; it was jus' a plain wooden shutter. De cabins was a long ways off from de big house, close by de big old spring whar de wash-place was. Dey had long benches for de wash-tubs to set on, a big old oversize washpot, and you mustn't leave out 'bout dat big old battlin' block whar dey beat de dirt out of de clothes. Dem Niggers would sing, and deir battlin' sticks kept time to de music. You could hear de singin' and de sound of de battlin' sticks from a mighty long ways off.

"I ain't never been to school a day in all my life. My time as chillun was all tuk up nussin' Mistess' little chillun, and I sho didn't never git nary a lick 'bout dem chillun. Mistess said dat a white 'oman got atter her one time 'bout lettin' a little Nigger look atter her chillun, and dat 'oman got herself told. I ain't never uneasy 'bout my chillun when Paul is wid 'em,' Mistess said. When dey started to school, it was my job to see dat dey got dere and when school was out in de evenin', I had to be dere to fetch dem chillun back home safe and sound. School didn't turn out 'til four o'clock den, and it was a right fur piece from dat schoolhouse out to our big house. Us had to cross a crick, and when it rained de water would back up and make it mighty bad to git from one side to t'other. Marster kept a buggy jus' for us to use gwine back and forth to school. One time atter it had done been rainin' for days, dat crick was so high I was 'fraid to try to take Mistess' chillun crost it by myself, so I got a man named Blue to do de drivin' so I could look atter de chillun. Us pulled up safe on de other side and den dere warn't no way to git him back to his own side. I told him to ride back in de buggy, den tie de lines, and de old mule would come straight back to us by hisself. Blue laughed and said dere warn't no mule wid dat much sense, but he soon seed dat I was right, cause dat old mule come right on back jus' lak I said he would.

"Us chillun had good times back den, yes Mam, us sho did. Some of our best times was at de old swimmin' hole. De place whar us dammed up de crick for our swimmin' hole was a right smart piece off from de big house. Us picked dat place 'cause it had so many big trees to keep de water shady and cool. One Sunday, when dere was a big crowd of white and colored chillun havin' a big time splashin' 'round in de water, a white man what lived close by tuk all our clothes and hid 'em way up at his house; den he got up in a tree and hollered lak evvything was atter him. Lawsy, Miss, us chillun all come out of dat crick skeered plumb stiff and run for our clothes. Dey was all gone, but dat never stopped us for long. Us lit out straight for dat man's house. He had done beat us gittin' dar, and when us come runnin' up widout no clothes on, he laughed fit to kill at us. Atter while he told us he skeered us to keep us from stayin' too long in de crick and gittin' drownded, but dat didn't slow us up none 'bout playing in de swimmin' hole.

"Talkin' 'bout being skeered, dere was one time I was skeered I was plumb ruint. Missy, dat was de time I stole somepin' and didn't even know I was stealin'. A boy had come by our place dat day and axed me to go to de shop on a neighbor's place wid him. Mistess 'lowed me to go, and atter he had done got what he said he was sont atter, he said dat now us would git us some apples. He was lots bigger dan me, and I jus' s'posed his old marster had done told him he could git some apples out of dat big old orchard. Missy, I jus' plumb filled my shirt and pockets wid dem fine apples, and us was havin' de finest sort of time when de overseer cotch us. He let me go, but dat big boy had to wuk seven long months to pay for dat piece of foolishment. I sho didn't never go nowhar else wid dat fellow, 'cause my good old mistess said he would git me in a peck of trouble if I did, and I had done larn't dat our mistess was allus right.

"Times has sho done changed lots since dem days; chillun warn't 'lowed to run 'round den. When I went off to church on a Sunday, I knowed I had to be back home not no later dan four o'clock. Now chillun jus' goes all de time, whar-some-ever dey wants to go. Dey stays out most all night sometimes, and deir mammies don't never know whar dey is half de time. 'Tain't right, Missy, folkses don't raise deir chillun right no more; dey don't larn 'em to be 'bejient and don't go wid 'em to church to hear de Word of de Lawd preached lak dey should ought to.

"Fore de war, colored folkses went to de same church wid deir white folkses and listened to de white preacher.

Slaves sot way back in de meetin'-house or up in a gallery, but us could hear dem good old sermons, and dem days dey preached some mighty powerful ones. All my folkses jined de Baptist Church, and Dr. John Mell's father, Dr. Pat Mell, baptized evvy one of 'em. Course I growed up to be a Baptist too lak our own white folkses.

"Slaves had to wuk hard dem days, but dey had good times too. Our white folkses looked atter us and seed dat us had what-some-ever us needed. When talk come 'round 'bout havin' separate churches for slaves, our white folkses give us deir old meetin'-house and built deyselfs a new one, but for a long time atter dat it warn't nothin' to see white folkses visitin' our meetin's, cause dey wanted to help us git started off right. One old white lady—us called her Aunty Peggy—never did stop comin' to pray and sing and shout wid us 'til she jus' went off to sleep and woke up in de better world. Dat sho was one good 'oman.

"Some of dem slaves never wanted no 'ligion, and dey jus' laughed at us cause us testified and shouted. One day at church a good old 'oman got right 'hind a Nigger dat she had done made up her mind she was gwine to see saved 'fore dat meetin' ended. She drug 'im up to de mourner's bench. He 'lowed he never made no prep'ration to come in dis world and dat he didn't mean to make none to leave it. She prayed and prayed, but dat fool Nigger jus' laughed right out at her. Finally de 'oman got mad. 'Laugh if you will,' she told dat man, 'De Good Lawd is gwine to purge out your sins for sho, and when you gits full of biles and sores you'll be powerful glad to git somebody to pray for you. Dat ain't all; de same Good Lawd is gwine to lick you a thousand lashes for evvy time you is done made fun of dis very meetin'.' Missy, would you believe it, it warn't no time 'fore dat man sickened and died right out wid a cancer in his mouf. Does you 'member dat old sayin' 'De ways of de Lawd is slow but sho?'

"Corpses was washed good soon atter de folkses died and deir clothes put on 'em, den dey was laid on coolin' boards 'til deir coffins was made up. Why Missy, didn't you know dey didn't have no sto'-bought coffins dem days? Dey made 'em up right dere on de plantation. De corpse was measured and de coffin made to fit it. Sometimes dey was lined wid black calico, and sometimes dey painted 'em black on de outside. Dere warn't no undytakers den, and dere warn't none of dem vaults to set coffins in neither; dey jus' laid planks crost de top of a coffin 'fore de dirt was piled in de grave.

"When dere was a death 'round our neighborhood, evvybody went and paid deir 'spects to de fambly of de dead. Folkses set up all night wid de corpse and sung and prayed. Dat settin' up was mostly to keep cats offen de corpse. Cats sho is bad atter dead folks; I'se heared tell dat dey most et up some corpses what nobody warn't watchin'. When de time come to bury de dead, dey loaded de coffin on to a wagon, and most times de fambly rode to de graveyard in a wagon too, but if it warn't no fur piece off, most of de other folkses walked. Dey started singin' when dey left de house and sung right on 'til dat corpse was put in de grave. When de preacher had done said a prayer, dey all sung: _I'se Born to Die and Lay Dis Body Down_. Dat was 'bout all dere was to de buryin', but later on dey had de funeral sermon preached in church, maybe six months atter de buryin'. De white folkses had all deir funeral sermons preached at de time of de buryin'.

"Yes Mam, I 'members de fust money I ever wuked for. Marster paid me 50 cents a day when I got big enough to wuk, and dat was plumb good wages den. When I got to whar I could pick more'n a hunnerd pounds of cotton in one day he paid me more. I thought I was rich den. Dem was good old days when us lived back on de plantation. I 'members dem old folkses what used to live 'round Lexin'ton, down in Oglethorpe County.

"When us warn't out in de fields, us done little jobs 'round de big house, de cabins, barns, and yards. Us used to holp de older slaves git out whiteoak splits, and dey larnt us to make cheer bottoms and baskets out of dem splits. De best cheer bottoms what lasted de longest was dem what us made wid red ellum withes. Dem old shuck bottoms was fine too; dey plaited dem shucks and wound 'em 'round for cheer bottoms and footsmats. De 'omans made nice hats out of shucks and wheat straw. Dey plaited de shucks and put 'em together wid plaits of wheat straw. Dey warn't counted much for Sunday wear, but dey made fine sun hats.

"Whilst us was all a-wukin' away at house and yard jobs, de old folkses would tell us 'bout times 'fore us was borned. Dey said slave dealers used to come 'round wid a big long line of slaves a-marchin' to whar dere was gwine to be a big slave sale. Sometimes dey marched 'em here from as fur as Virginny. Old folkses said dey had done been fetched to dis country on boats. Dem boats was painted red, real bright red, and dey went plumb to Africa to git de niggers. When dey got dere, dey got off and left de bright red boats empty for a while. Niggers laks red, and dey would git on dem boats to see what dem red things was. When de boats was full of dem foolish

Niggers, de slave dealers would sail off wid 'em and fetch 'em to dis country to sell 'em to folkses what had plantations. Dem slave sales was awful bad in some ways, 'cause sometimes dey sold mammies away from deir babies and famblies got scattered. Some of 'em never knowed what 'comed of deir brudders and sisters and daddies and mammies.

"I seed dem Yankees when dey come, but I was too little to know much about what dey done. Old folkses said dey give de Athens people smallpox and dat dey died out right and left, jus' lots of 'em. 'Fore dey got rid of it, dey had to burn up beds and clothes and a few houses. Dey said dey put Lake Brown and Clarence Bush out in de swamp to die, but dey got well, come out of dat swamp, and lived here for years and years.

"Granddaddy told us 'bout how some slaves used to rum off from deir marsters and live in caves and dugouts. He said a man and a 'oman run away and lived for years in one of dem places not no great ways from de slave quarters on his marster's place. Atter a long, long time, some little white chillun was playin' in de woods one day and clumb up in some trees. Lookin' out from high up in a tree one of 'em seed two little pickaninnies but he couldn't find whar dey went. When he went back home and told 'bout it, evvybody went to huntin' 'em, s'posin' dey was lost chillun. Dey traced 'em to a dugout, and dere dey found dem two grown slaves what had done run away years ago, and dey had done had two little chillun born in dat dugout. Deir marster come and got 'em and tuk 'em home, but de chillun went plumb blind when dey tried to live out in de sunlight. Dey had done lived under ground too long, and it warn't long 'fore bofe of dem chillun was daid.

"Dem old slavery-time weddin's warn't lak de way folkses does when dey gits married up now; dey never had to buy no license den. When a slave man wanted to git married up wid a gal he axed his marster, and if it was all right wid de marster den him and de gal come up to de big house to jump de broomstick 'fore deir white folkses. De gal jumped one way and de man de other. Most times dere was a big dance de night dey got married.

"If a slave wanted to git married up wid a gal what didn't live on dat same plantation he told his marster, den his marster went and talked to de gal's marster. If bofe deir marsters 'greed den dey jumped de broomstick; if neither one of de marsters wouldn't sell to de other one, de wife jus' stayed on her marster's place and de husband was 'lowed a pass what let him visit her twict a week on Wednesday and Sadday nights. If he didn't keep dat pass to show when de patterollers cotch him, dey was more'n apt to beat de skin right off his back. Dem patterollers was allus watchin' and dey was awful rough. No Mam, dey never did git to beat me up. I out run 'em one time, but I evermore did have to make tracks to keep ahead of 'em.

"Us didn't know much 'bout folkses bein' kilt 'round whar us stayed. Sometimes dere was talk 'bout devilment a long ways off. De mostest troubles us knowed 'bout was on de Jim Smith plantation. Dat sho was a big old place wid a heap of slaves on it. Dey says dat fightin' didn't 'mount to nothin'. Marse Jim Smith got to be mighty rich and he lived to be an old man. He died out widout never gittin' married. Folkses said a nigger boy dat was his son was willed heaps of dat propity, but folkses beat him out of it and, all of a sudden, he drapped out of sight. Some says he was kilt, but I don't know nothin' 'bout dat.

"Now Missy, how come you wants to know 'bout dem frolics us had dem days? Most of 'em ended up scandlous, plumb scandlous. At harvest season dere was cornshuckin's, wheat-thrashin's, syrup-cookin's, and logrollin's. All dem frolics come in deir own good time. Cornshuckin's was de most fun of 'em all. Evvybody come from miles around to dem frolics. Soon atter de wuk got started, marster got out his little brown jug, and when it started gwine de rounds de wuk would speed up wid sich singin' as you never heared, and dem Niggers was wuking in time wid de music. Evvy red ear of corn meant an extra swig of liquor for de Nigger what found it. When de wuk was done and dey was ready to go to de tables out in de yard to eat dem big barbecue suppers, dey grabbed up deir marster and tuk him to de big house on deir shoulders. When de supper was et, de liquor was passed some more and dancin' started, and sometimes it lasted all night. Folkses sometimes had frolics what dey called fairs; dey lasted two or three days. Wid so much dancin', eatin', and liquor drinkin' gwine on for dat long, lots of fightin' took place. It was awful. Dey cut on one another wid razors and knives jus' lak dey was cuttin' on wood. I 'spects I was bad as de rest of 'em 'bout dem razor fights, but not whar my good old mist'ess could larn 'bout it. I never did no fightin' 'round de meetin'-house. It was plumb sinful de way some of dem Niggers would git in ruckuses right in meetin' and break up de services.

"Brudder Bradberry used to come to our house to hold prayermeetin's, but Lawsey, Missy, dat man could eat more dan any Nigger I ever seed from dat day to dis. When us knowed he was a-comin' Mistess let us cook up heaps of stuff, enough to fill dat long old table plumb full, but dat table was allus empty when he left. Yes Mam, he prayed whilst he was dere, but he et too. Dem prayers must'a made him mighty weak.

"Marster Joe Campbell, what lived in our settlement, was sho a queer man. He had a good farm and plenty of most evvything. He would plant his craps evvy year and den, Missy, he would go plumb crazy evvy blessed year. Folkses would jine in and wuk his craps out for him and, come harvest time, dey had to gather 'em in his barns, cause he never paid 'em no mind atter dey was planted. When de wuk was all done for him, Marster Joe's mind allus come back and he was all right 'til next crap-time. I told my good old marster dat white man warn't no ways crazy; he had plumb good sense, gittin' all dat wuk done whilst he jus' rested. Marster was a mighty good man, so he jus' grinned and said 'Paul, us mustn't jedge nobody.'

"When marster moved here to Athens I come right 'long wid 'im. Us started us a wuk-shop down on dis same old Oconee River, close by whar Oconee Street is now. Dis was mostly jus' woods. Dere warn't none of dese new-fangled stock laws den, and folkses jus' fenced in deir gyardens and let de stock run evvywhar. Dey marked hogs so evvybody would know his own; some cut notches in de ears, some cut off de tails or marked noses, and some put marks on de hoof part of de foots. Mr. Barrow owned 'bout 20 acres in woods spread over Oconee Hill, and de hogs made for dem woods whar dey jus' run wild. Cows run out too and got so wild dey would fight when dey didn't want to come home. It warn't no extra sight den to see folkses gwine atter deir cows on mules. Chickens run out, and folkses had a time findin' de aigs and knowin' who dem aigs b'longed to. Most and gen'ally finders was keepers far as aigs was consarnt but, in spite of all dat, us allus had plenty, and Mistess would find somepin' to give folkses dat needed to be holped.

"When us come to Athens de old Georgy Railroad hadn't never crost de river to come into town. De depot was on de east side of de river on what dey called Depot Street. Daddy said he holped to build dat fust railroad. It was way back in slavery times. Mist'ess Hah'iet Smith's husband had done died out, and de 'minstrator of de 'state hired out most all of Mist'ess' slaves to wuk on de railroad. It was a long time 'fore she could git 'em back home.

"Missy, did you know dat Indians camped at Skull Shoals, down in Greene County, a long time ago? Old folkses said dey used to be 'round here too, 'specially at Cherokee Corners. At dem places, it was a long time 'fore dey stopped plowin' up bones whar Indians had done been buried. Right down on dis old river, nigh Mr. Aycock's place, dey says you kin still see caves whar folkses lived when de Indians owned dese parts. If high waters ain't washed 'em all away, de skeletons of some of dem folkses what lived dar is still in dem caves. Slaves used to hide in dem same caves when dey was runnin' off from deir marsters or tryin' to keep out of de way of de law. Dat's how dem caves was found; by white folkses huntin' runaway slaves.

"Now Missy, you don't keer nothin' 'bout my weddin'. To tell de trufe, I never had no weddin'; I had to steal dat gal of mine. I had done axed her mammy for her, but she jus' wouldn't 'gree for me to have Mary, so I jus' up and told her I was gwine to steal dat gal. Dat old 'oman 'lowed she would see 'bout dat, and she kept Mary in her sight day and night, inside de house mos'ly. It looked lak I never was gwine to git a chance to steal my gal, but one day a white boy bought my license for me and I got Brudder Bill Mitchell to go dar wid me whilst Mary's ma was asleep. Us went inside de house and got married right dar in de room next to whar she was sleepin'. When she waked up dere was hot times 'round dat place for a while, but good old Brudder Mitchell stayed right dar and helped us through de trouble. Mary's done been gone a long time now and I misses her mighty bad, but it won't be long now 'fore de Lawd calls me to go whar she is.

"I done tried to live right, to keep all de laws, and to pay up my jus' and honest debts, cause mist'ess larnt me dat. I was up in Virginny wukin' on de railroad a few years ago. De boss man called me aside one day and said; 'Paul, you ain't lak dese other Niggers. I kin tell dat white folks raised you.' It sho made me proud to hear him say dat, for I knows dat old Miss up yonder kin see dat de little Nigger she tuk in and raised is still tryin' to live lak she larnt him to do."

When the visitor arose to leave, old Paul smiled and said "Goodby Missy. I'se had a good time bringin' back dem old days. Goodby, and God bless you."

[HW: Dist. 1
Ex-Slave 102]

SUBJECT: EMELINE STEPNEY, A DAUGHTER OF SLAVERY
DISTRICT: W.P.A. NO. 1
RESEARCH WORKER: JOSEPH E. JAFFEE
EDITOR: JOHN N. BOOTH
SUPERVISOR: JOSEPH E. JAFFEE (ASST.)
[Date Stamp: MAY 8 1937]

EMELINE STEPNEY

Emeline Stepney, as she came into the office that July day, was a perfect vignette from a past era. Over 90 years old, and unable to walk without support, she was still quick witted and her speech, although halting, was full of dry humor. Emeline was clad in a homespun dress with high collar and long sleeves with wristbands. On her feet she wore "old ladies' comforts." She was toothless and her hands were gnarled and twisted from rheumatism and hard work.

Emeline's father, John Smith, had come from Virginia and belonged to "Cap'n Tom Wilson." Her mother, Sally, "wuz a Georgia borned nigger" who belonged to "Mars Shelton Terry." The two plantations near Greensboro, in Greene County, were five miles apart and the father came to see his family only on Wednesday and Saturday nights. The arrangement evidently had no effect in the direction of birth control for Emeline was the second of thirteen children.

Life on the Terry place was a fairly pleasant existence. The master was an old bachelor and he had two old maid sisters, Miss Sarah and Miss Rebecca. The plantation was in charge of two overseers who were reasonably kind to the Negroes.

No crops of any kind were sold and consequently the plantation had to be self-sustaining. Cotton was spun into clothing in the master's own spinning room and the garments were worn by the master and slaves alike. A small amount of flax was raised each year and from this the master's two sisters made household linens. Food crops consisted of corn, wheat (there was a mill on the plantation to grind these into flour and meal), sweet potatoes, and peas. In the smoke house there was always plenty of pork, beef, mutton, and kid. The wool from the sheep was made into blankets and woolen garments.

The Terry household was not like other menages of the time. There were only one or two house servants, the vast majority being employed in the fields. Work began each morning at eight o'clock and was over at sundown. No work was done on Saturday, the day being spent in preparation for Sunday or in fishing, visiting, or "jes frolickin'". The master frequently let them have dances in the yards on Saturday afternoon. To supply the music they beat on tin buckets with sticks.

On Sunday the Negroes were allowed to attend the "white folks' church" where a balcony was reserved for them. Some masters required their "people" to go to church; but Emeline's master thought it a matter for the individual to decide for himself.

Emeline was about 15 when her first suitor and future

husband began to come to see her. He came from a neighboring farm and had to have a pass to show the "patty rollers" or else he would be whipped. He never stayed at night even after they were married because he was afraid he might be punished.

The slaves were never given any spending money. The men were allowed to use tobacco and on rare occasions there was "toddy" for them. Emeline declares SHE never used liquor and ascribes her long life partly to this fact and partly to her belief in God.

She believes in signs but interprets them differently [HW: ?] from most of her people. She believes that if a rooster crows he is simply "crowin' to his crowd" or if a cow bellows it is "mos' likely bellowin' fer water." If a person sneezes while eating she regards this as a sign that the person is eating too fast or has a bad cold. She vigorously denies that any of these omens foretells death. Some "fool nigger" believe that an itching foot predicts a journey to a strange land; but Emeline thinks it means that the foot needs washing.

Aunt Emeline has some remedies which she has found very effective in the treatment of minor ailiments. Hoarhound tea and catnip tea are good for colds and fever. Yellow root will cure sore throat and a tea made from sheep droppings will make babies teethe easily. "I kin still tas'e dat sassafras juice mammy used to give all de chilluns." She cackled as she was led out the door.

United States. Work Projects Administration

[HW: Atlanta
Dist. 5
Ex-Slave #103]

2-4-37
Whitley
SEC.
Ross

[HW: AMANDA STYLES]

AMANDA STYLES

On November 18, 1936 Amanda Styles ex-slave, was interviewed at her residence 268 Baker Street N.E. Styles is about 80 years of age and could give but a few facts concerning her life as a slave. Her family belonged to an ordinary class of people neither rich nor poor. Her master Jack Lambert owned a small plantation; and one other slave besides her family which included her mother, father and one sister. The only event during slavery that impressed itself on Mrs. Styles was the fact that when the Yanks came to their farm they carried off her mother and she was never heard of again.

Concerning superstitions, signs, and other stories pertaining to this Mrs. Styles related the following signs and events. As far as possible the stories are given in her exact words. "During my day it was going ter by looking in the clouds. Some folks could read the signs there. A 'oman that whistled wuz marked to be a bad 'oman. If a black cat crossed your path you sho would turn round and go anudder way. It was bad luck to sit on a bed and when I wuz small I wuz never allowed to sit on the bed."

Following are stories, related by Mrs. Styles, which had their origin during slavery and immediately following slavery.

"During slavery time there was a family that had a daughter and she married and ebby body said she wuz a witch cause at night dey sed she would turn her skin inside out and go round riding folks horses. Der next morning der horses manes would be tied up. Now her husband didn't know she was a witch so somebody tole him he could tell by cutting off one of her limbs so one night the wife changed to a cat and the husband cut off her forefinger what had a ring on it. After that der wife would keep her hand hid cause her finger wuz cut off; and she knowed her husband would find out that she wuz the witch.

My mother sed her young mistress wuz a witch and she too married but her husband didn't know that she wuz a witch; and she would go round at night riding horses and turning the cows milk into blood. Der folks didn't know what ter do instead of milk they had blood. So one day a old lady came there and told em that a witch had been riding the cow, and to cast off the spell, they had to take a horse shoe and put it in the bottom of the churn and then the blood would turn back ter milk and butter. Sho nuff they did it and got milk.

Anudder man had a wife that wuz accused of being a witch so he cut her leg off and it wuz a cats' leg and when his wife came back her leg was missing.

They say there wuz a lot of conjuring too and I have heard 'bout a lot of it. My husband told me he went to see a 'oman once dat had scorpions in her body. The conjurer did it by putting the blood of a scorpion in her body and this would breed more scorpions in her. They had to get anudder conjurer to undo the spell.

There wuz anudder family that lived near and that had a daughter and when she died they say she had a snake in her body.

My husband sed he wuz conjured when he wuz a boy and had ter walk with his arms outstretched he couldn't put em down at all and couldn't even move 'em. One day he met a old man and he sed "Son whats der matter wid you?" "I don't know," he sed. "Den why don't you put your arms down?" "I can't." So the old man took a bottle out of his pocket and rubbed his arms straight down 'till they got alright.

He told me too bout a 'oman fixing her husband. This 'oman saw anudder man she wonted so she had her husband fixed so he would throw his arms up get on his knees and bark just like a dog. So they got some old man that wuz a conjurer to come and cure him. He woulda died if they hadn't got that spell off him.

My father told me that a 'oman fixed anudder one cause she married her sweetheart she told her he nebber would do her any good and sho nuff she fixed her so dat she would have a spell ebby time she went to church. One day they sent fer her husband and asked him what wuz the matter with her and he told them that this other 'oman fixed her with conjure. They sent for a conjurer and he came and rubbed some medicine on her body and she got alright.

During slavery time the master promised ter whip a nigger and when he came out ter whip him instead he just told him "Go on nigger 'bout your business." Der Nigger had fixed him by spitting as for as he could spit so the master couldn't come any nearer than that spit.

I know a Nigger that they sed wuz kin ter the devil. He told me that he could go out hind the house and make some noise and the devil would come and dance with him. He sed the devil learned him to play a banjo and if you wanted to do anything the devil could do, go to a cross road walk backwards and curse God. But don't nebber let the devil touch any of your works or anything that belonged to you or you would lose your power.

The nearest I ebber came ter believing in conjure wuz when my step mother got sick. She fell out with an 'oman that lived with her daughter cause this 'oman had did something ter her daughter; and so she called her a black kinky head hussy and this 'oman got fightin mad and sed ter her. "Nebber mind you'll be nappy and kinky headed too when I git through wid you." My Ma's head turned real white and funny right round the edge and her mind got bad and she used to chew tobacco and spit in her hands and rub it in her head; and very soon all her hair fell out. She even quit my father after living with him 20 years saying he had poisoned her. She stayed sick a long time and der doctors nebber could understand her sickness. She died and I will always believe she wuz fixed.

After relating the last story my interview with Mrs.

Styles came to an end. I thanked her and left, wondering over the strange stories she had told me.

www.ingramcontent.com/pod-product-compliance
Lightning Source LLC
Chambersburg PA
CBHW071650160426
43195CB00012B/1414